Dear Mr. Beckett

"James Laughlin was perhaps the canniest but not the bravest American publisher. That title goes to Barney Rosset of Grove Press. When a book that might make legal trouble (*Lolita* and *Tropic of Cancer*, for example) came his way, Laughlin would say, 'Let Barney do it.'"

—Dwight Garner, New York Times

"On the list, before *Lady Chatterley* were three volumes of Brecht, two each of Ionesco and Brendan Behan, and eight of Samuel Beckett, who in the process of publication by Grove became Rosset's friend. 'Barney and I go to the tennis matches,' Beckett said not long ago. 'We play games, and we talk politics. We don't talk literature. I don't talk literature with nobody. It's bad enough to have to write these books without talking about them too.'"

"'Grove is the American publisher closest to our views,' Lindon said the other day in his little office in an alley off St.-German-des Prés. 'And I like Barney because he is a very fine man. I always say, when the Americans are intelligent, they are very intelligent. Barney has a sense of liberty that is rare in Europe, he is extraordinarily young, and he has a taste for risk—literary risk, risk of good taste, political risk.'"

—Martin Mayer, The Saturday Evening Post

"[Rosset] is like the old guy in *Krapp's Last Tape* (by his favorite author, Samuel Beckett) who passes his life in endless soliloquy, pausing only to play back some fine moment from his past, some flash of passion or of beauty now forever lost."

"That's Barney Rosset, Grove Press' Rosset, the old smut peddler himself, turning his dubious attentions to home movies and the debauching of the American family. Good old Barney, always gnawing away at the props of middle-class morality, always springing trap doors under the square toes of the bourgeoisie. ...

You have to understand that this guy is a real plunger. He does everything on impulse and then figures out afterward whether he made a smart move or was just kidding. Sure he goofs. He buys books that don't sell, houses that flood, vehicles that brake down, movies that can't be shown, newspapers that don't reflect his views, wives that he can't live with—but sometimes he lucks one in there that makes him a millionaire, or, what is more important to a guy that has been a millionaire all his life, that makes him legendary.

—Albert Goldman, *Life Magazine*

Samuel Beckett and Barney Rosset, Paris 1986 © Bob Adelman

Dear Mr. Beckett

THE SAMUEL BECKETT FILE

BARNEY ROSSET

FOREWORD BY EDWARD BECKETT
PREFACE BY PAUL AUSTER
EDITED BY LOIS OPPENHEIM
CURATED BY ASTRID MYERS ROSSET

DEAR MR. BECKETT
The Samuel Beckett File: Correspondence, Interviews, Photos
By Barney Rosset
Preface by PAUL AUSTER • Edited with an Introduction by LOIS OPPENHEIM
Foreword by EDWARD BECKETT • Curated by ASTRID MYERS ROSSET

AN OPUS TRADE PAPERBACK ORIGINAL

Tuxedo Park, NY : Opus, [2017] | Series: Author file series. | Includes bibliographical references
and index.

ISBN: 978-162316-070-8

LCSH: Beckett, Samuel, 1906-1989. | Beckett, Samuel, 1906-1989--Correspondence. | Rosset,
Barney. | Rosset, Barney--Correspondence. | Dramatists--20th century. | Grove Press-- History.
| Writers, French--20th century--Biography. | Writers, Irish--20th century-- Biography. |
Literature, Modern--History and criticism. | Publishers and publishing--United States--History-
-20th century. | Publishers and publishing--United States--Biography. | Theater--Production
and direction--Sources. | Theatrical producers and directors--United States--Correspondence. |
BISAC: LITERARY COLLECTIONS / Letters. | DRAMA / European / Irish. | BIOGRAPHY
& AUTOBIOGRAPHY / Literary. | LITERARY CRITICISM / Drama.

LCC: PR6003.E282 Z48 2016 | DDC: 828/.91409--dc23

Permission credits are an extension of this copyright page, and can be found on page 463.

Book design by Jess Morphew & Florence Aliesch

A Division of Subtext Inc., **A Glenn Young Company**
P.O. Box 725 • Tuxedo Park NY 10987

Publicity: E-mail opusbookpubpr@aol.com
Rights enquiries: e-mail GY@opusbookpublishers.com
All other enquiries: www.opusbookpublishers.com

OPUS is distributed to the trade by The Hal Leonard Publishing Group
Toll Free Sales: 800-524-4425 • www.halleonard.com

FIRST EDITION
10 9 8 7 6 5 4 3 2

Printed in the United States of America.

"I am always in touch with you, Barney, even without visiting or hearing."

Letter from Samuel Beckett to Barney Rosset October 12, 1978

contents

Acknowledgments

We are grateful to a large number of people for their contributions to this volume, for their support and assistance. Interviewers and others generously supplied previously unpublished materials; photographers waived or substantially lowered their customary fees; special collections library personnel gave graciously of their time. It would be impossible to name them all. Among them, however, are Bob Adelman (photographer); Kevin Brownlow (historian, filmmaker, and author); Cora Cahan (President, The New 42nd Street); Paula Court (photographer); Geneviève Chevallier (Université de Nice); Nicolette Dobrowolski (Special Collections Research Center, Syracuse University Libraries); Nicole Dittrich (Special Collections Research Center, Syracuse University Libraries); Leo Edelstein (editor and author); Michael Feingold (theatre critic); Benjamin Formaker-Olivas (UCLA Library Special Collections); Marek Kedzierski (theatre director); James Knowlson (Professor Emeritus, University of Reading); Richard Kreitner (*The Nation*); Daniel Labeille (State University of New York); Brigitte Lacombe (photographer); John Larson (Museum Archivist, The Oriental Institute, The University of Chicago); John Minihan (photographer); Lisa Luna (Associate Editor, Harper's Bazaar); Laura Morris (archivist, Joan Mitchell Foundation); Lucy Mulroney (Special Collections Research Center, Syracuse University Libraries); Karla Nielsen (Rare Book and Manuscript Library, Columbia University); Mark Nixon (Beckett International Foundation, University of Reading); John Oakes (publisher, OR Books); Vahid Rahbani (theatre director); Cesar Reyes (UCLA Library Special Collections); John Shipley (Helen Muir Florida Collection, Miami-Dade Public Library

System); Dirk Van Hulle (University of Antwerp); and Rick Watson (Head of Reference Services, Harry Ransom Center, The University of Texas at Austin).

We would also like to thank several others who were of enormous help in a great variety of ways: Edward Albee, Michael Feingold, Leon Friedman, David Mamet, Estelle Parsons, and David Rieff.

Most especially, we thank Edward Beckett, Executor, Estate of Samuel Beckett, for his encouragement from the start and for his thoughtful suggestions; Tony Bly, our photo editor, for his technical expertise (and constant good will!); Christophe John deGrazia, Literary Executor, for his contribution to the editing of his father's interviews; Florence Aliesch whose final design was performed with great skill and grace, and our editor/publisher, Glenn Young, whose wit and intelligence enriched the very great pleasure we took in working together.

— *Lois Oppenheim and Astrid Myers Rosset*

foreword

EDWARD BECKETT

So soon after finally finding a French publisher, Samuel Beckett was happy to have an American publisher interested in his work. Happy but also worried that Rosset might not know what he was getting into. Fresh from problems with a Paris magazine that had excised a section of *l'Innommable* that it deemed offensive and well aware of the problems that Joyce had had with publication in America, he wrote in a letter to Barney Rosset dated June 1953 "With regard to my work in general, I hope that you realize what you are letting yourself in for."

At that time he may not have been aware that Rosset had already published *Lady Chatterley's Lover*, *Tropic of Cancer* and a good deal more and that he was a dogged character, not easily deterred once he had decided on what he wanted to do.

Once over this first hurdle, Sam and Barney formed a strong bond that over the years developed into firm friendship. This was plainly demonstrated by Sam's immediate response to Barney's request for something new to re-establish himself as a publisher when he was forced out of Grove Press. Thus began the *Eleutheria* saga that was to finish so unhappily five years after Sam's death.

This book is a valuable memento of the long enduring friendship and respect that these two men held for each other, as well as a tribute to the extraordinary achievements of Barney Rosset.

a life in art

PAUL AUSTER

I want to make this as personal as I can, so I will not apologize for what might sound hopelessly nostalgic in this world of no more record shops, fewer and fewer bookstores, and the possible extinction of publishing houses as we have known them for the past two hundred years, but for the people of my generation, those of us born in the late forties and early fifties and who came of age in the sixties, the literary boys and girls who were planning to devote themselves to a life in art, publishers were the ones who helped guide us toward the discoveries we would have to make in order to discover who we were and what we were hoping to become, and from our point of view there were only two American publishers worthy of our absolute trust, New Directions, with its essential list of modernist poets both from this country and abroad, and the younger, more energetic Grove Press, directed by a battling renegade named Barney Rosset, whose mission was to stir things up and challenge the status quo in any way he could, and the times were ripe for such a challenge, the world was waking up again after the dark years of economic depression and the long nightmare of global war, new ideas were suddenly in the air again, new artists were emerging, and Barney Rosset instinctively seemed to understand who the best of those new artists were, and as I worked my way through this lovely, enlivening scrapbook of letters, documents, and memories, I was astonished to discover the names of many people I have known, people who have been of immense importance to me throughout what has now been a long life in art, beginning with Joan Mitchell, Barney Rosset's fellow Chicagoan, schoolmate, and first wife, the brilliant, generous, indelible Joan, who became my friend when I moved to Paris in 1971 as a twenty-four-year-old beginner, who did the cover art of the first issue of a magazine called *Living Hand* that I helped launch with a couple of friends, and who was responsible for my meeting Samuel Beckett, and Joan's companion at the time, the French-Canadian painter Jean-Paul Riopelle, who also became my friend and once lent me his house for a month-long stay in the Laurentian Mountains and wound up illustrating the first book I ever published in France (even now, the five lithographs are hanging on a wall in my living room, as is the lithograph Joan made for the magazine), and Jean Genet, whom I met while I was still an undergraduate at Columbia when he visited the campus to deliver a speech in defense of the Black Panthers (such were the times, and such was the lure of Columbia after our mini-revolution in the spring of 1968), and because it was known that I could make my way around in French, I was enlisted to translate the speech and serve as his interpreter during the time he stayed with us, memorable hours spent in the company of one of Grove Press's most memorable authors, the beatifically smiling Jean Genet, who walked around with a small flower tucked behind his ear, and Alain Robbe-Grillet, whom I met in Hamburg in 1988, the two of us among the seven different writers from seven different cities who had been invited to celebrate Hamburg's 800th anniversary, Alain being the representative from Paris, I being the one from New York, and after three days spent in Germany together we remained friends to the last, and Harold Pinter, not just a Grove Press author but a Faber & Faber author in the UK, as am I, which led to an encounter at a Faber dinner in London and an unforgettable conversation about the relative merits of cricket and baseball, and Richard Avedon, the photographer, who did a portrait of me sometime in the mid-nineties and later apologized for having done such a bad job of it, and Richard Seaver, the former Grove editor whom I met after my return from Paris in the mid-seventies and who graciously cheered on my work over the ensuing decades, and the long friendships formed with some of the poets in Donald Allen's history-making anthology from 1960, in particular John Ashbery and Robert Creeley, who sat side by side in a class at Harvard the year I was born, and Susan Sontag, who appears in this book because of the production of *Waiting for Godot* she directed in Sarajevo during the siege, the intense and opinionated Susan who sometimes rubbed people the wrong way but never me—we were friends, we admired each other, we got along—and how not to remember the last time I saw her, the two of us sitting on a sofa together backstage at Cooper Union before participating in a human rights event for American PEN, sitting together holding hands and talking about the importance of friendship, and because she kept me in the dark about the return of the cancer that would eventually kill her, I didn't understand that she was in fact saying good-bye to me, and Edward Albee, who just last year sat with me in a stuffy room on the top floor of the Strand discussing the work of Samuel Beckett in a conversation moderated by Jeanette Seaver, Dick Seaver's widow, and then, of course, Samuel Beckett himself, whom I met in the early seventies because of Joan Mitchell, and how remarkable it is to think that the literary hero of my youth was sixty-seven years old then, which is precisely my age now, the great Samuel Beckett, who kept up a correspondence with me for many years after that initial meeting, a lifeline that helped sustain me through rough stretches of doubt and early despair, and decades later, when the one hundredth anniversary of Samuel Beckett's birth was approaching, I tried to pay back the debt I felt I owed him by putting together the four-volume centenary edition of his work, which was published by Grove Press in 2006, a project warmly encouraged by Edward Beckett, Samuel Beckett's nephew and literary executor, to whom I also owe a debt of gratitude, and then last of all, but really first of all, Barney Rosset, whose guts and wisdom made it possible for me to read Beckett and all the other writers published by Grove, the one-in-a-million Barney Rosset, whom I finally met during the last years of his life, late but not too late, for even old Barney was young, the youngest old man in all of America, and now America's bravest publisher is dead, Samuel Beckett is dead, Joan Mitchell is dead, Jean-Paul Riopelle is dead, Genet and Pinter and Sontag and Robbe-Grillet and Seaver and Avedon and Creeley are dead, but even if they are ghosts now, not a day goes by when I don't open the door of my room and invite them in.

December 3, 2014

Barney Rosset, Photo by Casey Kelbaugh

quelques parisien

introduction

LOIS OPPENHEIM

Dear Mr. Beckett pays homage—through letters, interviews, contracts, photos, and scribbles—to two extraordinary men of letters and the relationship between them: One definitively changed the world of publishing by his uncanny sense of who and when, by his courage and perserverance before the laws of censorship, and by being outrageous when it mattered most. The other revolutionized the theatre and the broader literary landscape by giving remarkable shape in word and image to the shapelessness of life.

Barney Rosset was indefatigable and voracious (whatever the arena!). He had a sharp wit and a devilish smile. Samuel Beckett was contemplative, introverted, at times seemingly aloof.

All red doodles are by Barney Rosset

But Rosset's world was labyrinthine—so much of 20th century culture related to him in one way or another—and when you entered it, you were there to stay. Beckett did and was.

Unknown in this country and little known abroad, Beckett was virtually introduced to the English-speaking world in the 1950s by Rosset, who published his work not only at Grove Press but in the literary magazine *Evergreen Review* where the author's work appeared almost continually from the first issue to the last. Rosset had purchased Grove's backlist of three books for $3,000 in 1951 and was on his way to creating a publishing house that would become a cultural icon. Sylvia Beach, who published James Joyce in Paris and owned the Shakespeare & Co. bookstore there, phoned Rosset one day to suggest that Grove publish *Waiting for Godot*, already rejected by Simon & Schuster and elsewhere. In agreeing to publish *Godot*, a tragicomedy written by an Irish writer first in French, Rosset made what was a determining decision for the press and for himself; he would remain Beckett's "main man" in the U.S. until the writer's death in 1989.

Repeatedly, Rosset depicted himself as an amoeba, an amoeba with tentacles that moved toward any unfilled corners and a brain at its center ensuring that it did so with intelligence. Grove was one such corner; the writings of Alain Robbe-Grillet, Eugène Ionesco, Jean-Paul Sartre, Simone de Beauvoir, Marguerite Duras, Harold Pinter, Brendan Behan, Bertolt Brecht, Henry Miller, D.H. Lawrence, Malcolm X, Allen Ginsberg, William Burroughs, Jack Kerouac, and Samuel Beckett were others.

His amoeba brain notwithstanding, Rosset had an impetuousness about him, a quality historian and biographer Laurence Bergreen also discovered in Beckett, whom Bergreen depicted in *Esquire* as "not simply a somber sage," but having within him

Selection of Grove Press covers

"passion and joy and even recklessness" contrary to the austere portrait so often painted of him. "Like many," wrote Bergreen in 1990, "I had assumed that he dwelt in the same barren and hopeless circumstances as the tramps and crones who populate his imagination." He discovered otherwise and it is perhaps this "otherwise" that engendered Beckett's deep affection for Rosset. Indeed, Rosset was similarly characterized by Bergreen as being "closer in spirit to Huckleberry Finn than the Marquis de Sade" in spite of "his reputation as the enfant terrible of American publishing." (Interestingly, Nobel Laureate Kenzaburō Ōe similarly referred to Rosset as "my Huckleberry Finn." He did so first in a letter and then repeatedly thereafter, which pleased Rosset enormously.)

Beckett was a quiet activist, whether by way of his involvement in the French Resistance during the Second World War, the dedication of his 1982 play *Catastrophe* to the imprisoned Czech President Vaclav Havel, or his by no means overtly political, but nonetheless radical writing: He challenged theatrical norms by creating a central character who never appears and another that is but a disembodied mouth. He challenged the norms of fiction by doing away with characters (as we knew them) and plot alike. Rosset's activism was anything but quiet: To bring the reader *Tropic of Cancer*, "he went to court in sixty separate state and local prosecutions, six state supreme court rulings, and a U.S. Supreme Court hearing," summed up fellow publisher John Oakes. He challenged American sensibilities beginning at age twelve, when he affirmed just how important he perceived Benito Mussolini to be—an affirmation that the FBI erroneously construed as admiration in the voluminous file it maintained on Rosset. As Oakes describes it, "laws, cultural mores, and finances could not stop him," and "Rosset was to become "*the* great cultural impresario of the postwar era," "the champion of what was once known as 'the underground,'" for which he endured the wrath not only of the FBI and many a U.S. court of law, but the U.S. Post Office and even other publishers. Asked by Oakes how he earned his reputation as a "subversive," Rosset replied he couldn't answer, that that was "a 'do you still beat your wife' question."

As if there weren't enough hazard in his professional life, Rosset not infrequently dreamt of being a circus aerialist— spotlight on him, appropriately attired—as Randy Sue Coburn revealed in *The Washington Star*. Yet there was this: He knew nothing whatsoever about being an acrobat! The dreamland trapeze bar suddenly swinging toward him, Rosset characteristically if illogically would reason, "This is obviously what I am, so I must know what to do." Not knowing how to prevent the worst, he was steadfastly confident that something would save him. Truth be told, this is how Rosset lived. And to this daring—that took the form of groundbreaking obscenity trials and a life on the precipice of bankruptcy—is owed the publication of *Lady Chatterley's Lover*, *Tropic of Cancer*, and a good deal more.

"How's my American rogue?" Beckett, eager to hear news of Rosset, fondly inquired in 1986 of Everett Frost, producer of the writer's radio plays. Rosset's roguish ways endeared him to some and infuriated others—prosecutors mainly—and, as Mike Zwerin reported in the *International Herald Tribune*, he basked "in the rogue role—continually reminding you how good he was at it." "When I started Grove Press in 1951," Rosset told Zwerin, "publishing *Tropic of Cancer* was my immediate objective. I only started with *Lady Chatterley's Lover* because it was more sedate. … I thought I'd lead with that and build up to *Tropic of Cancer*."

What he built up to first was being arrested! The judge, as most magistrates he encountered were wont to do, would eventually rule in Rosset's favor, but what Rosset referred to "with a killer smile" (Zwerin's observation) as "great trials" was not the only form taken by the many controversies in which he became embroiled.

The acquisition of Grove Press in 1985 by Ann Getty and George Weidenfeld provided many a reporter plenty of "dirt," courtesy of the court battle that followed Rosset's firing from Grove (that he would remain as President was essential to the contract he had signed). The coverage of Rosset's banishment went international. The French daily *Le Monde* reported on the 6th of June, 1986:

> L'homme qui, aux Etats-Unis, a publié Samuel Beckett, Jorge Luis Borges, Eugène Ionesco, Jean Genet, Marguerite Duras, D.H. Lawrence, J. Kerouac, H. Selby, Jean Cocteau, Alfred Jarry, André Malraux, Durrenmat, Pablo Neruda, François Truffaut, D.T. Suzuki, Alain Robbe-Grillet et Henry Miller vient de perdre tout pouvoir dans la maison d'édition qu'il avait créée voilà trente-cinq ans.

> [The man who, in the United States, published Samuel Beckett, Jorge Luis Borges, Eugène Ionesco, Jean Genet, Marguerite Duras, D.H. Lawrence, J. Kerouac, H. Selby, Jean Cocteau, Alfred Jarry, André Malraux, Durrenmat, Pablo Neruda, François Truffaut, D.T. Suzuki, Alain Robbe-Grillet and Henry Miller has just lost all power in the publishing house he created thirty-five years ago.]

A petition demanding that the new Grove owners remain independent with Rosset at the helm or be bought out by "*des propriétaries plus intéressants*" was circulated at a gathering of writers and agents celebrating Beckett's 80th birthday. The petition would have been newsworthy for simply bearing the signatures of William Burroughs, Allen Ginsberg, Hubert Selby, John Rechy, Robert Coover, Jim Caroll, Kathy Acker, Lawrence Ferlinghetti, Nat Sobel and Samuel Beckett.

So, too, the imbroglio that surrounded the publication of Beckett's *Eleutheria* was hardly insignificant. This battle, which took place in the early 1990s and remained out of court, pitted the Executor of the Beckett Estate (the playwright had died in '89) against Rosset who wanted to publish posthumously the work given him by Beckett some years prior. Not wanting to translate the play into English—Beckett was already 80 when the idea of publishing the work arose—Beckett had substituted *Stirrings Still* as a "gift" for Rosset instead. Ever determined to put *Eleutheria* in print, Rosset went so far as to form a new publishing house (together with John Oakes and Dan Simon)—Foxrock, Inc. (named for the Dublin suburb where Beckett was born)—and, like so many times before, the ever determined Rosset—Beckett's "American rogue"—prevailed.

If personality and the selection of titles to put in print were more conspicuously entwined than one typically finds in a publisher (an interviewer for *The Paris Review* called Grove "an extension" of Rosset's personality), it was not that his steadfastness and, indeed, his tendency toward the subversive were without encouragement. A student of the progressive Francis W. Parker School in Chicago (where, in an attempt to make known his c. 1938 antiwar feelings, he organized a revolution, attacked the school and put up a flag declaring the creation of a new country), he was part of a multi-year experiment tracking the results of a pedagogical environment wherein students had no entrance requirements (grades or other) for college or university. His inclination for dissident publishing showed itself early: Rosset and his eighth-grade friend, Haskell Wexler, put out their own newspaper. "First we called it the Sommunist—a combination of 'socialism' and 'communism,'" he told Oakes. "Then we got a little irritated with that and changed it to the Anti-Everything." That he was already thinking about publishing while at Parker is further evidenced by his having crossed out the G on all his textbooks published by Grosset and Dunlap.

As Rosset told theatre director Marek Kedzierski, "Although the idea of being defiant was certainly there, it wasn't quite as apparent to us as it maybe appeared from the outside. We were allowed and encouraged to take what one might think of as radical stances towards politics, towards personal relations; when it became defiance was after we left school and we faced the outside world. In order to keep on living as we had in high school we had to become quite defiant."

Joan Mitchell, the well-known abstract expressionist painter who would become the first of Rosset's five wives, was at Parker with him. "He ran his class," she once related. "Everybody looked up to him. He had a car before anyone else had a car, but that wasn't it. He was shy and he didn't talk well and he became class president; and he was a little guy and skinny, with thick glasses, and he became the football star." Clearly, there was something in Rosset that resonated with the lessons in free and independent thinking at Parker, something that already commanded the respect of his peers and set the stage for his doing ever after

Barney and Astrid visiting Beckett's birthplace in Dublin

exactly as he wished. And clearly this 'something' in Rosset resonated with the aesthetically defiant Beckett.

Like Beckett, moreover, Rosset was Irish at his core (though the former's exile to France was self-imposed while the latter's U.S. citizenship was a result of his Irish grand-parents transplanting to the Middle West). Trinity College Dublin, which Beckett had attended in the 1920s, invited Rosset to speak at a 50th anniversary celebration of *Waiting for Godot* in 2003. The long-awaited first trip to Ireland so consumed him that he obtained an Irish passport in recognition of his genealogy. Listen to Frank Shouldice in the *Irish Independent*, writing at the time of Rosset's visit to the homeland of his maternal grand-parents whose conversations in Irish he had listened to as a child: "[A]t Trinity Barney Rosset feels the emotion return in waves. He produces his Irish passport from an inside pocket. He's here, at last."

Perhaps more than anything, what they had in common was perseverance. "I can't go on, I'll go on" are the concluding words spoken by the Unnamable in the final novel of the author's celebrated trilogy. Rosset personified these words—in court and out: After being roughly bounced from Grove Press by Ann Getty (the oil heiress) and British publisher George Weidenfeld in 1985, Rosset established another publishing house, Rosset & Co., and then Blue Moon Books, which put into print Beckett's *Stirrings Still*, Marguerite Duras' *The Man Sitting in the Corridor*, Kenzaburō Ōe's *Seventeen and J*, among other books.

Rosset and Beckett individually earned numerous prestigious awards for their achievements. Beyond such accolades, however, it is the "unofficial" expressions of gratitude for the legacy of each—as expressed both in the personal statements and the creative work of so many—that drives home the global impact of both these men. As Oakes said of Rosset, "Whether they knew it or not, hipsters everywhere were under his sway. And some of us with soft hands, eager to join Barney's legions in battle, could never shake his influence." "He made publishing a romantic endeavor," he went on to explain. Told of this volume in progress, filmmaker D. A. Pennebaker wrote, "Barney was always interesting to me because he knew what would last and what was dross. I think he was born knowing. Very few are and he lived on the edge of that." Journalist/novelist Mike Golden commented, "Barney had the most amazing ability to like and respect most of his enemies, after acknowledging their transgressions." As for Beckett, over and above his revolutionizing of world literature, what greater testimony might there be than the many visual artists (Georg Baselitz, Charles Klabunde, Avigdor Arikha, Jasper Johns, Louis le Brocquy, and Edward Gorey among them) who strove to make visual Beckett's "painterly" writing? Choreographers (Anna Sokolow's dance version of *Act Without Words I* comes readily to mind), composers (Morton Feldman and Philip Glass, to cite but two), and a legion of writers have found in Beckett a unique legitimacy for their own creative endeavors. When "Waiting for Krazy" was aired in 1958 by CBS's Camera Three (and was shown at the Museum of Modern Art in a 1962 television retrospective), it was clear that Beckett's work had already infiltrated a whole other cultural level.

Rosset and Beckett's relationship extended beyond the traditional author-publisher dyad to a friendship vital to each, as the many unpublished letters and documents included here amply reveal. From "Dear Mr. Beckett" to "Dear Samuel Beckett" and then "Dear Sam," the shift from formality to familiarity in the opening of the letters is paralleled by the ever-increasing warmth of their contents. From "Sincerely, Barney Rosset" to "Love, Barney" and then "All our love to you and Suzanne, Barney," the even more conspicuous shift in the closing of the letters bears further witness to the bond they shared. Rosset, in fact, would go so far as to name his son "Beckett."

Rosset would disclose to his Irish friend the distress and joy that accompanied the defeats and successes of his professional as well as his personal life. As the vicissitudes of both steepened, the friendship only deepened. The previously unseen letters to Beckett leaves one not only with a fascinating insight into the literary and cultural history in which the two figures loomed so large, but the uncanny feeling that one has come to know both men – and know them intimately. Yet it is not just through the letters that we come to know both Rosset and Beckett, but through the myriad other documents offered here for the first time.

Barney Rosset saw himself, as he put it, as an "odd mixture

of Beckett, politics, sex... not academic, not non-academic, a sharp primitive..." In the spirit of his own self-image, this book has been shaped for the general reader. Scholars may gain insight from it, but it is not intended as an academic archive. Barney Rosset as publisher didn't tolerate a great many footnotes and Samuel Beckett didn't tolerate the literary critic (or "crrritic!" as Estragon famously assaults Vladimir in *Godot*). Thus a loosely structured but reasonably chronological compendium is the chosen format, albeit a theatricalized one for the theatre is surely an appropriate frame. The reader may come across the occasional repetition, for some tales were frequently re-recounted in Rosset's own writings and in the many interviews he gave to journalists, documentary filmmakers, potential biographers, scholars, and others. The reader might even encounter the occasional inconsistency, for as Rosset was called upon again and again to relate his experiences he did so as he remembered them at that moment. And not infrequently with a rum-and-Coke in hand.

editorial note

LOIS OPPENHEIM

All quotations following chapter titles are from the works of Samuel Beckett. The doodles are by Samuel Beckett and Barney Rosset; those not identified otherwise are by Rosset. Errors in facsimiles of letters remain, of course, uncorrected. Variant spellings (e.g., End Game, Endgame) appear throughout the volume as will happen with shifts between European and American practice or for reasons unknown (e.g., Eleutheria vs. Eleuthéria, which is not explainable by English vs. French as Rosset's Foxrock edition has the accent while the Faber & Faber edition does not). 'L'Inno,' which appears throughout the Rosset letters, refers to Beckett's novel *L'Innommable*. Titles are italicized as is customary, wherever possible, but underlined in typewritten material (or not, if Rosset neglected to do so) and other documents that pre-date computer usage.

Dramatis Personae

F. Murray Abraham: American actor. Appeared in the 1988, Lincoln Center production of *Waiting for Godot*

Joanne Akalaitis: Contemporary American theatre director

Edward Albee: American playwright; winner of numerous awards, including three Pulitzer Prizes for Drama

Donald Albery: British theatre producer

Donald Allen: Among the earliest and most influential editors at Grove Press and *Evergreen Review*

Deirdre Bair: American biographer; author of a biography of Beckett

Sylvia Beach: American-born bookseller and publisher who lived most of her life in Paris; proprietor of Shakespeare and Co. bookstore

Edward Beckett: Nephew of Beckett and Executor of the Samuel Beckett Estate

Albert Bermel: Theatre academic and translator

Tom Bishop: Florence Gould Professor of French Literature and Director, The Center for French Civilization and Culture, New York University

Roger Blin: French theatre director; directed first performances of *Waiting For Godot* and *Endgame*

Georges Borchardt: Literary agency, Georges Borchardt, Inc. Became Beckett's agent when Rosset removed as such by the Estate

John Bottoms: Beckett actor, played Clov in *Endgame*

Patrick Bowles: Collaborated with Beckett on English translation of *Molloy*

Charles Boyer: French actor who starred in many American movies

Barbara Bray: British translator; longtime friend and companion of Beckett

Bertolt Brecht: Twentieth-century German playwright

Michael Brodsky: Writer and English translator of *Eleutheria*

Louis le Brocquy: Twentieth-century Irish painter; illustrator of *Stirrings Still*

Robert Brustein: Founder, Yale Repertory Theatre and American Repertory Theatre; theatre critic for *The New Republic*

William S. Burroughs: American novelist, author of *Naked Lunch*

John Calder: Beckett's publisher in England

Ruby Cohn: Professor of Comparative Drama, University of California, Davis, who was a leading authority on Beckett's work

Kay Cicellis: Author who wrote in English and Greek; published by Grove

Joe Coffey: Cameraman on *FILM*

Michael Coffey: author and former journalist

Suzanne Deschevaux-Dumesnil: Wife of Samuel Beckett

Marguerite Duras: French writer, associated with the *nouveau roman* ("new novel"), and film director

Alvin Epstein: Beckett actor, *Krapp's Last Tape*, 1994

Jason Epstein: Editor and publisher; a founder of *The New York Review* and of the Library of America

Martin Esslin: English producer and scholar; coined the term "Theatre of the Absurd"

Tom Ewell: Actor who played Vladimir in 1956 American première of *Waiting for Godot* at Coconut Grove Playhouse in Miami, Florida

Faber: Faber and Faber Limited (usually abbreviated to Faber) British publishing house

Ray Federman: French-American academic; also novelist, poet, translator, and critic

Howard Fertig: Publisher, Howard Fertig, Inc.

Wallace Fowlie: Writer and professor of literature with whom Rosset studied at the New School

Martin Garbus: First Amendment lawyer, legal counsel for *Eleutheria*

Jeremy Geidt: Actor who played in *Waiting for Godot*, 1995

Jules Geller: Writer/Editor and a former director of *Monthly Review*

Jean Genet: French novelist and playwright; a political activist and avant-garde author

Bernard Gersten: Executive Producer of Lincoln Center Theater from 1985 to 2013

Niklaus Gessner: Writer and filmmaker

Allen Ginsberg: American poet and leading figure of the Beat Generation

Maurice Girodias: French publisher and founder of Olympia Press

Jerome Gold: Author and founding publisher of Black Heron Press

Mike Golden: Journalist, novelist, editor and publisher of the online magazine *Smoke Signals*

S. E. Gontarski: Professor and noted Beckett scholar

Edward de Grazia: Free-speech lawyer, professor, playwright; worked closely with Rosset and Grove Press in the 1960s

Dan Greene: Publisher, Weidenfeld & Nicolson and CEO, Wheatland Corporation's publishing division (Weidenfeld & Nicolson and Grove Press) 1985-1989

Graham Greene: Twentieth-century English novelist

Andre Gregory: American theatre director

Mel Gussow: American theatre critic for the *New York Times*

Ben Halley, Jr.: Played Hamm in *Endgame*

Hamish Hamilton: British book publishing house (founded by Jamie Hamilton in 1931)

Vaclav Havel: Czech writer and "absurdist" playwright; last President of Czechoslovakia, first President of the Czech Republic

Chris Hegedus: New York documentary filmmaker and wife of D.A. Pennebaker

Eugene Ionesco: Romanian-born playwright associated with the theatre of the absurd; lived in Paris and wrote primarily in French

Bill Irwin: American actor. Appeared in the 1988, Lincoln Center production of *Waiting for Godot*

Spoon Jackson: Serving prison term of life without parole since 1978; actor in San Quentin production of *Waiting for Godot*

Jan Jonson: Actor and director of the Royal Dramatic Theatre in Stockholm; staged *Waiting for Godot* at San Quentin and other prisons

Ken Jordan: New York writer and publisher; son of Fred Jordan of Grove Press

Fred Jordan: Editor at Grove Press and Managing Editor of *Evergreen Review*

Deborah Karl: Former literary agent

Boris Kaufman: Oscar-winning cinematographer who shot *FILM*

Marek Kedzierski: Polish writer, translator, stage director, and theatre critic

Franz Kline: American painter; major figure in the abstract expressionist movement of the mid-twentieth century

Wilhelm de Kooning: Dutch American abstract expressionist painter

Daniel Labeille: Producer of the world premiere of *Rockaby*, under the auspices of Programs in the Arts – State University of New York

Bert Lahr: Actor who played Estragon in American première of *Waiting for Godot* at Coconut Grove Playhouse in Miami, Florida, and in first Broadway production of *Waiting for Godot*

Jérôme Lindon: Publisher of Les Editions de Minuit and Beckett's French publisher

David Mamet: Contemporary American playwright

Steve Martin: American actor. Appeared in the 1988, Lincoln Center production of *Waiting for Godot*.

E.G. Marshall: Played Vladimir in first Broadway production of *Waiting for Godot*

Jack MacGowran: Irish Beckett actor

Barry McGovern: Irish Beckett actor

Marilynn Meeker: Editor, Grove Press

Deryk Mendel: Beckett performer and director

Joan Mitchell: Abstract expressionist painter; Rosset's first wife

Gregory Mosher: American theatre director and producer

MichaeMyerberg: Theatre producer; produced the first American production of *Waiting for Godot* which took place in Miami, Florida

John Oakes: Former Grove Press Editor and founding publisher of OR Books

Kenzaburō Ōe: Contemporary Japanese author; awarded the Nobel Prize in Literature in 1994

Harold Oram: Prospective American backer for English-language *Waiting for Godot*

Estelle Parsons: American actor

D.A. Pennebaker: New York documentary filmmaker; filmed Alan Schneider directing Billie Whitelaw in *Rockaby* (1981)

Harold Pinter: British playwright; Nobel Laureate

Jackson Pollock: American abstract expressionist painter best known for his "drip paintings"

Richard "Dick" Powell: American actor, film producer, and director

George Reavey: Publisher and translator; Beckett's first literary agent

Kenneth Rexroth: American poet, translator, and critic

Jean-Paul Riopelle: Canadian painter and sculptor

Alain Robbe-Grillet: French writer associated with the *nouveau roman* ("new novel")

Marion Saunders: New York literary agent representing Minuit and Beckett

Robert Scanlan: Professor of the Practice of Theatre, Harvard University; past Literary Director of the American Repertory Theater

Judith Schmidt Douw: Rosset's assistant at Grove Press

Alan Schneider: American theatre director of Samuel Beckett's work

Richard ("Dick") Seaver: Editor at Grove Press; Associate Editor, *Evergreen Review*

Jeff Sewald: Writer/filmmaker

Martin Siegel: New York attorney

Dan Simon: Editor and publisher; founder of Seven Stories Press

Susan Sontag: Writer; film and theatre producer

Patsy Southgate: Writer and translator

Patrick Stewart: English stage and screen actor. Appeared in 2013, New York production of *Waiting for Godot*

Tom Stoppard: Award-winning British playwright; knighted in 1997

Jerry Tallmer: Writer and theatre critic, early supporter of Beckett's work

Alexander Trocchi: Twentieth-century Scottish novelist; an editor of *Merlin*, magazine that first published Beckett in English

Austryn Wainhouse: American author, publisher, and translator

Lord George Weidenfeld: British publisher; together with Ann Getty (wife of Gordon Getty), acquired Grove Press in 1985

Shirley Wilber: Beckett actor, played Nell in *Endgame*

Walter Winchell: Newspaper and radio commentator (famously referred to *Waiting for Godot* as "a dramatic whatzit")

Billie Whitelaw: English actor and foremost female interpreter of Beckett's work

Thornton Wilder: American playwright and novelist; three-time winner of the Pulitzer Prize and winner of National Book Award

Robin Williams: American actor and comedian. Appeared in the 1988, Lincoln Center production of *Waiting for Godot*

Shelley Winters: American film, stage, and television actor

Irene Worth: Leading actor of British and American theatre

LA RECHERCHE
LES TIGRES
LES CHATEAUX CHIMONS
L'ELEPHANTS

prologue

ROSSET ON... ROSSET

On First Meeting Beckett

It was probably Sylvia Beach who first seriously talked to me about Samuel Beckett, in New York, in 1953. As the proprietor of Shakespeare and Co., the leading English-language bookstore for many years in Paris and close friend and publisher of James Joyce, she had known Sam Beckett for many years. She recommended him to me in the warmest terms as a coming writer of importance. When I asked Wallace Fowlie, who had been my professor at the New School in New York, to read Beckett and give me his opinion, he confirmed what Sylvia Beach had told me, and what I also felt myself. And so we got our most important author, and shortly after that my then wife Loly and I went to Paris for the first of many meetings with Sam.

We met Beckett at the bar of the Pont Royal Hotel on the Rue Montalembert almost next door to France's largest literary publisher, Gallimard. Beckett came in, tall, trench-coated and taciturn, on his way to another date, he told us. He said that he had only time for one quick one. "He arrived late," Loly remembered. "He looked most uncomfortable and never said a word except that he had to leave. I was pained by his shyness, which matched Barney's and, in desperation, I told him how much I had enjoyed reading *Godot*." At that, we clicked, and he became warm and fun. We went to dinner and to various bars, ending up at his old hangout, *La Coupole*, on the Boulevard Montparnasse at three in the morning with Beckett ordering champagne. Beckett wrote me a year later: "It's hard to go on with everything loathed and repudiated as soon as formulated, and in the act of formulation, and before formulation... I'm horribly tired and stupefied, but not yet tired and stupefied enough. To write is impossible, but not yet impossible enough."

On Corresponding with Beckett

Our correspondence, formal at first, warmed quickly. Sometimes Beckett typed, at my rather brash request, and sometimes letters were written in Beckett's almost inscrutable script. "You know, Barney, I think my writing days are over," Beckett writes in 1954. And later, "Sick of all this old vomit and despair more and more of ever being able to puke again." "Perhaps I can feel a little bit of what you are going through," I wrote the same year. In a world where writers switch publishers at the first shake of a martini pitcher, our trans-Atlantic communications seemed to float on a sea of tranquility and trust.

On Beckett

I think Beckett was a different person to every different person. To me, my image of Beckett was that he was a great psychiatrist, or a great psychoanalyst who had many patients. Let's say he was Freud. And to each patient he was the best friend of that person. And that person thought the only person who knew him as well was Beckett; there was nobody else. And also, therefore, it worked in reverse. Not necessarily true, but whoever Beckett was with, dealing with, the subject, he was in it 100% and could give you the impression that you were the only person. That came to me after a while because I couldn't believe how he could pay as much attention to everybody as he did to me. But I think I was wrong. He paid a lot of attention to everybody—to each person.

(Interview with Jeff Sewald)

On Beckett's Work

SEWALD: Albee has said that Beckett's work is written almost like music. The way it sounded was very important to him.

ROSSET: Absolutely. Two other playwrights, who are very much like Beckett even though the subject matter is totally different, are Pinter and Mamet. They are like an American baseball team, a double play combination. It was from Mamet to Pinter to Beckett and out. The important thing is the timing. The timing in Mamet and the timing in Pinter is, to me, very much like Beckett, even though the subject matter, the feeling, etc., can be totally different. There is a kinship, particularly between those three.

SEWALD: Do you think Mamet was affected by Beckett's work?

ROSSET: Tremendously. Absolutely, especially in timing. He can be talking about a real estate theft or something, but the spacing, the timing is absolutely all important in catching the feeling of the theatre.

Krapp's Last Tape was my favorite thing Beckett did. It's about a real life thing that happened. Beckett had a girlfriend whose father was a professor in Germany, but he was Jewish-Irish. It was right when Hitler was coming in; which was bad timing. But on the coast, France, Germany, on the north, he was in love with this young woman, he told me, and she left him and went off with somebody else. And I'd had a very similar thing with a very close young woman whom I'd grown up with and another student friend of ours. It was my best friend, Haskell Wexler, and she left me and married him. I don't think I ever recovered. How I stayed friends with Haskell, I don't know, but I did. And that story struck me as very similar, and it did Beckett too. There's another novel that's talked about in *Krapp's Last Tape*, a character named Effi from a novel *Effi Briest*, which I never read. I've looked for it. I don't know if it was ever translated. Beckett was very fluent in German, which I was not. So I never read *Effi Briest*, but he told me the story of that novel, it sounded like the same thing. And that story of this young woman in Germany seemed to me the crucial love affair of Beckett's life. That touched me very much.

SEWALD: *Krapp's Last Tape* is many people's favorite. Why do you think that is?

ROSSET: I don't know. Why is *Ulysses* good?

(Interview with Jeff Sewald)

On Waiting for Godot

I certainly think he was, in the good sense of the word, in the avant-garde of writing. He was the cutting edge of trying to find something new, a new kind of expression that wasn't built on a story line. When *Waiting for Godot* opened, for example, it seemed absolutely inscrutable to people. In a sense, it was like a Jackson Pollock painting. People could not understand; what is this about? Why doesn't he go from a to b to c? Why isn't there a climax? All of these various things and it seemed intractable to understanding and yet now, today, sports writers, for example, constantly refer to *Waiting for Godot* as if now, we… it seems part of our lives. He always probed further and further and further. Beckett also got more and more set on his directions but his were to get more and more sparse and visual, actually. He was really going from writing to the visual image and many of the last things he did were for television. He was a man of his times; he was not a throwback to the past. He was always going, trying something new and using the technological discoveries of today. There was a bit of the physicist in Beckett and yet there was a great deal of emotion.

When you see *Waiting for Godot* you can look at it many ways. There are many literary allusions, there are all sort of things, layers and layers of understanding and writing which make it very, you know, a great deal of fun for historians and academics of all kinds. But on the other hand, to me, there was one, very simple thing, one human relationship, which was between, in this case, Beckett and his wife, in a deserted area. It's specifically named in the play in the end. It's in the south of France where he and Suzanne were for quite a long time together and I get this whole thing of their being bored with each other, not knowing what to do, when the hell are they going to get out of there, not ever wanting to see each other again and she, in the play, she/he, he removed either of the sexual differentiations, she leaves and goes out and comes back the next day and all of their efforts to converse with each other at one point... Vladimir says, 'well, let's hang ourselves. At least that way I'll have an erection.' Which was censored in London.

That was one of Beckett's great fears...that all of his work would be censored for obscenity. And that, I think, was part of his using the French language; people wouldn't notice it in French, whereas in English we're all very familiar with various words that take on another feeling in an Anglo-Saxon environment. So that's what it was about. And he transformed that very real human situation which we've all known at one time or another and converted it into an eternal situation, you know, a great myth. A myth that's open to many, many interpretations but coming out of a very, very real thing where two people are just bored to death and there's no other human conversation possible with outsiders. On a farm, waiting. Waiting for many things; they could be waiting for the war to end; they could be waiting to get rid of each other; they could be waiting to have an affair with someone else; waiting to die. All of that. So Beckett goes from that very simple human thing to great universalities and along the way throws in his Irish background, his Joycean background, his great knowledge, which is Dante, etc.

(Interview with Patsy Southgate)

On a Production of *Endgame*

When Joanne Akalaitis, who had done some things of Beckett but not theatre as such, had taken prose material and converted it into dramatic form, asked Beckett if she could do *Endgame* and he said yes, apparently it didn't occur to him that she would also transform the play into something more following her own vision which was not the same as Beckett's. Oddly enough I never saw it, but I keep thinking I saw it because I dreamt of seeing it all the time. I dreamt of going to the theatre, I dreamt of the sidewalks, the streets, the theatre, the play, but I did send Fred Jordan of Grove and other people. I read all the reviews and so did Beckett and in this case Beckett reacted very strongly and called me, which was fairly unusual, in New York and demanded that I get it stopped, as if I had the power to get it stopped. We had made a contract with the theatre to put on *Endgame* making it implicit that they wouldn't change the play. So I set about trying to get them to stop and it was extremely difficult and I became sort of the messenger who gets killed trying to deliver the message. The theatre got the Harvard University lawyer and the State of Massachusetts to defend them and I had Martin Garbus and we tried. We offered to let the play go on if they would take Beckett's name off of it or if they would say it was an adaptation of Beckett and they refused those things. But we did get them to give in, I thought very significantly. They had to cease all advertising. They agreed to cease all advertising and they agreed to let us put two, two or three, pages of the text as written by Beckett into their program and a note from us saying, please, see what you see, and see what Beckett wrote—something to that effect. Which I thought was—chose to believe anyway—was quite a significant victory for us. One of the things they did was they cast a black man as the lead part in the play, as Hamm, which wouldn't have mattered if they had done it because he was a good actor but that was obviously not the case. They dressed him as an African king and also the mother and father, one of them was black, I've forgotten if it was the mother or father, which made the play take on overtones of being a play about misogynation and Beckett said that. If he'd meant that he would have written it that way and I said so and I was accused by Actor's Equity of being a racist and censored for it. Later they apologized to me but that did not get into *The New York Times*.

There is so much silence in Beckett's writing and the words are so spare that they almost invite people to think they could do it better, they could flesh it out, they could change it, transform it and take what they think was Beckett's outline and make it into something totally different.

(Interview with Patsy Southgate)

On FILM

I think Beckett was very interested in film but, unfortunately, it wasn't carried through. That was our own fault, in a way. We made a film, spent too much and then lost about a third of it. We tried to copy Orson Welles; I mean very deliberately and carefully and with people who were highly skilled. But the people who made the film were filmmakers that I didn't know. I liked their films and went and found them and hired them. I put them together, but not necessarily well. So I think we cut short his film career; we gave him an opening and then closed it.

We had tried Charlie Chaplin for FILM, but I got a letter saying Chaplin doesn't read scripts. I wrote back and said, "I'm sorry; I didn't know Mr. Chaplin couldn't read." That ended that.

(Interview with Jeff Sewald)

GELLER: How did you get Beckett to make a film?

ROSSET: I asked him. Nobody had ever asked him before.

(Interview with Jules Geller)

On Stirrings Still

SEWALD: Tell me a little bit about *Stirrings Still*. He dedicated that to you.

ROSSET: That was apologetically, really. Everything that Beckett had done in the past, that he gave to us to publish, he would then say, "I don't want it." So I had gotten used to that. It meant like two or three years would go by before he would say, "Well, okay, go ahead." That happened several times on several books. And the last time was the most important. When I left Grove, he gave me his play, *Eleutheria*, which I didn't really know too much about. And I liked it very, very much. And Beckett said, "I'm going to translate it for you." Then, "It's awful, terrible." But he had done that over and over again. So it didn't really bother me. And he said, "I will give you something else." I think he said he would write then. I never felt secure in that belief, but he said it was brand new and he would give me that and he did and we published it. But I was waiting, really, honestly, for *Eleutheria*. And I felt very confident that within two years, he would have said, "Well go ahead," but he died; so he didn't. *Stirrings Still*. It did mean a lot to me. ... It was reminiscent of a situation; which I think we had both talked about—somebody is dying and slowly becomes blind and loses all ability to have any touching, any sensual feeling for anybody; anything outside of himself. I'd had a dream myself, as a child, when I had a tonsillectomy or something. I was given ether; it was an ether dream, a terrible nightmare of becoming blind. You feel alive and you can hear, and so on but you can't touch anybody else. And that's what *Stirrings Still* was about, to me. So it was important, but it did not replace *Eleutheria*.

(Interview with Jeff Sewald)

It's very short, the whole thing, but it's divided into three sections. First he wrote two sections and he called it "Fragments." "Fragments I and II." In the meantime, I'd seen Marguerite Duras and she said, "I've got to give you something" and—a very sweet, a very nice acquiescence of Pantheon—she took back from them a 'novella' which was long enough to be published as a book in France. But so was Beckett's "Stirring Still" and to us it's a different kind of publishing; it's so short.

Marguerite Duras and Barney, 1967

So I had these two things and I got Barbara Bray to translate the Duras, and I think she did it very beautifully; I still have it, unpublished. But I had these two things and I puzzled and puzzled as to how to make them seem to have enough weight, so to speak, as a publishing venture, and it occurred to me that I would do each of them as a nice little hardcover book and then put them in a box together. And I told this to Beckett and he was not pleased. He didn't say that, he just didn't like the idea of being published with another author. So then, when I got back to New York I got a note from him saying, you know, "Dear Barney, if I write more for you, will you publish it by itself?" So I cabled him back saying, "yes indeed I will do it by itself" and he added a very short additional piece of like one page and that's part three, but he then gave it a different name, "Stirrings Still." I was still puzzled as to how to publish it and my English friend John Calder said, "Let's do a small, limited edition by itself, a beautiful thing." And that seemed to me to solve the problem nicely and it was to have an artist illustrate it and, naturally, I wanted Joan to be the person and as far as I can tell from anything she said, the answer was 'yes' and she was going to go ahead … [but] she didn't do it. An Irish painter, Louis le Brocquy—who I was pleased to have Joan tell me was good—was really unknown to me although he was apparently well known in France and in Ireland. It's a French name but he's very Irish; Irish with a French-sounding name. And it was done…

(Interview with Patsy Southgate)

On Joan Mitchell

JORDAN: Would you say Joan was important to you in your early development, intellectually and artistically?

ROSSET: Oh, artistically, totally. Not politically. I mean I almost destroyed her, made her into a communist. For a painter that was bad news, because that meant socialist realism. But you couldn't keep her down.

JORDAN: Her sense of aesthetics was something that she must have conveyed to you and opened your eyes to art.

ROSSET: Oh, it was an incredible experience. I had watched her change from being a realist to an abstractionist. Day by day. It was very exciting. The figures faded away. The Tour de France, the great bicycle race, went through our little town. We went and watched it and then chased it in a car. She did a beautiful painting. The bicycles all merged. The bicycle wheels went around together. If you saw it now you wouldn't think it was so abstract, but it was like Marcel Duchamp's *Nude Descending a Staircase*. It was absolutely key to her development, and I thought it was fantastic. Then she became more and more abstract, but that painting was key. Later I asked her about that painting, a number of times, and she said, Don't worry, I know where it is. It was in her parents' apartment. I have a photograph of us standing in front of it. It's the only evidence I have of that goddamn painting. I don't know what happened to it.

Joan Mitchell and Barney Rosset, 1948.

While all this was going on we were totally isolated. But

Joan had heard about the New York painters, Hans Hofmann and a little bit about Pollock. Hofmann had a school on Eighth Street, and I just felt maybe that's where she ought to be. I knew it was where I ought to be. So I said, finally, "We'd better go home." She said, "Who's going to carry my paintings—they're big!" I said, "I will, but only if you marry me." Big mistake! She said OK. We got married by the mayor. The ocean liner came and anchored offshore. The paintings went out by rowboat. All those goddamn paintings. We lived here, first on Eleventh Street, way west, almost to the White Horse Tavern—a little house in the back, a dollhouse. Later we lived on Ninth Street. Then Joan left.

JORDAN: She walked out?

ROSSET: She walked out and moved to Tenth Street, where she had a studio. I waited for her to come back. I said, "Joan, you've got to come back—if you don't come back, I'm going to get divorced." "Don't get divorced," she said, "I'll come back." I waited one year. So I finally said, I'm going to Chicago. In Illinois they have extremely liberal divorce laws if you're a resident, which we were not exactly. But her father, *my* father . . . So I went to Chicago. I called her. I said, "Joan, I'm getting divorced tomorrow." I charged her with desertion, and she agreed it was true. One paragraph was the whole divorce thing, and one other sentence. She kept the right to use her maiden name. That's all she wanted! That was the whole settlement.

(Interview with Ken Jordan)

On Dick Seaver

ROSSET: Dick and Alex Trocchi were in Paris together, and they had this magazine called *Merlin*. I never learned all the ins and outs of that, but *Merlin* was the first publisher of Beckett in English. Dick is one of the two people I know who translated anything of Beckett's that got published. Until Beckett said, "Fuck both of you." He loved both this other guy (Austryn Wainhouse) and Dick, but he thought it was better to do it himself. And Dick would be the first to say that. …

GOLDEN: When did you meet Dick Seaver?

ROSSET: I met him in Paris in '53. I had already started publishing *Waiting For Godot*, and I had never heard of Dick Seaver or *Merlin*, so they had no influence on me because I had never heard of them. But when I got to Paris I did hear and I made a big thing out of meeting Dick. I've forgotten how I heard of him, it may well have been Beckett who told me, I don't know. But that's when I met him, and I thought he was marvelous, and immediately wanted him to come to work with me. But it took years for that to happen.

GOLDEN: When did you actually start Grove Press?

ROSSET: '51. I started it in '51. But it was started before me. I think in 1947 on Grove Street by a man named Robert Balcomb, Robert Feltz, and Cynthia Balcomb who owned the house on Grove Street. They started a publishing company to do reprints. They did three books and then quit. Then I bought out Feltz. Bought out—we're talking $1,500. And a trunk full of books. And Balcomb, who I discovered I couldn't live with. So I bought out the remaining copies of these books. So that's when I started, but technically it was started on Grove Street by Balcomb and Feltz.

(From interview with Mike Golden)

On Censorship

The Soviet Union banned both Beckett's *Waiting for Godot* and Henry Miller. Miller, especially, they would use as an example of decadence, whereas he was actually a very good analyst of how monstrous American culture was. That they liked, but they wouldn't publish him. It must have been the sex, or perhaps it was more subtle than that. With Beckett it must have been the hopelessness, although Beckett was published in Poland early on, and successfully.

On . . .

Little did I know what lay ahead of me... I *did* know that Mr. Beckett was going to be a very important person in my publishing life and, as it turned out, in my entire life....

If you ever needed to prove that publishing is a cottage industry, I think the relationship between myself and Mr. Beckett proved it.

(Rosset self-interview)

It's finally gotten around to where it started. It started in my apartment on Ninth Street. Then we moved to Broadway at Eleventh Street, where we had a hot dog stand at the bottom. After that we moved to University Place, then we bought a building on Eleventh Street and built a theatre and a bar. All of my dreams came true. ...

I actually owned my own bar. ... [I]t turned out to be a nightmare. The lesson was, go to other people's bars. Running a bar and a publishing company just don't mix.

Interview with John Oakes

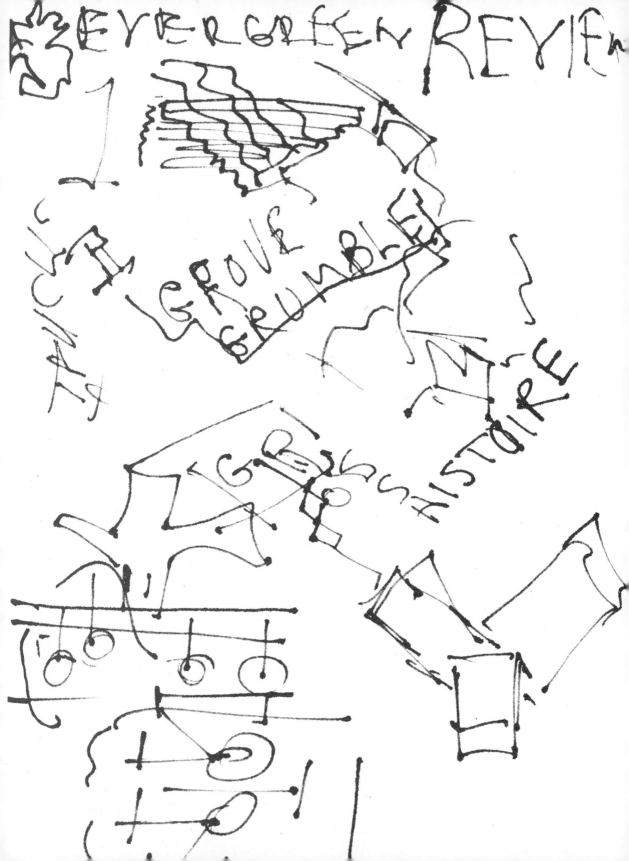

act one

THE EARLY LETTERS

"Words are all we have."

GROVE PRESS

795 BROADWAY, NEW YORK 3, N.Y. • GRAMERCY 3-7447

June 18, 1953

Dear Mr. Beckett,

It is about time that I write a letter to you—now that agents, publishers, friends, etc., have all acted as go-betweens. A copy of our catalogue has already been mailed to you, so you will be able to see what kind of a publisher you have been latched onto. I hope that you won't be too disappointed.

We are very happy to have the contract back from Minuit, and believe me, we will do what we can to make your work known in this country.

The first order of the day would appear to be the translation. I have just sent off a letter to Alex Trocchi telling him that the difficulties did not seem as ominous from here as they evidently do from there to him at least. If you would accept my first choice as translator the whole thing would be easily settled. That choice of course being you. That already apparently is a satisfactory solution insofar as the play is concerned. The agent here tells me that you have agreed to our proposal, and he is drawing up a sample letter contract now, which we will mail to you tomorrow.

I explained to Trocchi at great length, and probably with great density, why I thought it better for Merlin not to publish the first act in advance of book publication. It seems to me that a whole act hardly comes under the heading of an "excerpt" and might really serve to take a little of the edge off of the book publication. I suggested instead that they publish excerpts from the novels whenever pieces are ready, and join me in putting the play out as a book as soon as conveniently possible. I hope that you will join me in this idea. En Attendant Godot should burst upon us as an entity in my opinion.

As for translation of the novels, I am waiting first to hear from you, what you advise, and whether or not you will tackle them yourself. If your decision is no, and I do hope that it won't be, we can discuss between us the likely people to do it.

Sylvia Beach is certainly the one you must blame for your future appearance on the Grove Press list. I went to see her with your work on my mind, and after she talked of you in beautiful words I immediately decided that what the Grove Press needed most in the world was Samuel Beckett. I told her that, and then she suggested that I make a specific offer. I certainly had not thought of that up to the very moment she took out a piece of paper and pencil and prepared to write down the terms.

A second person was also very important. He is Wallace Fowlie. At my request he read the play and the two novels with great care and came back with the urgent plea for me to take on your work. Fowlie is also on our list. His new translation of Rimbaud's Illuminations, and a long study of them, is just now coming out. If you would like it, or any other book on the Grove list, please ask for them and they are yours. To go back—Fowlie has spent many years in France, has written books on Mallarme, a second on Rimbaud, his autobiography (Pantomimes), a book on surrealism, two volumes of poetry written in French, and so on. He does not usually speak in superlatives, but about your work he did, and that weighed a good deal with me. Then of course, I do happen to be the editor and owner of this publishing company, and I like your work too.

Chatto and Windus have not one single copy available of your book on Proust. If you ever come across one I would much appreciate it if you would let me borrow it. Proust is my particular passion and I would so much like to know what you have, or had, to say about him.

This would seem to be an already indecently long letter, so I will close. If you would give me your own address we might be able to communicate directly in the future.

Sincerely,

Barney Rosset

Sylvia Beach (center) with James Joyce and Adrienne Monnier

GROVE PRESS

795 BROADWAY, NEW YORK 3, N.Y. • GRAMERCY 3-7447

July 13, 1953

Dear Mr. Beckett,

It was nice to receive your letter of June 25 and then your letter of July 5.

First I must tell you that I have not received your translation of _Godot_. I am most anxious to see it. I would like to plan on publication of the play for 1954, either in the first or second half of the year, depending entirely upon completion date of the translation. I would think the ideal thing would be to coincide publication with performance, but that is ideal only and I would not think it wise to indefinitely postpone publication while waiting for the performance.

I made an appointment to see Mr. Oram, whom I met briefly some time ago, next Tuesday and we will discuss the whole matter. I was not aware of the fact that Mr. Oram was involved with the theatre and I am still somewhat wondering about it but perhaps I will know more after I have lunch with him. He told me that he was an intimate friend of yours and, of course, I was surprised to hear this.

As to the translation of the novels, I am naturally disappointed to hear that you prefer not to undertake translation yourself. I can well see your point, however, and it would seem a little sad to attempt to take off that much time to go back over your own books but I hope that you will change your mind. I note that _Murphy_ was published in England by Routledge and it does not seem completely out of the question that they would be willing to again publish your books. I will send on to you the first few pages of _Godot_ translated by my acquaintance here and I believe he will also undertake to do a few pages of _Molloy_. I would appreciate it very much if I could also see the specimens given to you by Trocchi provided they are acceptable, or nearly acceptable to you; otherwise there would not be much point in sending them on to me. Of course it would be easier to collaborate with a translator living in France but, on the other hand, correspondence would not seem to be an insurmountable problem.

As to the obscenities within the books, my suggestion is that we do not worry about that until it becomes necessary. Sometimes things like that have a way of solving themselves.

I do hope you locate a copy of _Transition_ with the fragments translated by yourself.

I do plan on going to Europe in the fall, and I will certainly look forward to meeting you then.

Yours Sincerely,

Barney Rosset

CABLE ADDRESS
SAUNDMAR NEWWORK

TELEPHONE
MUrray Hill
5-4667

June 18, 1953

MEMORANDUM OF AGREEMENT BETWEEN SAMUEL BECKETT, c/o LES EDITIONS
DE MINUIT, 7 rue Bernard-Palissy, Paris VI, France (represented by
Marion Saunders, Literary Agency) AND GROVE PRESS, 795 Broadway,
New York, N.Y., COVERING THE ENGLISH TRANSLATION OF EN ATTENDANT
GODOT.

1. Samuel Beckett hereby agrees to translate his play, entitled
in French EN ATTENDANT GODOT, into English, for Grove Press.

2. Grove Press will fully own this translation, and any book
publisher, magazine publisher, play, radio, movie, or television
producer, etc.., in any country, wanting to use that translation,
will have to apply to Grove Press for permission. However, this
shall not be construed as meaning that Grove Press have the right
to print and publish Samuel Beckett's translation of EN ATTENDANT
GODOT in any territories except the ones specified in clause (1)
of the Agreement dated June 2, 1953, between Les Editions de Minuit
and Grove Press, concerning EN ATTENDANT GODOT; nor that they
shall have the right to sell or license the actual publication or
production rights in the book, except the ones specified in clause
(6) of the Agreement mentioned above.

3. In full payment for the ownership of this translation, Grove
Press will pay Samuel Beckett the sum of $150.00 (one hundred
fifty dollars) upon delivery of the English translation, plus a
royalty of 2½% (two and one-half per cent) on the published price
of all copies sold of Grove Press's regular trade edition; payments
shall be made semi-annually, as for the regular royalties.

s/ Samuel Beckett
S/ SAMUEL BECKETT

s/ Barney Rosset
GROVE PRESS
Barney Rosset, Owner

795 BROADWAY, NEW YORK 3, N.Y. ● GRAMERCY 3-7447

July 31, 1953

Dear Mr. Beckett,

Your translation of Godot did finally arrive, and also
I received a copy from Oram. I like it very much, and it seems
to me that you have done a fine job. The long speech by Lucky
is particularly good and the whole play reads extremely well.

If I were to make any criticism it would be that one
can tell that the translation was done by a person more used
to "English" speech than American. Thus the use of words such
as bloody—and a few others—might lead an audience to think the
play was originally done by an Englishman in English. This
is a small point, but in a few places a neutralization of the
speech away from the specifically English flavor might have the
result of enhancing the French origins for an American reader.
Beyond that technical point I have little to say, excepting
that I am now extremely desirous of seeing the play on a
stage—in any language.

I am sending on the fragment of Godot translated by
the man here. You will have to decide from that if his work
interests you. I personally think that he did a rather good
job, but if you much prefer the person you have found then by
all means send me the sample you have. I read the fragments by
you in transition and again I must say that I liked them very
much—leading to the continuance of my belief that you would be
the best possible translator. I really do not see how anybody
else can get the sound quality, to name one thing, but I am
willing to be convinced.

By all means, the translation should be done with only
those modifications required by the change from one language to
another. If an insurmountable obstacle is to appear, let it
first appear.

I will look forward to hearing about progress towards
a translation.

Yours Sincerely,

Barney Rosset

795 BROADWAY, NEW YORK 3, N.Y. • GRAMERCY 3-7447

August 4, 1953

Dear Mr. Beckett,

      I am putting aside <u>Watt</u>, which I received this
morning, to write this letter. Fifty pages poured over me
and I will inundate myself again as soon as possible. One
irritation did jut out at me and that is the lack of good
proofreading in the pages I went through. I do hope that the
misspellings, inverted letters, etc., are dealt with before
the printing is done. To find one word deliberately distorted
and the next botched by the typesetter can spoil the tone
so easily. Also it is a shame that the typeface used is so
scrubby and ugly. Good writing can also look well without
losing any of its intrinsic value—or so it would seem to me.

      After the sample of <u>Godot</u> went back to you, the first
part of <u>Molloy</u> arrived and I was most favorably impressed with
it. I remember Bowles' story in the second issue of <u>Merlin</u> and
it does seem that he has a real sympathy for your writing. If
you feel satisfied, and find it convenient to work with him,
then my opinion would be to tell you to go ahead. Short of
your doing the work yourself the best would be to be able to
really guide someone else along—and that situation you seem to
have found.

      Again a mention of words. Those such as skivvy and
cutty are unknown here, and when used they give the writing
a most definite British stamp. That is perfectly all right if
it is the effect you desire. If you are desirous of a little
more vagueness as to where the scene is set it would be better
to use substitutes which are of common usage both here and in
Britain.

      Watt came here through the good graces of the Marion
Saunders agency. I would think that <u>Merlin</u> would have leaked a
copy out to me, but it did get here so I cannot complain too
bitterly. My suggestion on <u>Watt</u> is that part of the edition
bear the imprint Grove Press on the title page, that the
reverse of the title page say Copyright 1953 (or 54) by Samuel
Beckett, and we will undertake to copyright it for you in this
country. The Grove Press part of the edition, at least, should

be printed on good paper and put in a binding up to American
standards. The books should be sold to us at cost by <u>Merlin</u>
and the profit to you and them (whatever your arrangement with
them is) will come out of royalties on which we will make a
small advance. This will keep the price of the book at the
lowest possible figure and give it a fighting chance to get
sold.

I am happy to be reading Watt and I hope to see more
of <u>Molloy</u> soon.

With Best Regards,

Barney Rosset

October 19, 1953

Dear Samuel Beckett,

Loly and I were sorry not to see you again, but I think our memories of our last visit will last us a while. Loly finished reading Malone Meurt last night and she liked it exceedingly much. Now on to L'Innommable.

This morning I was summoned to the office of one Marion Saunders, literary agent, and was told by same that due to me the New York production had not proceeded. Somehow this was because I have a letter contract with you (drawn up and presented to me by the Marion Saunders office I might add) which necessitated my approval of New York production, plus the implication that I might like to be paid something. It seems that Oram feels that he cannot go around getting permission from two people (you and me). I told Saunders that in the first place I thought it ridiculous to say that our contract had deterred Oram, but that if it actually did I would be only too happy to tell him, in writing, that if he obtained your permission to any production, my permission would automatically go along with yours. My only concern would be to be sure that any cuts, changes, or additions to the script were passed upon and approved by you. That seems both fair and reasonably simple. As to payment, I suggest that I get 1% of the proceeds. I also think that to be fair, but if any violent objections are raised I am certainly not going to stop any serious attempt at production. Incidentally, that 1% would in no way affect anything you are to get.

We like the Molloy translation very much, and we are looking forward very keenly to seeing more. My congratulations to you and Patrick for the good work.

Best,

Barney Rosset

MEMORANDUM OF AGREEMENT made this 2nd day of June 1953, between Les Editions de Minuit, 7 rue Bernard-Palissy, Paris VI, France, represented by Marion Saunders Literary Agency, 104 East 40th Street, New York 16, N.Y., (hereinafter called the Proprietors) of one part, and Grove Press, 795 Broadway, New York, N.Y., (hereinafter called the Publishers) of the other part.

WHEREBY IT IS AGREED by and between the Parties hereto as follows concerning the work entitled in French:

MALONE MEURT by Samuel Beckett

which is hereinafter referred to as the said Work.

1.   The Proprietors grant to the Publishers the sole and exclusive license to print and publish the Work in book form in the English language in the United States of America and its dependencies, and Canada, and the Philippine Islands; and the non-exclusive right to sell it in all other parts of the world outside the British Commonwealth (except Canada). In consideration of the above license, the publishers agree to pay the following royalties:
(a) on the published price of all copies sold of the regular trade edition a royalty at the rate of 7½% (seven and one-half per cent) on the first 3,000 (three thousand) copies; 10% (ten per cent) from 3,000 to 6,000 (three thousand to six thousand) copies; 12½% (twelve and one-half per cent) from 6,000 to 10,000 (six thousand to ten thousand) copies; and 15% (fifteen per cent) thereafter.
(b) 10% (ten per cent) of the sums received where copies of the said Work are sold at special discounts of 50% or more of the retail price. No royalty shall be paid for copies given away for advertising purposes, or for remainders, or damaged copies sold below cost.

2.   The Publishers shall pay to the Proprietors a sum of $400.00 (four hundred dollars) in advance and on account of royalties, this sum to be paid on completion of this agreement.

3.   The Proprietors represent and guarantee to the Publishers that they are the sole owners of the said work, and that they are the owners of all the rights in this agreement granted to the Publishers.

4.   Accounts and payments: Semi-annual statements of accounts for the six months' period ending January 31st and July 31st of each year shall be furnished by the Publishers to the Proprietors on the succeeding May 1st and November 1st, respectively, and settlement of such accounts shall be on or before the following June 15th and December 15th; provided, however, that if during any semi-annual accounting period fewer than 25 copies of the said Work have been sold by the Publishers, the Publishers shall not be required to account to the Proprietors until the next semi-annual accounting date upon which unaccounted-for sales aggregate 25 copies or more.

5.   First serial rights, within the territory covered by this agreement, and dramatic, movie, and television rights when sold to a U.S. firm or producer, will be handled by the Proprietors' agent, Marion Saunders. Net proceeds of any sale shall be divided 10% to the Publishers and 90% to the Proprietors.

6.   The Publishers shall have the exclusive right, after book publication, to arrange for the sale of the following rights within the territory covered by this agreement, and if any such rights are sold by the Publishers, the net proceeds shall be divided equally between the Proprietors and the Publishers: reprint, second serial, digest, anthologies, and Book Club.

7.   The Publishers shall present to the Proprietors at the time of publication of the original edition six free copies of the American edition of the said Work.

8. All rights not specifically mentioned in this agreement are reserved to the Proprietors.

9. The Publishers guarantee that the said work shall appear in book form in the English language in the U.S.A. within twelve months of the date of publication of the American edition of MOLLOY, unless prevented by circumstances beyond their control. It being understood, however, that should Samuel Beckett take more than two months to look over and revise the Publishers' English translation, this twelve month period would be increased to the extent of the additional delay. The Publishers agree to let Samuel Beckett make whatever changes he deems necessary in their English translation of the Work.

10. If at any time the Work shall be out of print and is allowed to remain out of print for one year, and the Proprietors shall notify the Publishers to this effect, all rights granted hereunder shall terminate and revert to the Proprietors unless the Publishers shall within thirty days of receipt of such notice declare their intention to publish a new edition of the Work, and within six months of receipt of such notice publish such new edition. The Work shall not be considered to be out of print if it is on sale in a cheap edition or in any other edition in the United States.

11. If the Publishers shall, during the existence of this agreement, default in the delivery of semiannual statements or in the making of payments as herein provided and shall neglect or refuse to deliver such statements or make such payments, or any of them, within thirty days after written notice of such default, this agreement shall terminate at the expiration of such thirty days without prejudice to the Proprietors' claim for any monies which may have accrued under this agreement.

12. No assignment shall be binding on either of the parties without the written consent of the other party to this Agreement and the terms and conditions shall be binding upon the successor XE of the corporation, parties hereto and upon the executors or administrators of the individual or the individuals constituting a firm party hereto and also the permitted assigns of any of the parties hereto.

13. Regardless of the place of its physical execution, this agreement shall be interpreted under the laws of the State of New York and of the United States of America.

14. For the considerations expressed herein and the publication of the book hereunder, the Proprietors hereby grant to the Publishers the irrevocable option to accept for publication the next two novels written by Samuel Beckett and published in France by The Proprietors, on terms to be arranged. The option, however, shall not apply to the second of such novels if not exercised by the Publishers with regard to the first. The Publishers shall have sixty days after the submission of the work for the exercise of such option.

15. The Proprietors hereby authorize their agent, Marion Saunders, 104 East 40th Street, New York 16, N.Y., to collect and receive all sums of money payable to them under the terms of this agreement and the Proprietors declare that the receipt of the said Marion Saunders shall be a good and valid discharge in respect thereof and the said Marion Saunders is hereby empowered to act on the Proprietors' behalf in all matters arising out of this agreement.

IN WITNESS HEREOF WE HAVE HEREUNTO SET OUT SIGNATURES FOR AND ON BEHALF OF:

PROPRIETORS *Jérôme Lindon*
Les Editions de Minuit

PUBLISHERS *Barney Rosset*
Owner
Grove Press

GROVE PRESS

795 BROADWAY, NEW YORK 3, N.Y. • GRAMERCY 3-7447

15 November 1954

MEMORANDUM OF AGREEMENT BETWEEN SAMUEL BECKETT, 6 rue des
Favorites, Paris XVeme, France and GROVE PRESS, 795 Broadway,
New York 3, N. Y., U.S.A., COVERING THE ENGLISH TRANSLATION OF
MALONE MEURT.

1.   Samuel Beckett hereby agrees to translate his novel
written by him in French and entitled in French MALONE MEURT
into English for Grove Press.

2.   Grove Press will fully own the rights to this translation in the United States and its possessions and in Canada
and the Philippine Islands, and any book publisher, magazine
publisher, play-, radio-, motion picture-, or television-
producer, etc., in these countries, wanting to use that translation, will have to apply to Grove Press for permission to
do so. Samuel Beckett retains the rights to England and
its dominions (or member-countries of the British Commonwealth), excluding Canada. For Europe and the rest of the
world, the rights are shared equally in open market between
Samuel Beckett and Grove Press.

3.   In payment for the rights herein agreed on, Grove Press
will pay to Samuel Beckett a sum of money to be computed at
the rate of $4.50 (four dollars and fifty cents) per $1,000
(one thousand) words of translation, plus a royalty of 2.5%
(two and one-half percent) per copy for each copy of the
hardbound trade edition sold in excess of 3,000 (three thousand)
copies; and upon signing of this memorandum by Samuel
Beckett and Grove Press, Grove Press will pay to Samuel
Beckett an advance of $150.00 (one hundred and fifty dollars);
and upon delivery to Grove Press of the completed translation
Grove Press will pay to Samuel Beckett any and all additional
money owed to him under the terms of this agreement.

Signed:
FOR AND ON BEHALF OF GROVE PRESS:

Signed: *Barney Rosset*
                            Barney Rosset, Proprietor
                            DATE: *Nov. 29, 1954*

_____
Samuel Beckett   *Samuel Beckett*
DATE: *November 9th 1954*

THE CHASE NATIONAL BANK
OF THE CITY OF NEW YORK

NO. 45—1948

NEW YORK, 12/16/54

U. S. $ 150.00

ADVISED BY AIR MAIL

WE CONFIRM HAVING SOLD
YOU OUR CHECK IN FAVOR OF SAMUEL BECKETT *****

FOR ONE HUNDRED FIFTY AND 00/100 *****

UNITED STATES DOLLARS

PAYABLE AT THE BUYING RATE FOR SIGHT DRAFTS ON NEW YORK. NO DUPLICATE ISSUED

DRAWN ON CHASE NATIONAL BANK OF THE CITY OF N.Y.
PARIS FRANCE

THE SALE OF THIS CHECK IS MADE SUBJECT TO THE
CONDITIONS STATED ON THE REVERSE SIDE HEREOF.

WE CHARGE YOUR ACCOUNT

WE HAVE YOUR CHECK

PLEASE SEND US YOUR CHECK

Orre # 3567
Beckett - advance MALONE

PROTECTED THROUGH
CHASE NATIONAL BANK PARIS FRANCE

TO

GROVE PRESS 3567

ISSUED WEST 14TH STREET

BRANCH

	AMOUNT OF CHECK	CHARGES	TOTAL	
F.X. 131 6-52	$150.00	$1.15	$151.15	

GROVE PRESS

795 BROADWAY, NEW YORK 3, N.Y. • GRAMERCY 3-7447

January 16, 1954

Dear Samuel,

You will probably have the proofs of <u>Godot</u> before
you get this letter. I hope that you do not find them too bad-
both as to design and as to errors. Loly and I are spending
our first nights in our new home at East Hampton and the
galleys arrived after we left New York, so we have not yet
seen them. It would help a great deal if you would correct
them just as soon as you conveniently can and ship them off
to us airmail-we are already behind schedule for our planned
publication date and I do want to see the book this spring so
that we may capitalize on the <u>New World Writing</u> piece.

One of the fine photos from Germany is being used for
the jacket and we will send you copies as soon as we get
them. We tried to pick the picture you suggested-may it be
that we guessed correctly.

Two baffling letters have arrived from Lindon
of Minuit. He seems to be pressing me to go ahead with
<u>L'Innommable</u> now, and not to wait for the completion of
<u>Molloy</u> and <u>Malone Meurt</u>. He says that another firm (English I
believe, but I am not certain) has made him a high offer for
the book. I have replied saying that I have all intentions
of publishing <u>L'Innommable</u>, but that it is an academic
question at the moment because I first have to wait to get the
translation of the first two books.

If you could clarify this situation for me I would
appreciate it very much-also, where does <u>Merlin</u> now stand on
publishing <u>Molloy</u> and the other two books? Lindon does not
seem satisfied with what I have to say, and it seems to me
that he does not understand that one book logically follows
the other-or maybe I am not comprehending his letters.

It is so nice where we are-snowed in, quiet, sootless,
that I think you might like it. Let's hope that you can pay
us a visit some time.

Yours,

Barney Rosset

February 5th, 1954
East Hampton

Dear Samuel,

A copy of the jacket is on its way to you—I hope that you find it satisfactory.

Perhaps I can feel a little bit of what you are going through—not being able to get things flowing again. No nice clichés will help, but I remember our evening together very clearly, and especially when you spoke of your reasons for writing in French. I have been wondering if you would not get almost the freshness of turning to doing something in English which you must have gotten when you first seriously took to writing in French. A withdrawal from a withdrawal—English.

Murphy impressed me tremendously—More Pricks Than Kicks (or is it reversed) I have never seen—and perhaps the road from L'Innommable could lead to another kind of symbol—English. Anyway, that is my contribution—plus an invitation to visit us.

And all of this translating—it is nice for us, and it means some additional income for you—but it must surely inhibit new feelings from rising to the surface. It is like always being caught in the old puddle—getting brackish and no new rain. If it were not for our own skin being involved I could more wholeheartedly urge you to throw it all aside and sleep some new sleep. But then—why is it necessary to pour out more right now. Maybe the trying is what does the stopping.

Yours,

Barney Rosset

GROVE PRESS

795 BROADWAY, NEW YORK 3, N.Y. • GRAMERCY 3-7447

April 14, 1954

Dear Samuel,

    Waiting for Godot seems to be finally ready to come off
the press. Quite a wait it has been—in fact so long that we
have decided to postpone publication date until next fall.
We expect the book to be a handsome one and copies will be
dispatched out the instant they arrive—we hope they will gain
your blessing.

    It has been so long since we have heard from you.
What has been happening with the translation . . . I'm almost
afraid to ask, but we would like to know.

    Very warmest greetings from Loly and myself—

    Yours,

Barney Rosset

We are still hoping to have you pay us a visit one of these
days—noted in *The New York Times* that Godot will be put on in
London. Hope it is true.

GROVE PRESS

795 BROADWAY, NEW YORK 3, N.Y. • GRAMERCY 3-7447

May 5, 1954

Dear Samuel,

If there is anything more difficult to get translated
than Molloy it must be a handwritten letter by Beckett.
After a few hours' struggle Loly and I do think that we have
discerned certain words pertaining to the English language
drifting across to us but we would be hard put to testify
under oath to that belief.

First then—to the translation of Molloy. We had
thought that things might be going slowly. As for you either
giving it over entirely or doing it all yourself—my strong
desire was always that you do it yourself, and my feelings
still run that way.

We have a contract with Bowles whereby he was to
translate Molloy for us and be paid at the rate of $3.50 per
1000 words of translation plus a royalty of 2.5% per copy
for each copy sold over 3000 copies. We paid him $180.00 thus
far and I would be very happy to switch the same terms over
to you. I do not know whether the sections translated cover
the advance paid or not. We have the first 108 pages here and
you mention having done the first few pages of part two with
Bowles. That should come fairly close to the mark. Let me know
as to what you plan to do—we of course will hope that you
wither renew contact with Bowles or plough on by yourself.

The censoring of Godot is incredible. I don't know
what to say—except a plague on the lord chamberpot.

We hope that the book has arrived and that it does not
annoy you too much. We put off the publication date as you
know, but if we want to do Molloy in the foreseeable future
you must get on with the translation. Hope you see your way
clear to getting it done, with or without Bowles.

Warmly yours,

Barney

Hey, man, which way to Grove Press?

GROVE PRESS

795 BROADWAY, NEW YORK 3, N.Y. • GRAMERCY 3-7447

June 8, 1954

Dear Samuel,

I am terribly sorry not to have answered you sooner—but a hideously annoying accident delayed me on everything. I lost a briefcase containing—in addition to my Leica camera, etc., books, contracts, one short manuscript, and much correspondence. Numbered among the fallen were the last two letters from you plus what seems to be our only extant (now extinguished) copy of the contract made with Bowles.

All of this was being carried to East Hampton from whence I was going to write to you about the translations. Now I am slightly at a loss, both as to what you said and as to what exactly our arrangements with Bowles were. A letter is also going off to him to type off a copy of the contract and send it to us post haste. Enclosed with the plea was a check for $60.00, representing the translation fee for the New Amer Lib [New World Writing] bit, and which we promised to him for collecting material on Godot.

The exact gist of what you said is not with me, but I do know that you wanted terms for doing the translation which differed from Bowles' or yours on the Godot work. Samuel, I am not trying to cry my way into your heart, but the way of a small publisher of good books in this country, one who has not extra lines such as children's books, who has no best sellers, and practically no income from reprints, etc., is a hard way indeed. We are not having an easy time of it and it is hard enough for us to faithfully follow up all of our commitments without creating any new "lump sum"s to be passed out. I will be happy to pay you along the same lines as laid out either in the Godot contract (advance of $150.00 against 2 Ð % royalty, or a similar advance against so many dollars per thousand words). As for you being a better translator than Bowles—no argument, and I am very pleased to know that you want to do the job yourself, but it is not exactly a situation where better gets paid better. If you had agreed to do the work in

the first place on Molloy the payment would have been the
same.
Molloy should be known a little by the time it comes out now
that excerpts have appeared almost simultaneously in New World
Writing, Paris Review and Merlin. Are you planning on any
more?

And what about plans for more work? Is the man
prowling further into the rock, or is he preparing for a new
peek out.

An interesting theatrical group here of high
professional standards asked for a copy of Godot—perhaps
something will come of it. I believe we mentioned that a copy
went off to London as you asked. Let us know what happened. A
copy of our new catalogue is on its way to you.

Best regards from Loly and myself. We are still
hoping to see you in East Hampton one of these days, morosely
putting around the sand dunes.

As Ever,

Barney

GROVE PRESS

795 BROADWAY, NEW YORK 3, N.Y. • GRAMERCY 3-7447

July 7, 1954

Dear Samuel,

We are terribly sorry to hear about your brother—and we
only hope that things will work out for the best. And perhaps
Ireland will offer some compensation.

Is there any new development about a London production
[of Godot]?

Do tell us what you think about the translating jobs,
etc., and the status of Molloy.

Loly and I send our warmest greetings and the deep wish
that your brother will make a good recovery.

Yours,

Barney

P.S. If you stay in Ireland long enough I will be tempted
to ask you to look up the family of my grandmother and
grandfather on my mother's side—the Tanseys.

GROVE PRESS

795 BROADWAY, NEW YORK 3, N.Y. • GRAMERCY 3-7447

August 18, 1954

Dear Samuel,

Time must be very drearily and sadly dragging
along for you these days—and we can only offer our sympathy
which seems so little and so thin to say, but there it is.

Somebody by the name of Jacqueline Sundstrom, who reportedly is a part owner of the Babylon theater in Paris, told
somebody else here that Alec Guinness has bought the English
performing rights to Godot. I am writing about this because
we have interested three separate groups in putting on the
play here and we would very much like to know what the actual situation is. One group, the most definite at the moment,
has leased the Cherry Lane theater. This is a famous little
theater in Greenwich Village that has just been refurbished in
new decor, seats, etc. The group, professional in background,
is going to start their season with Congreve's Way of the
World (not done here for many years) and the second play will
be one by Anouilh not previously done in America. Then they
would like to do Godot. We don't know what the fees would be,
but if the rights become free it would be possible to enter
immediate negotiations because the fall is upon us. Do let us
know what is happening, because if Guinness or somebody else
does not have any plans for America I would think it a shame
to pass up other opportunities that we might recover.

On to Molloy. How is the translation coming along? It
is terribly important to know when we will have the completed
manuscript (and we would very much like to have any additional sections which are ready) so that we may plan for publication. Also I do hope that Merlin and Grove won't come out with
two separate editions. That seems such a waste of productive
energies. We could sell our copies to them or vice versa—but
anyway, be that as it may, I hope that we get the completed
manuscript at no worse than the same time Merlin does so that
we may have a fair chance to get the book out simultaneously.
I notice that they are already advertising it.

Your work is attracting attention here and I feel
certain that some day your merit will gain its place. Loly
received from Germany a handsome folder put out by the German
publisher. Very nice indeed.

Kindest regards and affection from us both.

Yours,

Barney

Grove Press Office 1954,
Loly and Barney Rosset

795 BROADWAY, NEW YORK 3, N.Y. • GRAMERCY 3-7447

February 15, 1955
Mr. Samuel Beckett
6 Rue des Favorites
Paris 15
FRANCE

Dear Samuel,

One success after another rolling up in Europe—and
nothing on Broadway. Poor Mr. Albery is going to have the
greatest mountain of blame ever piled up if something is not
forthcoming within a reasonable time here in New York.

Maybe the new work, from a distance of some little
time, may not turn out to be so bad as you now think it is.
Don't throw away the wastepaper basket. This is my advice.
Poor Lindon must be hard up trying to get a book out of you.
Maybe you will give him something more substantial yet.

What you have to say about Malone sounds perfectly
satisfactory. All I ask is that when you actually do get
around to doing the book, we would terribly appreciate it if
you would give us a section to read now and then.

This afternoon I received a book from Lindon entitled
Roberte Ce Soir. Do you know anything about it? And if you
do, what do you think?

Sincerely,

Barney

GROVE PRESS

795 BROADWAY, NEW YORK 3, N.Y. • GRAMERCY 3-7447

August 31, 1955

Dear Samuel,

  Loly and Peter and I have been whiling away our summer hours in East Hampton. Peter seems to be accomplishing the
most, being engaged in rapidly increasing his size. Also his
lungs seem to be improving in power as time goes by.

  We would be terribly interested in knowing what kind
of a reception Godot received in London. No word has come to
our attention here. Do let us know.

  Our edition of Molloy has finally come off the press
and two copies are on their way to you by now. As the books
came in last Friday I have not yet seem them myself but I am
told that the total effect is not too bad, considering what
we had to start with. We altered our original plan to bring
the book out simultaneously in a hard and soft bound edition,
and we are now publishing the hardbound edition only, at least
for the moment. My attorney here in New York felt that that
was much the wiser course to pursue because he felt that we
might run into censorship problems and by steering clear of
the paperbound book for awhile at least we might avoid a lot
of unnecessary trouble. We shall see. Copies have already gone
out to all of the important newspapers, magazines and critics.

  I am very happy to know that the translation of Malone
is coming along so well and I very much look forward to seeing
it.

    With very best wishes,

Barney

GROVE PRESS ✳

795 BROADWAY, NEW YORK 3, N.Y. • GRAMERCY 3-7447

September 24, 1955

Dear Samuel:

Thank you very very much for sending on the clippings. I find them to be completely fascinating. They are certainly extremely good and if they cannot help the play then nothing can. I would like to hold them for a while if that is possible, but if you very much want them back immediately, let me know and they will go back. I am very anxious to know how things are going in the new theatre. What is the news?

Rosica Colin asked me if I would sell my translation rights for England for Godot to Faber for L50 and I said yes. I will let you know what comes of that.

Enclosed is one of the first reviews of Molloy. It appeared in a recent copy of the New Republic magazine.

I am certainly looking forward to seeing the text of Malone. You asked me what the final date can be and I find that an unanswerable question. I can only say that I would like to have it as soon as possible and that I am very much looking forward to it.

Copies of Molloy are in all the New York City bookstores that wanted them but distribution across the rest of the country has not yet gone out. The post office is now examining the book and I am sure their decision will be very amusing if not pleasing. As soon as it comes I will let you know.

I do hope that all goes well with you, and Loly and I send our warmest greetings.

Yours,

Barney

GROVE PRESS, INC.
64 UNIVERSITY PLACE
NEW YORK 3, NEW YORK
OREGON 4-7200

CONTRACT

June 23, 1960

MEMORANDUM OF AGREEMENT made this 23rd day of June 1960, between Les Editions de Minuit, 7 rue Bernard-Palissy, Paris VI, France, (hereinafter called the Proprietors) of one part, and Grove Press, 64 University Place, New York 3, N. Y., U.S.A. (hereinafter called the Publishers) of the other part.

WHEREBY IT IS AGREED by and between the parties hereto as follows concerning the work entitled MOLLOY, MALONE DIES and THE UNNAMABLE: Three Novels by Samuel Beckett, (hereinafter referred to as the Work).

1. The Proprietors grant to the Publishers the sole and exclusive license to print and publish the Work in book form in the English language in the United States of America and its dependencies, and Canada, and the Philippine Islands; and the non-exclusive right to sell it in all other parts of the world outside the British Commonwealth (except Canada). In consideration of the above license, the Publishers agree to pay the following royalties:

    (a) on the published price of all copies sold of the hard bound edition: seven and one-half per cent ($7\frac{1}{2}$%) on the first 5,000 copies; ten per cent (10%) on the next 5,000 copies; twelve and one-half per cent ($12\frac{1}{2}$%) on all copies sold above 10,000.

    (b) the following royalties shall be paid on all copies sold of the paper bound edition: six per cent (6%) on the first 20,000 copies; seven and one-half per cent ($7\frac{1}{2}$%) thereafter.

    (c) ten per cent (10%) of the sums received where copies of the said Work are sold at special discounts of 50% or more of the retail price. No royalty shall be paid for copies given away for advertising purposes, or for remainders, or damaged copies sold below cost.

2. The Proprietors represent and guarantee to the Publishers that they are the sole owners of the said Work, and that they are the owners of all the rights in this agreement granted to the Publishers.

3. Accounts and payments: Semi-annual statements of accounts for the six months' period ending June 30th and December 31st of each year shall be furnished by the Publishers to the Proprietors and settlement of such accounts shall be made sometime within four months thereafter; provided, however, that if during any semi-annual accounting period fewer than 25 copies of the said Work have been sold by the Publishers, the Publishers shall not be required to account to the Proprietors until the next semi-annual accounting date upon which unaccounted-for sales aggregate 25 copies or more.

4. Proceeds of first serial rights, within the territory covered by this agreement and dramatic, movie, and television rights sold to a U.S. firm or producer shall be divided 10% to the Publishers and 90% to the Proprietors.

GROVE PRESS ✳

October 20, 1955

Dear Samuel,

We have received numerous inquiries concerning the
production of Godot. Now we have been informed that a Michael
Myerberg is purchasing American production rights from Albery.
Myerberg is a reputable American Broadway producer who has
put on a least two important productions, including one by
Thornton Wilder. Beyond that Yale University and some one
at Harvard have announced productions. Permission for these
certainly did not in any way come through us and if you
have not had a hand in the matter I strongly suggest that
these people should not be allowed to go ahead. Mr. Myerberg
evidently feels the same way. I have also written to Lindon
reminding him of our written agreement whereby I was to
receive 10 percent of the gross from any English production,
said 10 percent to come from Lindon's share.

I am very happy to see this bubbling up of interest
and my strong feeling is that your work is going to be
more and more known as time goes by. There definitely is an
underground of interest here, the kind of interest that slowly
generates steam and has a lasting stock. Godot has definitely
been picking up in sales the past few weeks and I also
attribute this to the London production.

If the play is to be put on in this country, with a
Broadway production, why don't you come over and take a look
at it? We would love to have you here. Give this a little
thought and then tell me your reaction.

Best regards,

Barney

Bert Lahr and E.G.
Marshall in *Waiting
for Godot* production,
courtesy of Harry
Ransom Center,
University of Texas

GROVE PRESS

795 BROADWAY, NEW YORK 3, N.Y. • GRAMERCY 3-7447

October 25, 1955

Dear Samuel,

Just spoke to the would be producer of Godot, Michael
Myerberg, who says he would like you to come here and to that
end he will pay all expenses of the trip. Of course to me
this sounds wonderful. He adds that Garson Kanin might be the
director and that Kanin wants you to be here to advise him. SO
! ! What is your reaction? I certainly hope you accept-it is
just in line with what I said in my last letter.

That certainly is enough for one letter-I do not want
to soften the impact of the above. However your request for
two more copies of Molloy has been received and they will go
off today.

We very much look forward to getting Malone. I know
the final agonies of the last revision and typing, but it
seems to be so very NEAR. Interesting reviews, some hilarious
(unintentionally) are coming in on Molloy. Unfortunately the
big papers have not taken any cognizance of it yet, but I feel
confident that you have been launched well into the American
mish mash, and every month and year will see more interest and
sales of your work.

I will say hello to Loly for you and whisper to Peter
Michael that he may see a French Irishman, one M. Beckett,
before he, Peter, can speak French or Irish.

Yours,

Barney

GROVE PRESS

795 BROADWAY, NEW YORK 3, N.Y. • GRAMERCY 3-7447

November 3, 1955

Mr. Samuel Beckett
6 rue des Favorites
Paris 15
France

Dear Samuel:

Now Mr. Myerberg informs me that Godot is due to open, providing that contracts get signed, in Miami, Florida, on January 3rd and then make two additional stops en route to New York. This all sounds very wonderful and I will keep my fingers crossed until all arrangements are completed.

If all goes well I will print a new edition of the play, to look like the old one excepting that it will be done with a paper jacket and will sell for something like $1.00.

Do think seriously of coming over. We would very much like to see you here.

Best,

Barney

GROVE PRESS

795 BROADWAY NEW YORK 3, N.Y. - GRAMERCY 3-7447

November 15, 1955

Dear Samuel,

Your letter and the answer to my cable arrived
simultaneously this morning. First, as to my cable, Myerberg
(whom I have not met but spoke to quite a few times on the
phone) asked that I send it. Apparently the director is to
be this Alan Schneider. He directed the Paris performance of
Wilder's Skin of Our Teeth, which was put on a few months
back. After you [see] him you will undoubtedly know more about
everything than I do. You will see what sort of a fellow he is
and then you may have a more final idea as to whether or not
you can work with him. I hope he will turn out to be somebody
you like and that he will make you inclined to come here and
help put the play together. Myerberg assures me that you would
not be bothered by journalists, fool questions, etc. And we—
Loly and I—would be more than happy to spirit you away to a
quiet place on the ocean where most people would be too lazy
to follow. Of course Peter Michael is getting inquisitive, but
we would get you your own place and not tell him the address.
So, I hope you reach a decision after meeting Schneider and we
will hope for the affirmative.

Myerberg has been a little vague about some things
and this has kept me from leaping into print with a cheaper
edition of Godot. However I am talking to the printer tomorrow
and we will see what size printing it would take to bring
out a nice paperbound edition at $1.00. The play is supposed
to open in Miami (hilarious idea) the first few days of

January and then come here around the 22nd of January. No theater has been named and Myerberg never has asked for my formal approval and I remain to be convinced that everything is settled. Perhaps things sound so good that my natural propensities push me into thinking that nothing will ever come of it. Both The New York Times and the Herald Tribune had short statements yesterday, so my fears are most likely unfounded.

Lindon keeps pestering me about L'Innommable. I repeatedly tell him that I will take it as soon as you are ready to proceed—what more can he want. And as for Malone Dies, I am very happy to know that the typing of the final version is really coming along—don't let a new translation into the Greek or Sanskrit editions hold you up. And that brings to mind the fact that our Greek writer (the girl who is Greek, brought up in France, and writes English thus reversing someone else), Kay Cicellis, writes from London that Godot is wonderful. A great play. Just another vote—but from la famille.

Yours,

Barney

GROVE PRESS

795 BROADWAY, NEW YORK 3, N.Y. ● GRAMERCY 3-7447

November 29, 1955

Dear Samuel,

By now you have met Schneider and accordingly you must know a great deal more about the New York plans for Godot than I. My hope is certainly that you hit it off with him and that we will have a good report from you in the immediate future. However no matter what your decision or feelings are, they will be the right one insofar as we are concerned.

Enclosed is a little piece which ran in the Sunday New York Times (November 27th) Book Review section. It is a particularly widely read column and it will do its bit to bring some attention to Godot.

I do look forward to having the manuscript of Malone. It will be a good day when it comes in. I quite understand how you do not want to plunge into L'Innommable right now. One has to have a break.

And now, just to wait for some news.

Yours,

Barney

"This summer Grove Press published with little fanfare a small book, a tragi-comedy in two acts, called 'Waiting for Godot,' by Samuel Beckett. . . . [We] took the little book up in our own time. . . . Then as we moved into the little play, we found ourselves surprisingly pinned down by the most sardonic vision we'd come up against in a long time. . . . When we finished, we thought, 'This is Hell, upper case—and lower case, too.' And another, more dogmatic self of ourself said, 'This is life.'"

—Harvey Breit, *The New York Times*

"'To me,' says Rosset,' *Godot* is the story of Sam and Suzanne living together during the war. Like the tramps, they were desexualized and bored out of their minds, just waiting for the fucking war to end.'"

—Laurence Bergreen, *Esquire*

"I read the play and decided to do it. I won't claim that I saw it as a turning point in 20th-century drama: that came later. And it certainly took a month of intensive rehearsal for me to realise that the play was a masterpiece. But from the very beginning, I thought it was blindingly original, turning the undramatic (waiting, doubt, perpetual uncertainty) into tense action. It was exquisitely constructed, with an almost musical command of form and thematic material. And it was very funny. It took the cross-talk tradition of music hall and made it into poetry."

—Peter Hall, *The Guardian*

GROVE PRESS

795 BROADWAY, NEW YORK 3, N.Y. • GRAMERCY 3-7447

December 6, 1955

Dear Samuel,

Malone arrived in fine order and I find the translation
perfectly splendid. As far as I am concerned the manuscript
is ready to go to the typesetter. I think I noted a few minor
mistakes, but they were very few in number and they can be
picked up in the galleys. I did feel after reading the book
that it was a terrible shame not to have L'Innommable to go
along with it and I hope that you will see your way clear to
getting started on that before too long. The books really do
go together and when all are available it will be a fine day
indeed.

Trying to count words in a manuscript is a maddening
enterprise. As far as can see it comes out to something like
fifty-one thousand words. If you have any unemployed rats
why don't you set them to work on verifying that totally
irresponsible figure.

An extremely annoying procedure has taken place
here over contracts, rights, and everything else you can
think of. Yesterday I was called by the most difficult woman
in the world, one Marion Saunders,* who proceeded to so
thoroughly confuse and infuriate me that I will not even try
to recapitulate our conversation. Anyway, Lindon in several
separate letters, and Myerberg on the phone, both agreed with
me that it would be perfectly fine and lovely for me to get ten
percent of the money accruing to Lindon. This is all I was
asking for in order for me to give my permission to Myerberg.
However, not trusting these fellows, I asked that I receive
some written assurance of this from the producer. The latter,
instead of sending me some simple form, sent my request to

London where it was finally transferred back to Miss Saunders.
Now the madcap queen is supposed to straighten things out.
All she did was demand that I pay her something for all the
work she was going through on somebody's behalf. I told her
that all she had done for me was cause me trouble and so
the conversation went. A moment ago a man walked in here
who wants to put on a special showing of Godot for agents,
actors, etc.

This fellow informed me that he had seen a statement
in the newspapers to the effect that Thornton Wilder was
going to write an adaptation of your play and that that would
be the one to be put on Broadway. By now you have met the
director, etc. etc., and perhaps that won't disturb you. It
certainly annoys hell out of me and my first reaction is to
say—let Mr. Wilder write his own play, talented as he may
be, and let yours go on a la Beckett. I certainly am anxious
to hear your views on this subject. It seems that agents,
producers and the like can never go from one point directly
to another.

So I have spent some intense moments reading Malone
and some infuriated ones listening to Miss Saunders. Now I
really look forward to hearing from you.

Best,

Barney

Marion Saunders, who gave Beckett's current agent Georges Borchardt his first job
in publishing, while respected in the field was an irritant to others besides Rosset.
Simone de Beauvoir referred to her as a "real old horror" (*Margaret Mitchell's Gone
with the Wind: A Bestseller's Odyssey from Atlanta to Hollywood*, Ellen F. Brown and
John Wiley, Jr., Lanham, MD: Rowman & Littlefield, 2011, p. 78). And her handling
of author royalties apparently didn't do much to improve her reputation. —ED.

GROVE PRESS

795 BROADWAY, NEW YORK 3, N.Y. • GRAMERCY 3-7447

June 18, 1953

Dear Samuel,

This morning two GOOD developments. First, I got
sick of waiting for Myerberg to tell me that everything was really set and I gave the printer orders
to proceed with a new edition of Godot, to sell at
$1.00. I hope this pleases you. If Myerberg does
not come through with a new photograph I will simply use the existing jacket which I like anyway.

    Secondly, yesterday's letter to Myerberg
finally produced results. His attorney called my attorney this morning and apparently they had a long
and agreeable conversation. It ended by Moselle's
(Myerberg atty) saying that he would produce all
the information we want by the end of next week,
and it seems that after that we should be able to
make an agreement. My fingers are crossed—but my
attorney is a close personal friend of mine and he
is not and has not been obstructing things. I do of
course put great faith in his advice on procedur-
al problems and I sort of found myself between you
and him the other day, but if we keep going along,
my feeling is that everything will work out well. I
am only swearing at myself for delaying so long in
activating the new edition of Godot.

       Yours,

       Barney

waiting for godot

samuel beckett

a tragicomedy in two acts

AN EVERGREEN BOOK $1.00

PUBLISHED BY GROVE PRESS

December 7, 1955

Dear Samuel,
Your cable arrived this morning and a reply went back—both to
London care of Albery and to you in Paris. Cable came from
London.

Believe me, I want to do what you want, but why in
God's name must it be you who has to guarantee me something,
and not the people who take in the money at the box office.
If everybody agrees on everything, why cannot this Myerberg
put something into writing. I am not a mad ogre waiting
here to gobble him up. In fact the opposite has been true—I
have tried to help him in any way possible, and what is most
important, I have been waiting for him to give me the go ahead
signal on putting out the paperbound edition of Godot—at my
expense, and he has not even come through on that. He said the
new edition should have a new photo on the cover, using the
American actors. That seemed perfectly reasonable to me, but
no photograph has ever been forthcoming. Deviousness has never
been my forte, but I am certainly getting some lessons.

Myerberg disturbed me when he said that the English
version of the play was not well translated, and that
disturbance was heightened when I was told about the Wilder
story in the paper (he to do an adaptation) but I infer from
your cable that all is okay along those lines.

I do appreciate your cable of assurance, and you can
know that I want to do as you desire, but let's not get into
a situation where you and I are the only ones who put our
cards on the table. They must tell you that I am putting up
"opposition." Opposition my Galway grandfather's ass, I am
only making the perfectly ordinary request that they have
their agreement with me on a little piece of paper, just as
all of the cross agreements with Albery, Lindon, Curtis Brown,
Myerberg, Saunders, et al, are.

While I am looking for my contract, as was Moran for
Molloy, Malone has gone off for a suit of type, and I am
rapidly developing a penchant for calling myself Morose. Not
really.

Best,

Barney

December 13, 1955

Dear Samuel,

Today Myerberg called me, and that is what provokes this letter. He is all amicability and charm, but no photograph is forthcoming until at least the end of the month, which of course is ridiculous if the book is to be ready for any part of the production. So I am going ahead with the old jacket, as is. No copy-just photo front and back. It did seem strange to me however and I do hope everything is all right.

Then I asked if you were coming, and he said you wanted to come, but it seems there was a problem of money to pay your way. This astounded me in view of what I had been told previously and also in view of the fact that Myerberg asked me to write to you, offering you a free trip, etc. He also said, in what now seems scrabbled in my mind, that the whole production would cost only about $15,000.00 to $25,000.00 (very low for a production these days), and that most of the money was his. I asked him why nobody every asked me for money, if it was in short supply, and he said he would send over the papers showing how the production is set up. He said that all costs might be paid for by the time the production got to Broadway. That would be wonderful for everybody. Anyway, the whole thing was sort of circuitous-although I hope all for the better-BUT do you really want to come, and is there now a problem of expenses being paid, or did Myerberg interject that for the first time when he spoke to me. Because if that is the situation I certainly think something can be worked out and we should decide how immediately.

Myerberg says the play is in rehearsal. Hope that is also true.

No word from you since setting up of meeting with Schneider. I would very much like to hear from you-do send word, any word.

Yours,

Barney

JOAN NIELSEN, SOCIETY EDITOR

Miami Memos

Words On Play

Any lack of activity on the party front yesterday was taken care of by words on the play (or a play on words) which opened the night before at the Coconut Grove Playhouse.

We'll call it "sit-home-and-figure-out-the-message-of-"Waiting For Godot-night." Never heard so many self-appointed drama critics stir up so much conversation about a single production ever launched in this area. There may be many more reservations pouring in to see if "Godot" ever shows.

Folks didn't wait long to call and ask, "Did you get it?" One man insisted he smelled smoke as he left the theatre, only to have his wife remark, "They're probably burning the script." Some staunch intellectuals commiserated with one another about the lack of understanding of symbolism, upholding some fierce allegorical reasons. Others stayed because they figured if the play made Broadway, they'd have had the first shot at seeing it.

We'd hate to see legitimate theatre go wanting because of some waiting.

Oh well, plays are like Streetcars. If one misses, (or if you miss one), a better is sure to come along.

GROVE PRESS

795 BROADWAY, NEW YORK 3, N.Y. • GRAMERCY 3-7447

December 28, 1955

Dear Samuel:

I do hope that the sackcloth and ashes arrived in time for Christmas. They would make such a timely and cheerful offering. Mr. Spencer Curtis Brown also intimated that you were the one to blame for everything, but he went far, far out of his way to tell me that all must be forgiven because you are a great writer and with great writers one cannot quibble about minor blemishes. Personally I do not hold you responsible for anything but I do agree, at least on the surface, with Mr. Spencer Curtis Brown's estimate of your work.

And to that end, the printing order has been given for the $1.00 edition of Godot. After it would have been too late to change anything anyway, I was very happy to get your letter saying that you could not imagine any photo you would like better than the one we used in the first instance and the one that we are again using. We did lose the negative of the photograph of you, which graced the back of the book, and so this time we are substituting a few words stolen from the review in The London Times. Hope that goes down well too. We are truly sorry that you have decided, at least for the moment, not to come over here now, but I do hope that your Marne mud dries up and drives you out into the moist air of Paris and that the latter causes haunting hankerings for New York. The ocean is salty and beautiful.

And on to big news. I am going to the Miami opening on January 3rd. I could not control my desire to see the production as soon as possible and I certainly did not want to take any chance of never seeing it, just on the chance of the dreary eventuality that it would never be able to gather itself together and leave Miami. My opinion is that there is only one worse city in the United States than Los Angeles and that one is Miami, but anything for Godot. I will certainly write to you immediately after the performance and let it not be said that I waited for Godot in New York. I went to him.

Yours,

Barney

GROVE PRESS

795 BROADWAY, NEW YORK 3, N.Y. • GRAMERCY 3-7447

January 6, 1956

Dear Samuel,

On Tuesday morning I put on my best summer raiment, and packed my little bag, I rode a taxi to the airport, I raced into the proper ticket counter and that is as far as I went. A dense and dismal fog covered up all of the proceedings and Godot in Miami was not destined to see me that evening. A few moments ago a friend called to read to me a review that appeared in the Miami Herald on Wednesday morning.

As yet I have not actually seen it but from what I remember of the phone conversation it would appear that the critic liked the play and the audience hated it. If I get an extra copy I will send one on to you but the man said that the audience was expecting something altogether different and that the play simply sailed and zoomed over their heads. He said it was an extremely well to do, well-dined and wined audience and that you could fairly hear the mink stoles howling with dismay at what was going on before them. He also went on to say that he had seen the play in London and that he thought the English cast was better. Here I would interpolate my own opinion that perhaps the critic should not be taken too seriously on this count.

Anyway he went on to say that he was very dubious about a Broadway opening and he thought it would be much wiser if Godot were to enter the New York scene via one of the good off-Broadway places now going. This of course has been my feeling all along, a feeling which I have sincerely and deeply hoped would turn out to be wrong. I still hope it will be but I have been truly puzzled as to how one could expect an ordinary American audience for a commercial theatre to make a hit of Godot. After all, such was not the case in Paris nor in London. It was introduced to a small and select group and through word of mouth made its way to success. Here the opposite is being tried by thrusting it immediately upon a large audience and hoping it will sink in rapidly.

Well. I still hope Mr. Myerberg is one hundred percent correct in his viewpoint and there is nothing to do but go along with him—so I am waiting and hoping.

Very best regards,

Barney

GROVE PRESS

795 BROADWAY, NEW YORK 3, N.Y. • GRAMERCY 3-7447

January 6, 1956

Dear Samuel,

Since writing the enclosed letter the enclosed story appeared in the Times, confirming what was already suspected. It is terribly unfortunate, but it really was hoping for the impossible to think that a Miami audience would put up with Godot. When I get the Florida review I will send it on to you—a whole life unto itself.

Certainly all is not lost—the printing of the inexpensive edition forges ahead, and my cable referred to an extremely hopeful situation that I have kept alive for months.

The Theater de Lys, with producer directors Carmen Capalbo and Stanley Chase is far and away the nicest off-Broadway theater. For many months it has had a marvelously successful production of Threepenny Opera by Brecht. Everything—acting (including Lotte Lenya), staging, direction, music, has been of a uniquely high caliber, and everything about the place points it up for Godot. It is a refurbished theatre, in the heart of Greenwich Village, it has three hundred seats, an excellent reputation, and, best of all, Capalbo and Chase are dying to put on your play.

I am enthusiastic, because I truly know this particular theater is absolutely the best chance in this era for Godot to be successful in this country. Exactly the same thing happened with Threepenny Opera—opened in a big theater, great reviews, no audience. Went to this theater—great reviews, great audiences, money and satisfaction. Samuel, believe me, this is a GREAT chance, better than the other ever could have been.

Yours,

Barney

GROVE PRESS

795 BROADWAY, NEW YORK 3, N.Y. • GRAMERCY 3-7447

January 11, 1956

Dear Samuel,

After sending you the clippings from The New York
Times and the Herald Tribune, plus the cable, the following
day's Herald Tribune and New York Times carried stories
saying that Myerberg still intended to open Godot in New
York in February even though he had lost the theater and had
decided that the whole cast would have to be changed with the
exception of Bert Lahr. All of this is totally confusing and
I still hope very much that some way can be found through the
welter of contracts and quasi-contracts, etc., to get an off-
Broadway theater for Godot. *

Please do discuss this matter with Albery and see if
you can't either get Myerberg to let a topnotch off-Broadway
production be put on, or eliminate him from the scene somehow.
At this moment I feel very cynical about his reports of a
Broadway production in February, but I am willing to be
pleasantly surprised.

Yours,

Barney

January 13, 1956

Dear Samuel,

A morning of frustration—first pleasure in getting a
letter from you and then ABSOLUTE RAGE at not being able to
read it beyond the third line.* Please do write again—right
away, and use that ugly mechanical aid to self-expression—the
typewriter.

A newspaper man came in the other day and said he was
writing a story on Ewell for a Kentucky paper and that he
wanted a copy of Godot. He said the Myerberg office would not
let him see it, saying that it was going to be changed???????

Wonderful to hear that you are writing another play—
slog away at it. I would love to come to Paris myself—who
knows, perhaps the urge will become irresistible one of these
days—I think that when the plan failed to go to Miami I could
easily of been persuaded to have meandered to a Paris-bound
one. Our Greek girl, Kay Cicellis, keeps writing from London
of the wonders of Godot, so there is even inter-love within
the Grove Press catalogue.

Malone is at a printer, and as soon as he comes back
for a moment I will employ a mouse to count the words again

Barney

For an example of the hand-writing to which Rosset refers,
see page 266. —ED.

GROVE PRESS

795 BROADWAY, NEW YORK 3, N.Y. • GRAMERCY 3-7447

January 27, 1956

Dear Samuel,

　　　　Alan Schneider called me this morning and we had a
long and cordial conversation.

　　　　I would like to try to summarize what he said to me.
It rather went as follows:

• Myerberg is not the man to produce Godot.

• Godot should be put on off-Broadway, preferably at the
Theater de Lys.

• Schneider would like to direct it, but beyond that, he would
like to see Godot put on as well—that means no Myerberg and no
Bert Lahr.

• Bert Lahr and Ewell played against each other. Lahr is a
good vaudeville comedian. He does not play for the play but
for himself.

• Myerberg plans to turn the play into a vehicle for Lahr.
This will be disastrous. In Miami Lahr and Ewell played two
different plays. Ewellat least tried to work for the play.

• Godot should not be put on at the Phoenix theater.

• The London production should not be brought over here. It is
inferior to American standards.

• Godot should not be based on "stars" à la Myerberg, but on
good unknown actors who will make an entity of the production.

• The London performance lacked clarity—and without redeeming
elements such as lyricism or humor.

• The Myerberg contract does not provide for an off-Broadway
production.

And so it went. Obviously what Schneider had to say was music to my tinny ears. It is all getting a bit tiring, but here is our combined political platform:

1. Off-Broadway production—preferably Theater de Lys, and absolutely not Phoenix Theater.
2. New producer.
3. Cast not built around a "star."
4. Do not bring over English production.

On other things we may also agree, but on the above I believe every intelligent citizen of New York who knows your work and who knows the theatrical world, will agree with Schneider and myself. I do hope you will pass along Schneider's opinions to Albery. Schneider says he believes the play to be a great one—and even if he does not direct it, he wants very much to see a good production in the right place. I told Schneider that I feared I was being thought of as the village crank by you and Albery because I have conducted this monotonous diatribe about off-Broadway, etc., but after listening to him I could not help but write again.

Yours,

Barney

795 BROADWAY, NEW YORK 3, N.Y. • GRAMERCY 3-7447

February 6, 1956

Dear Samuel,

I must say that I am more or less in accord with your
letter of February 2nd.

I am very happy that you have instructed Albery to
write Myerberg and tell him that there can be no unauthorized
deviations from script. Myerberg once told me on the phone
that he considered the translation to be a poor one and that
he would very much like to have Thornton Wilder redo it. I
think it entirely possible that he may be messing around with
it but I also think that word from Albery would stop him from
doing anything without your permission. It also pleases me to
know that you want an original American production. The paper
bound edition is already printed and we expect to have bound
copies this week. I will send one on to you the moment we get
them.

I did not know that all editions of Molloy have been
banned in Ireland. Has this helped or hurt Godot?

And if it is ever possible, give me a little inkling
about the places the new play is taking you.

Best,

Barney

GROVE PRESS

795 BROADWAY, NEW YORK 3, N.Y. • GRAMERCY 3-7447

March 8, 1956

Dear Samuel,

Much commotion and pleasantly so, milling around Godot. Time magazine has had a man in to see us and he spent much time mulching the reviews, English, French, American and so on. Also, Kenneth Rexroth, a dragon slayer out on the West Coast, is going to do an essay on the Author Beckett in a forthcoming issue of Nation magazine.

AND Theater Arts magazine wants to reprint whole text of play in issue this summer. Fee is not large but I am inclined to agree with them that it will help book sale not hurt, AND, paper bound edition has already sold over 1900 copies, in its brief weeks of existence, while the hardbound has more or less run its course at 800. I suddenly realize that we have not sent you a file of American reaction to Godot and Molloy, but we have been so busy letting people like Myerberg and other itinerant merchants look at it that we have not had a chance to send you anything. We will and what we send you can keep. As I wrote to Albery, owners of the ideal New York theater called (de Lys once again) and said they very much wanted the play—and to my surprise, said they leaned towards bringing over the English director. What is your feeling about that? They do not want the English cast—just the director. They would aim for next September if allowed to do so.

Malone is here, both from you and from the proof reader in Mexico. Where there was a divergence on corrections I have told the compositor to follow you. He will now make up page proofs, which I will whisk off to you and Mexico. I will send your corrected galleys to Mexico so that they can be matched with the proofreader's and he can send them back to you. Am very happy that you agree on paperbound edition and we will proceed with that plan. In addition I am taking the remaining unbound sheets of Molloy and fixing them up as an *Evergreen* paperbound.

Happy to know that the Faber edition is going so well—for your sake, not particularly theirs because they turned it down flat before the play became a success. As for memoirs, if

you take up their request I hope you certainly know that I
will be VERY happy to follow suit and publish them here. Let
me know.

And as for the new play, qu'est ce que on peut dire
(I had better visit Paris in order to do better than that). I
look forward to reading it VERY VERY much. If it wasn't for
Beckett and one or two more little gasps of pleasure, which
occasionally float in, I would drop this whole publishing idio-
cy, believe me.

Which leads to L'Innommable—merveilleux! (I must go
to Paris). Can we send you the same translation contract and
also write to Minuit for the contract with them? Anyway I will
do the latter thing immediately and soon as I hear from you I
will fix up the translation agreement.

Since starting this letter a card bounced in through
the door from Eric Bentley, a leading drama critic in these
parts, saying that hopes are still good for a Broadway Godot,
a trip to Paris, a hit on the head, and so forth.

Yours,

Barney

P.S. Kenneth Rexroth
This is the fellow writing about you—already called Molloy
a modern classic, etc., and now is trying very hard to get
together a Beckett library. Could you get Minuit to send
him all the French volumes? Rexroth is eccentric, voluble,
sometimes hilarious, afraid of nothing, and I think worth a
little attention from us.

The Point Is Irrelevance

By Kenneth Rexroth

ALTHOUGH Samuel Beckett has been around for a good many years, Roger Blin's production of *Waiting for Godot—En Attendant Godot—*at the Theatre Babylone, two years ago in Paris, catapulted him into an international reputation. Tennessee Williams is reported of the opinion that *Godot* is the greatest play since Pirandello's *Six Characters in Search of an Author.* Right off let me say that I agree with him. Furthermore, I think *Molloy* is the most significant —laying aside the question of greatness—novel published in any language since World War II.*

Beckett is so significant, or so great, because he has said the final word to date in the long indictment of industrial and commercial civilization which began with Blake, Sade, Holderin, Baudelaire, and has continued to our day with Lawrence, Céline, Miller, and whose most forthright recent voices have been Artaud and Jean Genet.

Now this is not only the main stream of what the squares call Western European culture, by which they mean the culture of the capitalist era; it is really all the stream there is. Anything else, however gaudy in its day, has proved to be beneath the contempt of history. This is a singular phenomenon. There has been no other civilization in history whose culture bearers never had a good word to say for it. Beckett raises the issue of what is wrong with us with particular violence because his indictment is not only the most thorough-going but also the sanest. It is easy enough to write off Lautreamont, who seems to have literally believed that the vulva of the universe was going to gobble him up, or Artaud, who believed that bad little people inhabited his bowels. The cyclone fence around the mad house is certainly a great

comfort. The trouble is, Beckett is on this side of the fence. He is not only an artist of consummate skill who has learned every lesson from everybody who had anything to teach at all—from Lord Dunsany to Marcel Proust and Gertrude Stein. (Compare the plot of *Godot* with that little theatre chestnut of Dunsany's, *The Glittering Gate.*) He also has a mind of singular toughness and stability—a mind like an eighteenth-century Englishman, as sly as Gibbon, as compassionate as Johnson, as bold as Wilkes, as Olympian as Fielding. I don't mean that he is "as good as" a mixture of all these people. I mean he is their moral contemporary. "Courage, sir," said Johnson to Boswell.

BECKETT refuses to run off to Africa and die of gangrene, or write childish poems to prostitutes, or even see angels in a tree. When a prophet refuses to go crazy, he becomes a problem, crucifixion being as complicated as it is in humanitarian America. When *Godot* was put on in Miami, *Variety* and Walter Winchell instantly recognizing themselves as two of the leading characters in the play, turned on it with a savagery remarkable even for them. Nevertheless, one of the most promising things about the reception of Beckett in America is the large amount of favorable notice he has received—not just in the quarterlies and *The Nation,* the *New Republic* and *Commonweal,* but in small-town book columns scattered over the country. The European recep-

*Molloy. Grove Press. $3.
Waiting for Godot. Grove Press. $1.

KENNETH REXROTH, author of many books of poetry, will bring out this year translations of Japanese, Chinese, Greek and French poems. He conducts a radio book-review program on KPFA, San Francisco.

April 14, 1956

tion of Beckett in the last couple of years, as you know if you keep up with things over there, has been dizzying. He has become an international public figure like Lollabrigida or Khrushchev.

Beckett's first published work was a six-page pamphlet, *Whoroscope* (Nancy Cunard, the Hours Press, Paris, 1930). This is a poem, like the poems we were all writing then—at least I was, and Louis Zukovsky, and Walter Lowenfels and a few other people—very disassociated and recombined, with two pages of notes. Its point is that although René Déscartes separated spirit and matter and considered man an angel riding a bicycle, mortality caught up with him and the spirit betrayed him —the angel wore out the bicycle and the bicycle abraded the angel. This has remained one of Beckett's main themes—what is mortality for? And the point of view has never changed. That is, he has carefully pared away from what they call his universe of discourse everything except those questions which cannot be answered. He gives plenty of answers—Pozzo and Lucky in *Godot* —the sempiternal master and man, are of course an answer. And, of course, an irrelevant answer. They owe their existence, as does all the "matter" (in Aristotle's sense) of Beckett's art, to their irrelevance.

In 1931, he did for Chatto and Windus a seventy-two-page guide to Proust, a masterpiece of irascible insight worthy to rank with Jonson on Savage. It is one of the very best pieces of modern criticism and somebody should certainly resurrect and reprint it. It is difficult to resist quoting it extensively. In the concluding pages, he says,

> The quality of language is more important than any system of ethics or esthetics . . . form is the concretion of content, the revelation of a world. . . . He assimilates the human to the vegetal. . . . His men and women are victims of their volition —active with a grotesque, predetermined activity within the narrow limits of an impure world. . . . But shameless. . . . The . . . stasis is contemplative, a pure act of understanding, will-less, the "amabilis insania." . . . From this point of view, opera is less complete than vaudeville, which at least inaugurates the comedy of an exhaustive enumeration. . . . In one passage, he

describes the recurrent mystical experience as a purely musical impression, non-extensive, entirely original, irreducible to any order of impression—sine materia . . . the invisible reality that damns the life of the body on earth as a pensum and reveals the meaning of the word defunctus.

The most cursory reading of five pages of *Molloy* or *Godot* will reveal the present significance of these words in the practice of Beckett himself.

Murphy (London 1938, Paris 1947) went unnoticed in the blizzard of "social" literature. It is the story of the quest for the person in terms of the quest for a valid asceticism. At the end Murphy has not found himself because he has not found what he can validly do without or safely do with. He may be on the brink of such a discovery, but mortality overtakes him. It is as though Arjuna had been poleaxed in his chariot while Krishna rambled sententiously on.

Watt was written in 1945 but published in Paris in 1953. "What" in Irish is pronounced "watt." It is a step forward in the best possible medium for Beckett's vision—the grim humor of *Iphigenia in Tauris, Lear*, Machiavelli's *Mandragola* and Jonson's *Volpone*. Its concern is the problem, who is who, and its corollary, what is what.

> Looking at a pot, for example, or thinking of a pot, at one of Mr. Knott's pots, of one of Mr. Knott's pots, it was in vain that Watt said, Pot, pot. Well, perhaps not quite in vain, but very nearly. For it was not a pot, the more he looked, the more he reflected, the more he felt sure of that, that it was not a pot at all. It resembled a pot, it was almost a pot, but it was not a pot of which one could say, Pot, pot, and be comforted.

I hope you noticed the sentence, "Well, perhaps not quite in vain, but very nearly." Because that is the gist of the matter and the plot of the novel, the point, so to speak. And it is the point of a good deal of Beckett.

Molloy is the story of two journalists, two keepers of personal, disorganized journals in the dark, light-years beyond the end of night. Molloy, a cripple, is left eventually on his belly in the gloom, clawing his way forward with his crutches. Possibly he is seeking his mother—at least at times that is the impression.

Eventually he crawls to a room somewhere where "they"—the "they" of Edward Lear's limericks—bring him food and writing material and take away for their own purposes his narrative as he writes it week by week. It is a grim revery of empty progress through time and space, punctuated with dog-like sex and paretic battle.

Moran, the subject of the second half of the novel, is a more recognizable literary figure—the hunter with all the characteristics of the hunted: Inspector Maigret with the personality of Gregor; the inspector in *Crime and Punishment* replaced by Smerdyakov from *Karamazov*. At the orders of a hidden boss whom Beckett, with a minimum of effort, invests with terrors of Fu Manchu, Moran hunts Molloy. In the process he loses his son and all the appurtenances of his personality, and becomes indistinguishable from his quarry. At the end he possibly encounters and kills Molloy without knowing it. On crutches himself, in the night, in the rain, he discovers a voice, and writes in turn his narrative.

Molloy is the drama, totally devoid of event, of relevant event, of the seekers and the finders, of whom it has been said: "Finders keepers, losers weepers."

The other two novels, yet to be translated from the French, are *Malone Meurt* (Paris, 1951), and *L'Innomnable* (Paris, 1953). Malone is another lonely writer, locked in a room and fed like a beast. He is trying to find his own existence by, as it were, describing his anti-self, by describing a hero who will be progressively differentiated from Malone. But he cannot do it. He cannot even keep track of the other's name, and he finally comes to write a story that sounds like an exhausted Sade, and which is, of course, the story of Malone.

L'Innomnable is exactly what its title says—the narrative of someone without a name who cannot find a name, who never does.

Waiting for Godot is that rare play, the distillation of dramatic essence which we have been talking about for the whole twentieth century, and about which we have done, alas, so little. Its peers are the Japanese Noh drama and the American burlesque comedy team. It is not just a play of situation—a situation which, in the Japanese Noh drama, reveals its own essence like a crystal. It just is a situation. The crystal isn't there. Two tramps, two utterly dispossessed, alienated, and disaffiliated beings, are waiting for somebody who is never going to come and who might be God. Not because they have any faith in his coming—although one does, a little—but because waiting requires less effort than anything else. They are not seeking meaning. The meaning is in the waiting. They are interrupted by the eruption into their contemplative lives of "The World," "Western Civilization"—or anything else like that that might be put in capital letters—in the persons of Pozzo and Lucky, Master and Man—two cacophonous marionettes of stunning horror. On their second appearance Pozzo and Lucky grow even more horrible and considerably less stunning. Otherwise, time does not pass. Today cannot recall yesterday, and tomorrow is not coming. The meaning is in the waiting. And in the tree, which overnight, between the acts, manages a few flimsy leaves. In the void, Beckett's tramps idle, analogues of Kanzan and Jitoku, the clown saints of Zen. Vladimir says, "Well, shall we go?" Estragon says, "Yes, let's go." Beckett says, *"They do not move. Curtain."*

Theatrically speaking, in terms of an evening's entertainment, I have given a falsely bleak picture. The play is hilariously funny. All the traditional business that has come down from the Romans through Italian comedy to burlesque, to the red-nosed, derby-hatted, baggy-pantsed burlesque clown is exploited. But it is not exploited in its own terms. Each passage of business worthy of Chaplin or Buster Keaton at their best is transmuted by a terrible light, like the deadly rays of unimaginable colors that shine in science fiction.

I think this summary of his achievement to date and its meaning has been fair to Beckett. Now there is nothing left, since I have already implied that he is an artist of consummate attainment, but an attempt to answer the question, since he is a moral artist, is it true? Do these books represent a valid judgment of the human situation? I do not like to sound like an editorial in *Pravda,* but I doubt it, partly. It is not absolutely true at its most superficial level. The world ill, *le mal mondiale,* is not only limited in time to the last two hundred years, but it is limited in space to that very little peninsula, Europe, and to the new lands Europe has overrun. I realize that it is imbecilic to say, "Why doesn't Beckett (or Artaud or Céline or Miller) sing the glories of our Stakhanovite workers and collectivist farmers and tractor drivers, or of our jet pilots and cobalt atom splitters? Where is the New Man, the Hero of the Twentieth Century?" And all critics who object to Beckett reduce themselves eventually to this level, the level of Zhdanov, *Variety,* Mac-Leish. But the light is never spent. Heroism is only smoldering and will flame up after these dark ages are over. The society in which we live is destroying the person and the communion of persons. First we self and the other (not the anti-humanist, Kafka-Kierkegaard, Godot —the "utterly other"—but Buber's "I and thou" on a purely secular plane). That is the current problem, the superficial "message" of Beckett's books, and it is, historically, superficial and temporary.

As for the permanent one, not superficially: this is Beckett's main subject, and here his judgment is not invalid, because it is the judgment of Homer, of the literature of heroes. The world is blind, and random. If we persist in judging it in human terms it is malignant and frivolous. Only man is loyal and kind and brave. Only man loves. Zeus thunders like the empty sky. Aphrodite ruts like her pigeons. If we refuse to accept the world on secular terms, Godot isn't coming. If we accept it for ourselves, the comradeship of men, whether verminous tramps with unmanageable pants or Jim and Huck Finn drifting through all the universe on their raft—the comradeship of men in work, in art, or simply in waiting, in the utterly unacquisitive act of waiting—is an ultimate value, so ultimate, that it gives life sufficient dignity and satisfaction. So say Homer and Samuel Beckett and everybody else, too, who has ever been worth his salt.

The Nation (April 14, 1956, p. 325-328)

795 BROADWAY, NEW YORK 3, N.Y. • GRAMERCY 3-7447

March 26, 1956

Dear Samuel,

Many thanks for sending back the page proofs of Malone
so quickly. They arrived this morning and are on their way to
the printer.

Thanks also for the signed contract for L'Innommable.
I quite understand how you may have put it aside for the
moment and please don't let that cause any anxieties insofar
as I am concerned. Do let us take a look at the new play when
you feel it is fit for human consumption.

We were in the process of digging large holes in our
garden when some 14 inches of snow collapsed on it the other
day. We are not sure at the moment as to whether or not we
will ever see it again.

George Reavey uncovered one Watson Pierce who still
had clutched to his bosom a copy of More Pricks Than Kicks. I
have now temporarily secured said copy and as soon as I finish
reading Murphy for the second time I will begin on this one.
It occurs to me that the stories are completely unknown in
the United States and if I had somebody make a typed copy of
each it might well be possible to submit them to some American
publications and perhaps achieve a sale or two. Would you
object to my doing this?

Our paper edition of Godot has now sold well over
2,000 copies and if Myerberg ever puts it on or lets somebody
else go ahead I am sure that we will have a fresh burst of
activity.

Best,

Barney

GROVE PRESS

795 BROADWAY, NEW YORK 3, N.Y. • GRAMERCY 3-7447

May 22, 1956

Dear Samuel,

      Something in the way of money must be percolating
through to you from London—or at least they are busy counting
up what is owed to you, because the Myerberg office called
today saying that Curtis Brown wrote that we had been overpaid
$100.00. This happens to be true (last January they paid us
10% of the advance from Myerberg and we did not make a proper
note of the fact) and the money will now be deducted from
whatever we have coming. So they are counting your dollars
carefully and I hope that you will have the use of them to get
some good manure for your Arbor Vitae.

      Along the same commercial but soothing lines, we
sent off a check or cheque yesterday directly to Lindon
(look, no agents) for the sum of $400.00 as an advance for
L'Inno. 3T1F*3T I hope that your proper share arrives chez vous
most promptly.

      Advertisements now have the run going through June
9thand if business holds I am sure that they will continue.

      Would you be available for an aperitif with a visitor—
namely me—sometime during the first two weeks of June if I
should take it into my head to want to eat dinner aboard an
Air France plane bound for you know where? After all, if you
won't come here (I wanted to say something in French but the
knowledge deserted me), ANYWAY, do let me know.

      Best,

      Barney

GROVE PRESS

795 BROADWAY, NEW YORK 3, N.Y. • GRAMERCY 3-7447

July 25, 1956

Dear Samuel,

Finally I at least sit down to write a note-it all seems so difficult these days. No trouble at all to run from one end of Manhattan to the other for some silly boring lunch date, but to get off something to you, or Joan, or anyone important, c'est autre chose.

Anyway-to at least comment on your most appreciated missiles. I would love to do the Proust book and your letter goaded me into action. I snatched it off the shelf in East Hampton and handed it to the printer today for a printing estimate. My idea is that we will bring it out, at $1.00 if possible, in February or thereabouts of next year. This time ALL of the royalties can go directly to you. If this meets with your approval, let me know and I will send you a letter of confirmation and even dredge up some sort of a modest advance.

It would seem that reappearance of Godot on Broadway is now in state of usual confusion. First it was announced for October at same theater. Then another play was name for same theater. Then Myerberg gave new theater for Godot, now another play for that theater. Soooo. Also he said that it could go on only if they could get original cast.
AND NOW FOR SOMETHING REALLY IMPORTANT.
First, read the enclosed letters. They give the idea-a program of readings of the writings of one SAMUEL BECKETT. I am absolutely terrified at the idea of being in charge of it and being expected to say something, so you must help me.

We need-A program

Readings from poetry - Echo's Bones
Whoroscope

Others things which I may not know about. Perhaps a French poem or two if either Marshall or Epstein can read in French.

Prose - Proust
Anything else which I may not know about.

Stories - More Pricks Than Kicks
Other stories unbeknownst to me

```
Novels - Murphy
         Watt
         Molloy
         Malone Dies
       L'Inno
```

And other things such as Fin de Partie, Texte de Rien and so
forth.

So out of all this richness we must put together something to
take up about 1hr and 45 minutes, including whatever little
words I may have to contribute—which means some kind of biographical background on you and some sort of setting for each
piece.

      Naturally it would be wonderful if any section of
something not yet published could be read because that would
help to draw attention to the whole affair—and if if IF IF I
could persuade you to stop in at a recording studio, either
for tape or disque, and read a section of something yourself,
then I think we would have something of truly great interest to the people here. I mentioned this to the Poetry Center
people and they were completely captivated by the idea. The
little piece Joyce read is blurred and almost unintelligi-
ble, but it is so treasured, and I know the same would be true
of anything you did. If you did read a piece, and then were
completely dissatisfied with it—well just junk it, otherwise
we could play it here—in French or English, or even better, a
bit of both. Do consider it—get Suzanne's opinion—and if it is
only a matter of arrangement, we could do that from here, although I am sure that somebody like Roger Blin, or undoubtedly you yourself already know, of some simple studio facility.
And I would very much demand to pay for any costs involved.
R.S.V.P. If you do not want to go into a studio then all you
need is a friend with a tape recorder. I have one, many of my
friends do also, so the same thing must exist in quantity in

Paris—as a matter of fact I had one there in '48. Had the silly idea I could write by speaking to the damn machine and then type it off.

That's all for the program for the moment—but I am counting on you like a man waits for that last drink two minutes before the pub closes.

And the BBC 3rd programme—merveilleux. I do hope something comes of it. Sounds like the same project for which our Greek girl, Kay Cicellis, has been asked to write a play. And the mime for TV, again the same hopes.

Nice sort of fat royalty payment on Godot book coming up in week or so.

And me. Loly is living apart, in East Hampton, nearby, we see each other, even get along better, and who knows where it goes—and as one said, even Noel Coward couldn't have written it. She sends her love, which I send, with mine, to you and Suzanne. J'attends, yrs.

Barney

August 20, 1956

Dear Samuel,

First for the addenda-enclosed:

     New Grove and *Evergreen* catalogues

     Beckett brochure

Second-for what is important-The Reading.

All constantly on my mind since I got your MOST welcome letter. I was very happy to get your concurrence and your views. Perhaps I could go back over your letter in the same order you mention things.

I certainly do want you to make suggestions on the readings. Please give me as many as you can dredge up.

In Murphy the "Amor Intellectualis etc." would be fine, even though I think that perhaps more of the quality of the writing comes out in other parts.

What about "Dante and the Lobster" from More Pricks than Kicks?

And for the recordings-both Poetry Center and I extremely happy and pleased that you will do something yourself-text in English and one in French sounds perfect-CROAK ON.

First week in September will be fine.

For Martin and Blin, Poetry Center says no-I think they are wrong and if you could possibly get them to do what you suggest in your letter I think that later we might have material for a disque-I would certainly give my share of the reading money to them and later if we found a way to get some income out of their efforts we would pass along part of the money. I am very strongly in favor of the idea and I do hope to get a tape with all three of you on it.

Alvin Epstein told me that he would like to read something in French-perhaps some poetry. What would you suggest?

A passage from L'Inno (translation in progress) would be very good idea-and also newsworthy.

Am looking forward to seeing the English text "From an Abandoned Work." What is a TCD magazine? We certainly might get some USA periodical to use it.

Proust is in the works-will publish it in first half of 57.

You might use the enclosed biographical notes as a starting point for what I might say about you (including correcting or throwing the whole thing out).

So that is for the reading. Your letter of approval has been best thing to happen since I got back from Paris.

So—Myerberg et al. Told later via secretary to trundle along a slug of disques. Hope he did so. Also hope you have heard recording of Godot. We have not and will very much like to know your reaction. They have a monstrous poster for it, but that should not prejudice the spoken woid [sic].

If Godot can run walk or crawl until the end of September I suppose that I can too —although I pass through doubts. Domestic situation is not settled. Is that good or bad.

Can't read the inked in work about the Limes Verlag trilingual poems. Encore une fois. Anyway I wear my lovely leather slippers and smoke an occasional Gaulois.

3rd Radio script — incroyable — and only hope I can see it one of these dreary months. Don't be careful and thus let something come of it. And j'attends the Fin de Partie script.

Perhaps will turn out my own *Evergreen* Magazine. Brings to mind Cioran. Was there any essay in particular you would recommend? Have all sorts of ideas for Beckett material.

Only intense thing I have done since leaving Paris has been to play my ambidextrous no talent tennis. Vacuous-drifting—played chess the other night with someone and started dreaming—finally was moving opponent's pieces. Unfortunately he ultimately noticed and woke me up—otherwise outcome would have been interesting.

Crash death of Jackson Pollock in East Hampton week or so ago was depressing - even though he had been trying to wind himself around a tree for several years and was probably only to be congratulated for having accomplished it so neatly. A last coherence out of chaos.

Anyway, Peter Michael thrives, walks, is obstinate, generous, is frustrated by Albertine the Cat, mutters a goodly number of sounds and prefers nothing to walking across the tennis court when his poor father is trying to have a set or two of adolescence.

Best to you both,

Barney

GROVE PRESS

795 BROADWAY, NEW YORK 3, N. Y. • GRAMERCY 3-7447

September 17, 1956

Dear Samuel:

Everything you have to say about the reading is clear, and I received sections of The Unnamable and From an Abandoned Work, excepting that I do not know if the later was originally written in English or French. Also, you do not mention Whoroscope. Do you wish us to look at that or do you want it skipped?

I certainly do hope very much that you go ahead with the recording and naturally I would also very much like to have something done by Blin and Martin.

The payment made to Saunders on behalf of you as translator should come directly to you and not to Lindon. It merely means that Maid Marion is still hoarding the funds.

I am now very much intrigued with the idea of bringing out Murphy and I recall Routledge claiming to still have the rights to it. I also note that they did not copyright the book. Please let me know what you feel about the whole matter and I will carry on from there.

We have written to Niklaus Gessner about the Godot piece and I very much hope that he sends it to us. If you or someone else let us have a copy we could make a photo of it here and return it the same day.

Will write about the other things later.

Best regards,

Barney

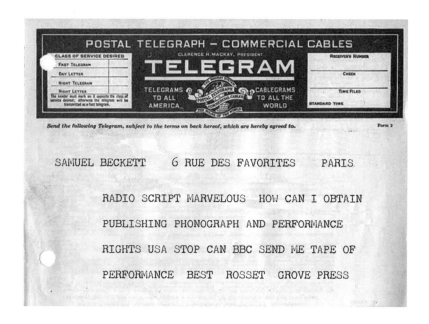

SAMUEL BECKETT   6 RUE DES FAVORITES   PARIS

RADIO SCRIPT MARVELOUS HOW CAN I OBTAIN

PUBLISHING PHONOGRAPH AND PERFORMANCE

RIGHTS USA STOP CAN BBC SEND ME TAPE OF

PERFORMANCE BEST ROSSET GROVE PRESS

Irish actor, Barry McGovern (Left), Billie Whitelaw, and Director, Everett Frost, relax during recording sessions for Samuel Beckett's play for radio, *Embers*. (Photo: Scott Kraft).

January 14, 1957

Dear Samuel:

The Boston production went off very well. To me the new Vladimir is incomparable—better than Marshall, and this greatly changes the whole play. The new Lucky is absolutely different from the other one and the descriptions of the Boston critics, wherein they say he is "astounding," is about the best adjective available. Estragon has some lamentable Negroisms, which disturb me and I hope they somehow tone him down before it opens on Broadway.

Still waiting to hear about All That Fall. Please send me The Gloaming.

We are planning a Mexican issue of the Evergreen Review and it seems to me we might very well be able to use something from the translations you did. Could we possibly get a look at the manuscript even though it is unpublished?

Please do write to John Morse telling him that Grove Press would like to both publish All That Fall and would also like to make a phonograph record of it, either using the BBC broadcast itself, or making a new version here.

I do look forward to getting Fin de Partie and am very happy to know that you may translate it immediately. I do hope you can manage to get the play put on in London without letting the English producer control the American rights, and this goes no matter who the American producer is—Myerberg or somebody else. It also seems to me that it would be very good if you could let more than one American producer read the play.

Yours,

Barney

ALL THAT FALL

a play by

Samuel Beckett

With Best Wishes for the Holiday Season

from

GROVE PRESS

GROVE PRESS

795 BROADWAY, NEW YORK 3, N.Y. • GRAMERCY 3-7447

March 23, 1957

Dear Sam,

Delighted to know that Fin de Partie and mime will be done at Royal Court. If only I could be there to see it—and I assure I would if only these infamous regulations were not in effect.

And am even more delighted to know that we can expect to have Fin de Partie by August. I certainly would like to purchase the translation—under any terms or agreement acceptable to you. Am looking at the agreement of the first translation, one which gave unforeseen benefits to me. The necessity to obtain permission for use from me actually became a small royalty deducted from Lindon's share and this royalty has amounted to a goodly number of hundreds of dollars and will undoubtedly continue to do so. I can see no earthly reason why I should deserve to have such a clause in the new agreement.

Sam, PLEASE don't hesitate to disagree with any suggestion I make. Believe me, you have meant a great deal to me and to Grove Press, and if any proposal I make does not coincide with your wishes I will certainly not be upset.

The first problem is to know exactly what rights you have already given to the Royal Court. Naturally I hope they have only performance rights for England but I await clarification from you. I am terribly interested in who gets the American performance rights. As far as those are concerned I would naturally be delighted if I were to have the same royalty arrangement as I do on Godot (only this time excluding England) and get what I believe is 10% of the amount due to you and Lindon combined. I think I can justify the royalty by the fact that we exercise a constant supervision on performances (especially amateur ones), get all requests for performance to the proper channels here, and I would like to act in some consulting manner as your representative here when a production is being prepared and staged, and at least be in a good position to transmit to all progress, etc. If either the royalty or the official consulting capacity seems a mistake to you—tell me, and we forget it.

Also I would very much like to have the right to do a phonograph or tape recording for commercial sale. At least I would like to have first crack at it and I would certainly give up this right if it became apparent somebody else could do it better. In my opinion we could do the record and sell it successfully. On the record I would make a separate contract with Lindon and you and pay separate advances, etc.

If you sell the translation to me—for which I would pay you an advance and a royalty—I presume I would then be free to sell it to Faber, proceeds of which would be divided with you. And any other sale I made, outside of our own publication, would be divided with you.

That about covers the matter of the translation—as soon as you approve the idea or change it in any way you desire, I will draw up a contract and zip it on to you.

Hope you were not displeased by *Evergreen* Review. Will certainly want to use something by you in issue number 3. One idea is From An Abandoned Work—or have you another suggestion?

And we must certainly have our collected poetry of Beckett. Echo's Bones, Whoroscope, and various our snitchets on hand. Will make out our listing and then have you add to it.

Loly is in course of doing final two weeks in Reno, Nevada. All a sort of barbarism and what follows next I do not know. I am afraid we are both fearful of looking ahead. Link continues to be the pillar holding the works up.
Last week we went out to East Hampton where I got in a bit of tennis, much to my amazement. Last year the same day was marked by a blizzard. This year the croci (croak who) are in bloom—and a few weeks back we skied a bit in the silly hills of Vermont. I cannot say that Loly is out of my mind, and how the summer will work with her a few houses away is at the moment a mystification.

At last, or at least now, I have a good and experienced man to be a co-runner of things, at least the administrative side, and he plus the others seem to be jelling into a sort of decent organization. We actually showed a profit for the months of January and February, first such signs of hope since the beginning some years ago—and the more than 8000 Beckett volumes which have gone out during the days since January 1st have certainly been a terribly important factor. Advances on royalties against both Proust and Murphy have certainly been covered and if ever you wish payments ahead of regular times, do just say the word. Otherwise the money will be computed for the six months and then sent thereafter.

It's a lovely day again—my wishes are that I could be there, in London or Paris (and why cannot a little jaunt to New York ever be arranged) and I am waiting for the day when at least you take the phone from hook and dial our new phone number.

Very best to you and Suzanne, to Roger Blin and the others. Fingers are snarled in hopes of Fin de Partie success.

Yours, as ever,

Barney

GROVE PRESS ✳

795 BROADWAY, NEW YORK 3, N.Y. • GRAMERCY 3-7447

[no date, but part written
Easter Sunday night 1957]

Dear Samuel,

Many, many thanks for the splendid letter—really managed to push up a rather murky Manhattan ceiling. I do hope
you get to water the greenery a bit and take a moment to recover from the London soup. Life magazine has been buzzing the
ears off the phone, asking questions about you. Probably use
three words in the end. Anyway it does appear as if an article might erupt. Did you meet John Calder in London? I met him
here and he has written saying that he will do Molloy,
Malone, and L'Inno all at one smack.

To go back to your letter for the moment. I am so
touched by words about me—contracts, performance rights, etc.
If by any chance I should be put in charge of Endgame here I
should try to pick out the right producer from amongst the
entrants I would endeavor to round up, and then try to follow
events with him as they progressed. I feel that this would be
my greatest area of helpfulness, but one way or the other, I
am happy you have thought of the possibility, and as I say
above, the contract for the translation will make no mention
of performance.
Anyway, if you offer me the thing—I will accept.

Certainly do not have Cascando, the American bitch—
have had others but not she. Do send her on. Judith is com-
piling our list and we will buck it over to you for further
items.

Proust is already being reprinted—first printing was
3000 and so is second—and it is outselling Murphy, this frankly stumps me. Reviews have been widespread and excellent on
the old boy, but the market seems to lie in the paperbound
books. He will get there, but I am trying to milk the other
first.

So really there is a great deal of activity—all done
with a fair amount of dispatch and perhaps even efficiency. I
fear that my dilatory actions in answering your letter, the
most important thing, may give you the idea that either we
are hopeless go to sleepers, or that I am not interested in

having rights to do the play. Actually everything that is not
personally involving to me gets done immediately, but reply-
ing to you is such a real thing to me, one I cannot trust to
dictation, or carrying out by someone else, that I sit on it
and brood and reread and mix up with Loly (now we are legally
divorced) and Peter and Link and everything else that confuses
and stops me and puts the core of me into a sort of state of
atrophy, lets the outward manifestations of life joggle along.
The new man at Grove Press is fine, administration moves on,
etc., etc., but I snarl my poor insides-brooding about Loly,
strangling myself with jealousy, glooming about Peter, saved
continuously by Link, and all that goes with it.

     The day here was lovely-play tennis, as atrocious-
ly as ever, dazzled by idea you even mention possibility of
coming here, pet the pussycat Albertine (and now she is what
has been with me the longest, some ten years), irritate myself
with getting my house in New York furnished, and so on. I have
given myself a study in my house there and I hope to shortly
start spending a good part of the day in it, perhaps inducing
myself to doing the important things first, like answering your
letters. The house is only two or three blocks from the office
and phones are hooked up directly (and so happy to know you
have one of the devils, its number shall not be spread by me)
and people will not be annoyed by my looking over their shoul-
ders while they work and so on. All hypothesis of course

     And that is it Samuel. My head seems like packages of
wires ripped open and twisted, misconnected and short cir-
cuited. Sometimes a message reaches some center, only to get
annihilated on its way to the next plug in point. Am hoping
for Paris Fin de Partie-and New York one. Hello and all that
is good to Suzanne.

    Yours,

    Barney

May 7, 1957

MEMORANDUM OF AGREEMENT BETWEEN SAMUEL BECKETT, 6 rue des Favorites, Paris XV, France, and GROVE PRESS, INC., 795 Broadway, New York 3, N.Y., U.S.A., COVERING THE ENGLISH LANGUAGE PUBLICATION RIGHTS OF FIN DE PARTIE.

1.   Samuel Beckett hereby agrees to sell to Grove Press, Inc., the world English language publication rights of his translation from the French, of his play FIN DE PARTIE. Grove Press, Inc. will fully own these publication rights and any book publisher, magazine publisher, etc., in any country, wanting to use this translation for publication purposes, will have to apply to Grove Press, Inc. for permission.

2.   In full payment for the ownership of these publication rights, Grove Press, Inc. will pay Samuel Beckett the sum of $150.00 upon delivery of the English translation, this sum to be considered as an advance against a royalty of two per cent on the published price of all copies sold of the Grove Press regular trade editions. Payment shall be made semi-annually, as regular royalties.

3.   In the event that Grove Press, Inc. sells these publication rights to any other publisher in any country, for any purpose whatsoever, one-half of any such income shall be paid to Samuel Beckett, the other half to be retained by Grove Press, Inc.

SAMUEL BECKETT

                                        BARNEY ROSSET, PUBLISHER
                                        GROVE PRESS, INC.

August 23, 1957

Dear Sam:

This is given over the phone from East Hampton.

I was delighted to get the *End Game* translation and we
have already had galleys set. A more or less corrected copy
will be on its way to you almost momentarily.

I have also spoken twice to Alan Schneider and I am sure that
he and I can proceed to set up a production. Your desire to
see the mime as a film gave me the idea that if we could have
the film made in France—with Mendel, of course—we could show
the film in the theatre here along with the play. I discussed
this with Schneider and he was quite enthusiastic about the
idea. This would not be a completely new procedure and I think
it might be very intriguing audience-wise. Perhaps Lindon
could investigate time and cost problems as concerns making
the film. When the film was not used with the play, it could be
shown separately in theatres.

I do plan to visit Europe this fall and I will write
more later.

Best,

Barney

November 11, 1957

Dear Sam,

This one hell of a time to finally write to you—seems I
go into a state of paralysis insofar as doing anything that
really counts. Perfectly able to tell? Tilford Tellingheusen
that I do not want his book on German spear carrying or
Alfonso Bastardo that his new grape vine book won't do—but I
simply find myself stymied when I try to do those things I want
to do. Anyway—had lunch with Alan and I promised I would write
to you immediately about a situation which is bothering him
very much—the apparent possibility that a production of Godot-
off-Broadway, will be put on shortly before we open *End Game*.
I agree with Alan, and our producer to be, that this could
easily be injurious to the new play by taking the publicity
and freshness from it.

The last evening is still much with me, not only the
hilarious blackout but also your feelings about what there
is to come now—writing in English. Alan remains the same fine
fellow and win or lose I think he is a good choice. I met his
wife and baby and tomorrow Alan is coming to my house for a
drink and to meet John Calder—do hope that all goes well with
you and Suzanne—and that the last of the damned translation
business gets out of the way soon.

Yours, as ever,

Barney

795 BROADWAY, NEW YORK 3, N.Y. • GRAMERCY 3-7447

Friday, January 10, 1958

Dear Sam,

I am terribly sorry about the letter business. Alan gave me
the copy to read and to forward on to you—and evidently he
also wrote to you asking for your approval, or the opposite.
It is or was meant for an article—to be signed by Alan—for The
New York Times drama section, and it is something with which
I have absolutely nothing to do. Quite often the director of
a new piece is asked to write something and of course this is
considered to be good publicity. You will remember the mis-
leading piece, which appeared before Godot—the story about the
men in the sand, etc. Alan came up with the letter idea and of
course he would wish to go through with it—but I am sure that
any strong objection voiced to him would cause him to abandon
it and come up with something else. An inconvenience—but there
are lots of them in the theater.

Many of your letters to me are not even in the Grove
Press files—but are stuck away in a drawer at home. I believe
that is an indication of how I would feel about the matter—but
there are many things about the theater and this promotion
business which escape me, and I strongly feel that Alan values
your friendship and confidence extremely highly and if he felt
that this public display of what is private were to make you
fear to speak freely to him in the future—he will stop the
piece. Believe me—I am not planning to broadcast anything said
to me personally, unless you specifically ask me to. I tried
to reach Alan this morning but was unable to—I will say that
you are not happy about the matter, that you would prefer he
not have the letters published—but that if the thing is of the
greatest importance to him, then you would reluctantly let him
do it.

Yours,

Barney

GROVE PRESS

795 BROADWAY, NEW YORK 3, N.Y. • GRAMERCY 3-7447

February 17, 1958

Dear Sam,

This is just the scratchings of a real letter, but
I did want you to know that I am still about and kicking.
Reviews of the play have gone to you—and our ad in the paper,
etc. Business at the theater does not seem to be good enough
to keep the producer happy and we are hoping that yesterday's
piece in The New York Times will help. Unfortunately we also
had the worst blizzard of the last few years yesterday and
so the damned paper had only half its usual circulation. The
advertising of the theater has created a severe pain in my
neck—I feel it is very poor in that it is not appealing to
the people likely to come to the theater (their big quote is
"loonier than Godot")—however the theater is the right one,
Alan has done his very best, the Hamm is quite acceptable,
the Clov not quite good enough, and the ash canners quite
adequate—the set marvelous (and it is a result of a suggestion
by Link)—the book is buzzing along quite nicely. I am about
talked out on the play before I even write to you, but Alan I
am sure has handled describing it to you much better than I
could anyway. All I know is that personally the play continues
to have tremendous appeal to me, always different, shifting
its surfaces—and some people have really been deeply affected
by the play. It is going to have a lasting life here.

But—I am very excited about the progress of L'Inno. It
looks like the day approaches when this accursed translating
can reach some sort of a stopping (almost, not quite, maybe)
and a new blossom can come forth. I suggested to Alan, and I
guess he to you, that we commission you to do a new work. This
would certainly mean that we take anything—or nothing—which
came forth. Of course I hope at least as much that some prose
piece may gurgle up from down below—perhaps even in English.

The tapes NEVER arrived. Have you any way to trace
them. I am hopeful of putting End Game on a disque. Sent off
1500 copies of paperbound Murphy to Calder—although we will
not sell it here that way until next fall. Will have final
sales figures for last six months of all Beckett books in the

near future. I believe they show continued good sales of
everything. Proust is a real surprise—new printing getting
ready. I would urge you and Lindon to take Calder as English
publisher whenever possible. He is a bit odd, but I like him,
we are doing many things together, he likes your work very
much, and although he may be a risk he may also end up a much
better publisher for you than someone like Faber.

Is there any chance of your coming this way—I became
a bit annoyed because the theater boys seemed to think that
your landing on American soil would boom the box office—and
this scratched me in several ways. However they are dying to
mail you a ticket (round trip) for you and Suzanne or you
alone, and if you would accept the offer I for one would be
extremely happy. Meeting Peter and Vicky might be worth the
trip. The latter is already half way to being an important
personage and she is not yet three.

Went skiing up on a mountain and managed to remain
intact. Would much prefer trying it in Suisse to here—but I
seem to be here (sometimes).

Yours,

Barney

March 28, 1958

Dear Sam,

For God's sake DON'T give up drink. Ex-drinkers are
more than I can put up with. And for Krapp—we shall pickle
him first in the *Evergreen Review*. Both Alan and my Ev Rev
coeditor are krapping their hands in joy over Krapp. I have
sent out the script to two prospective putter-onners and Alan
has promised to get an actor to give us a private performance
here. I will even lend my Krapp recorder for the tapes.

Said one fly to another as he surveyed his dismal pay
allowance, "the situation is getting grave" (grave not grove).
See what Krapp is doing to me, I practically dug my own grave.

Best,

Barney

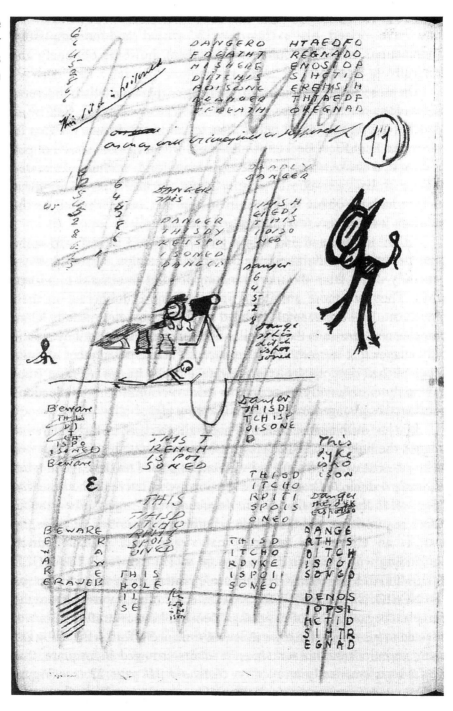

March 26, 1958

Dear Barney,

Thanks for letters, cheques and cuttings.

I'm glad you like poor old Krapp.

I must write even more stupidly and confusedly than I thought about rights and business. But if you redirect all your ingenuity on my Krappp letter I believe you will find it to mean what follows.

You (B. Rosset) have all and exclusive publication and performance rights In US, Canada and wherever else you normally exercise them.

You are therefore free, without consulting anyone, to publish Krapp and have it performed in US, Canada, etc., when, where, how, with whom, by whom, under whom and before whom you please. If this is not clear I'll give up drink.

Ever

Sam

October 20, 1964
Paris

Dear Barney,

    I have broken down halfway through
galleys of <u>More Pricks than Kicks</u>. I simply
can't bear it. It was a ghastly mistake on my
part to imagine, not having
looked at it for a quarter of a century, that
this old shit was revivable. I'm terribly
sorry, but I simply have to ask you to stop
production. I return herewith advance on
royalties and ask you to charge to my account
with Grove whatever expenses
whatever entailed by this beginning of
production. I'll be talking to John today to
the same humiliating effect. Please forgive
me.

        Yours ever,

Sam

entr'acte

Every newspaper—print newspaper—has what are called fillers: Short half-inch or 3/4 inch items to plug a space at the bottom of a column. (It was one such one-inch filler in The New York Times that in [the] 1950s would draw the attention of a Chicago-born rebel named Barney Rosset to a strange new play in Paris called "Waiting for Godot"—a play that, as it happened, a young New Yorker named Howard Fertig would actually have seen, in London, before he showed up at The Village Voice one day to write about it.)

—Jerry Tallmer, The Villager (Nov. 25, 1960)

 **books**

WAITING FOR GODOT

A play by Samuel Beckett. Grove Press, $1.

by Howard Fertig

Last summer, in England, I went to one of the strangest and most eloquent plays I have ever seen. "Waiting for Godot" (now published by the Grove Press, and opening this week on Broadway) had already been acclaimed in Paris, and it is still running, nine months after its opening, in London. At the London opening there was a great sound and fury from the critics. Some attacked it, others were enthralled by it; no one dismissed it. Possessing that quality of all original works of art—the Mona Lisa smile that chides both enemies and friends for their presumption and their arrogance—the play demanded discussion, reconsideration, and even acquiescence.

On second thought, hostile critics allowed a grudging admiration for this or that element of it, but still insisted: "It's not a play. Nobody does anything. Nothing happens." "That's precisely the point," its adherents answered, not quite sure whether this was so or not, but having seen the play as with the eye of faith, quite willing to include this in their vision of it.

In a sense, I suppose, nothing does happen. Two men are seen on the stage. Two tramps. They have been waiting for several days by the side of the road for a man who has promised to help them but has not appeared. What that help might be, we are never told. He keeps sending word that perhaps he will come the next day.

He never does. He probably never will. We feel this and so do the two men. But still they wait and hope, argue and complain. Twice during the play two other characters come along the road, thrust their own terrible lives at us, and then are gone. The two tramps are again alone and go on waiting, talking, and hoping as before. That is all. That is the play. And, as E. M. Forster once said, " 'Moby Dick' is about a whale."

The Traveler Adrift

The image of the traveler adrift, the lost voyager, the searcher—really as old as Homer—often seems the monopoly and the invention of the twentieth-century writer. What he has done, though, is to reverse the older meaning of the image by reading into it our modern nightmare. Ulysses finally returns home; Stephen Daedalus never does. Dante, when he finds himself "in a dark place, astray" at the beginning of the "Inferno," has made only the first of many discoveries which will finally lead him back to the light. When Kafka's heroes fully realize that they are astray, it is only at the close of the book and as a final discovery—the end of the journey, the sum of knowledge.

Estragon and Vladimir, the two waiting men, have taken their first step out of the darkness by convincing themselves that hope exists. "What are we doing here, that is the question," remarks Estragon to his companion, "and we are blessed in that we happen to know the answer. Yes, in the immense confusion one thing alone is clear. We are waiting for Godot to come." So, quite stranded on a road, exhausted, and with a lifetime of suffering behind them and most likely before them as well, they create their triumph by creating a certainty. It is a certainty the name of which they are not even sure;

Continued on page 5

WAITING FOR GODOT

Continued from page 4

Village Voice
(August 29, 1956,
p. 84)

they think it is Godot, they think that he may be able to help them, and they think that he is to meet them, here where they wait. If it should all turn out to be an illusion, it is still a little sublime. For at this moment they stand for that stubborn, proud spirit in human beings which, in the face of no matter what defeat, always insists on resuming the struggle.

Of Human Bondage

But have they not been placed in a subtle bondage by this very spirit in them that insists they endure? The question of human bondage recurs in many ways throughout the play. "Don't touch me! Don't question me! Don't speak to me! Stay with me!" cries Estragon, caught in a fury of confusion and misery; and in that cry is caught the whole dilemma of mutual need and opposing desire, as old as humanity itself.

A little later in the play an hallucination appears upon the stage. Two men enter—one tottering, loaded down with valises, a basket, a chair, and a rope around his neck, which is held by the second, who drives him forward with a whip. Here is the truth, one thinks, not knowing yet what truth it is the author has revealed, but knowing that this must always be its form, startling, hideous, with neither grace nor euphemism to make it more palatable. The two apparitions stand there, the one like some obscene enormity, the other looking as if he contained all the pain that man ever suffered. And then follows a chilling scene in which the master puts the slave through his paces as one would show off a trained dog.

Does Not Sentimentalize

Yet Beckett does not sentimentalize about the virtue of victims or the evil of masters. The two are not a separate breed, but each equally capable of the other's cruelty or abjectness. The accident of position is all. Estragon, given the opportunity, kicks at the fallen slave—who, in unknowing terror, had struck him before. When Pozzo the master returns in the second act, blind and helpless, begging for aid, he still goes off afterward, whipping his slave before him. Victim tears at victim, and Beckett tells us not to berate man's cruelty as "inhuman," but rather to see it as all too human.

And what, finally, is the play about? What are we finally to make out of this rich mixture of pity and terror? God only knows (might we say, perhaps, that only Godot knows?). Or would it be best after all to say that "Waiting for Godot," like "Moby Dick," is about a wail?

Barney Rosset and John Calder interview with Jules Geller

CALDER: I came across Robbe-Grillet when I went skiing in France and I bought *The Erasers* (*Les Gommes*) in the local bookstore, and read it, and liked it, but didn't do anything very much about it. But then I was after a girl, it was an American opera singer, and spent a lot of time in Paris. I would go to Paris to see her and I'd go around to all the publishers. And I went to see Editions de Minuit about Beckett, and I saw *Les Gommes* there, and I said, "Oh, I read that book. I liked it very much." "He's got a new one out now." So I took that away and read it too. And then I wanted to make a contract. In the meantime, I corresponded with Barney, and I was coming to New York every so often. So Barney said, "Well, if you do it, we'll do it too." Then you wanted to change it. You didn't want to do *The Erasers*, you wanted to do the other book first, *The Voyeur*, because it's shorter and sexier. It's about a violent rape and a murder. So we did that first, and then we went on to . . .

ROSSET: That's one way of looking at it. If you were to read the two books, I think nobody else would say those things, even though I agree with what John just said. *The Voyeur* is almost an abstract piece of writing. If you saw what you just saw in it, all right. *The Erasers* was written in more of a traditional kind of prose as a mystery story, and nothing particularly difficult about reading it, although it's strange and it's in the plot style. *The Voyeur* is really the "new novel."

CALDER: But it was because of you that we did *The Voyeur* first.

ROSSET: And I said that the title *The Voyeur*, and it's true, was more intriguing. Also, you couldn't even translate the other title.

CALDER: *Les Gommes.*

ROSSET: *The Erasers* is no good. What it meant was "gumshoe." The American term, maybe British, a detective, in other words a double entendre, and it's impossible to translate.

CALDER: Yeah, but it's in an eraser rubbing a...

ROSSET: Yeah, but it's also a detective.

CALDER: But it's the Oedipus legend retold in modern terms. On this eraser you've got the name half rubbed off, because it's been "Oedipe," which is a clue.

ROSSET: But it's a detective doing it. In French it has a double meaning, and there's no way to translate it into English. But it's also much more straightforwardly written, whereas *The Voyeur* is the breakup of writing, as we knew it. More like abstract expressionism. There's no straight plot in *The Voyeur.*

CALDER: Well, I think there is.

ROSSET: There may be now.

GELLER: That shows you the power of objectivism, you see. You saw it.

CALDER: It's a man on an island. He goes to an island. He's only there for a day. He reads about a rape and a murder in the paper, and then the reader gets the impression that he did it, but having read about it, maybe he's in his imagination living those events.

GELLER: So you don't know.

ROSSET: You don't know. It's very ambivalent.

CALDER: You just don't know.

ROSSET: But they were both good anyway.

CALDER: But everything in Robbe-Grillet is what happens in the mind.

ROSSET: Also, the book became much more famous in France, and made him sort of the head of the nouveau roman. The Voyeur is much more intriguing.

GELLER: When you both published the book, you didn't publish for Barney or vice versa?

ROSSET: No. Did we even use the same translator?

ROSSET: Yes. Who was the translator then?

Calder: No.

ROSSET: Richard Howard.

Calder: Exactly. But you know, it's after.

ROSSET: You used our translation.

CALDER: We didn't get a translator until we'd agreed to do it. And at that point you had more money than we had anyhow, so we let you pay for the translation and then we bought it from you.

GELLER: Very wise decision.

CALDER: We were never affluent, you see.

GELLER: Yeah, I know.

CALDER: We did everything much more on a shoestring. But there were a lot of people like that.

ROSSET: If you'd seen a Grove Press office, I don't think you would have said it was more than a shoestring.

CALDER: I can remember you taking a whole page in *The New York Times* and all it said was, I think, Evergreen Books, or it might have been Grove Press, but it had nothing but the imprint. A whole page of *The Times Book Review*. I said, "Barney this is crazy!" This was costing $15,000 in those days. I said, "$15,000 for just the name?"

ROSSET: John, John. I disagree. Much more like $4,000.

CALDER: Well, whatever the figure was. I remember to me it was astronomical.

ROSSET: Three.

CALDER: I said, "You're not advertising a book or an author. You're just putting on..." Barney said, "Oh, but you never know, you never know." So. But we had a lot of collaboration and we got to be closer together, you know and we got to be friends as well. I was in New York every so often.

CALDER: Barney occasionally came to London. Then we began to import and distribute Evergreen Books in Britain, and we were doing a pretty good job, but were also putting a lot of our energy into it, which meant we were publishing less ourselves because books that we might have simply taken the rights and done a British edition, we simply were bringing in the American edition. And we were roughly multiplying what it cost us by two and one-half times which was not nearly enough. A lot of the time we were doing it for no profit but we were certainly getting the volume.

GELLER: It gave you an extended list for a period.

CALDER: But also we were sort of falling behind in the payments, and then Weidenfeld came along and said "We can do a better job." And then we had all of those meetings with Maxwell about starting a British company in which we were all going to collaborate?

ROSSET: Maxwell?

CALDER: No, not Robert Maxwell. Remember...? The law publisher. Maurice Maxwell.

ROSSET: Yeah, that's right. Another Maxwell. Very nice person.

CALDER: Well, this was... He met Barney somewhere and he wanted to get involved in trade publishing, and the first thing he wanted to do was take Grove distribution away from us. Actually, he would have been doing us a great favor. However. We didn't see

Display Ad 85 -- No Title
New York Times (1923-Current file): Oct 16, 1957;
ProQuest Historical Newspapers: The New York Times (1851-2010)
pg. 33

New York Times
(Oct. 16, 1957)

Only Grove Press brings you the works of

SAMUEL BECKETT

"The most remarkable writer since World War II . . . one who must be ranked — and I weigh my words — along with Kafka and Joyce."
—SATURDAY REVIEW

JUST PUBLISHED!

ALL THAT FALL. "The new play by the author of *Waiting for Godot* takes hold on the attention as compellingly as did its theatrical forerunner in what seems a no less despairing search for human dignity."—THE LONDON TIMES. "It has the true ring of something original and intensely alive." — MANCHESTER GUARDIAN. *Clothbound $2.50*

WAITING FOR GODOT. "One of the most noble and moving plays of our generation."—THE LONDON TIMES. "Broadway's most controversial play."—LIFE. *Cloth $3.00; Soft-cover Evergreen edition $1.00*

MURPHY. "The funniest of his novels. It evokes a ferocity of terror and humor that shames most well-made novels of our time."—N. Y. TIMES. *Clothbound $3.50*

MOLLOY. "The most significant novel published in any language since World War II."—THE NATION. *Clothbound $3.00; Soft-cover Evergreen edition $1.45*

MALONE DIES. "A masterful achievement."—N. Y. HERALD TRIBUNE. "More powerful and important than Godot."—N.Y. TIMES. *Clothbound $3.75; Soft-cover Evergreen edition $1.25*

PROUST. "One of the most brilliant pieces of writing I have ever read on Proust."—SATURDAY REVIEW. *Clothbound $2.50; Soft-cover Evergreen edition $1.00*

GROVE PRESS
**795 Broadway
New York 3**

Send for free catalog of other distinctive GROVE PRESS and EVERGREEN titles.

entr'acte   153

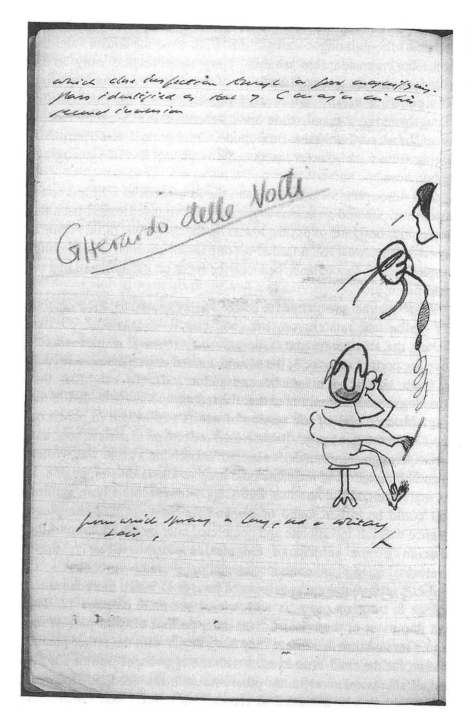

Dear Mr. Beckett

it that way at the time. Then they said, wouldn't we come into a group? So we talked about forming a group.

There were various meetings in London. They came to absolutely nothing at all. And then

Weidenfeld came along and said, "Why don't you let me distribute the books? I'll do a lot better than Calder." And he took them over, and they did a lot worse.

ROSSET: He did do it for a while?

CALDER: Yes.

ROSSET: I'd forgotten.

CALDER: After about six months, the results were so dismal, you gave them separate assignments.

GELLER: Did you do some of the playwrights that Grove worked on?

CALDER: Practically all of the French ones—Ionesco, Arrabal, Pinget, and of course his novels.

GELLER: Beckett, of course.

CALDER: No, we didn't do Beckett's plays. Faber did them.

ROSSET: Faber, that's right.

CALDER: There was a complicated reason for that but it has nothing to do with this.

GELLER: Any British playwrights?

ROSSET: Not much in the way of plays. There wasn't much of a crossover in drama.

GELLER: What about the British playwrights?

Calder: Ionesco and Arrabal were the principal ones.

ROSSET: Not even in Britain.

GELLER: Pinter?

ROSSET: No, no.

CALDER: We were meant to do Pinter and then … That went wrong.

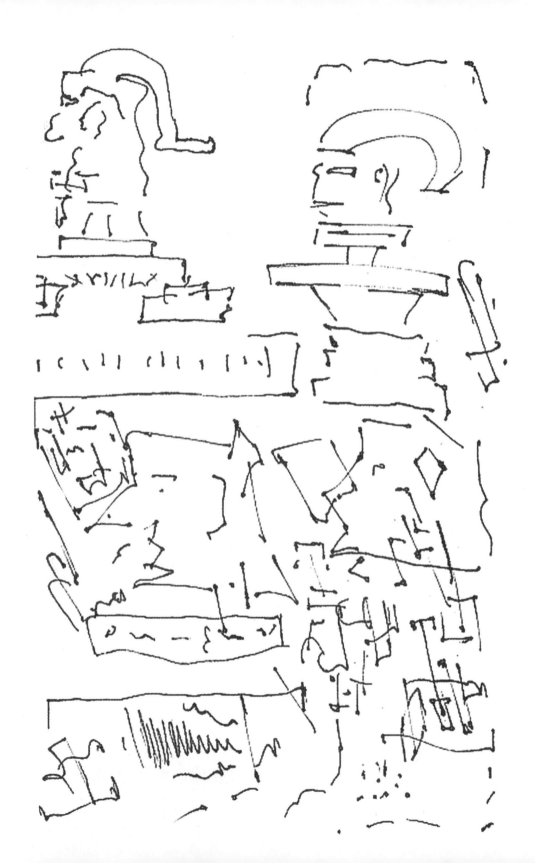

ROSSET: And so did Stoppard.

CALDER: See, we often had to hold back because we just didn't have the money to do things, so other people got them. I think what we got from you was Trocchi, primarily. Oh yes, then there was the musical series we collaborated on. Well, a French paperback series, that was partly musical, partly historical. They were little illustrated paperbacks.

GELLER: I remember those too.

ROSSET: They were nice books. They were hopelessly French.

CALDER: Well, I got involved with them mainly because I liked the musical series. Barney said, "Okay" because there was one on jazz he liked. But it was the stars that really interested me. And that got you into a whole series. And then they became Evergreen Profile Books; we had one series we published ourselves, and we had another one that we distributed, but that fell apart in the end, although we carried on with the musical ones. And there was... We got involved in the Gallery Books, Evergreen Gallery Books. We also distributed Evergreen Press in Britain, ran a subscription system for it. All this was late fifties and early sixties. Until the war broke out over Tropic of Cancer. And we never really got back to the same sort of close collaboration after that. We did Hubert Selby, which you had done, but it was actually sent to us by an agent. There must have been lots of individual titles. We sold you Green Henry, of Gottfried Keller, which you bought us out in copy as hardback with no great enthusiasm, but you did it. Now we've published it in paperback. It's out here now. You had a fight with Pinget because you compared him to Beckett and he wasn't happy about that. Said he wasn't anything like Beckett, so then he just stopped publishing. But there was quite a lot of collaboration.

GELLER: Oh yes, it sounds like it. But the same process is going on over there as over here. The big ones have swallowed up most of the...

CALDER: That's right. And a lot of people have gone bust in the last year. And I'm still struggling. I would take Henry Miller away from you now.

CALDER: We did a lot of political books, and we did a lot of books about colonial affairs, a big book on the South African appeasement trial. Then in the late fifties we did a lot of books about the Algerian War, both of which sold quite well, and about what the British were doing in Cyprus, Kenya, and so on. I was getting constant threats to kidnap me, boil me in oil, lynch me, and so on. Then during the sixties it was not a time for reading, there weren't that many political issues really affecting people... But I did publish quite a number of books about corruption in public places in the seventies, and that got me into a lot of hot water. Big libel cases. Of course we also had a big case over *Last Exit to Brooklyn*, which cost great deal of money, and got a public subscription to help pay for it. That took two years in the courts.

GELLER: How did you happen to be interested in publishing these political books?

CALDER: Because I was a political person.

GELLER: You were a political person as a student?

CALDER: Yeah.

ROSSET: You see, John and I, we'd say we were much more political than Maurice. Maurice arrived at whatever he arrived at from a very different...

CALDER: He's an anarchist.

ROSSET: I'd agree with that.

CALDER: Maurice is very quirky, and very self-destructive.

GELLER: Yeah. Well, so is Barney.

CALDER: True, true. Not in exactly the same way, but there are lots of similarities.

GELLER: I was reading an autobiographical book by Graham Greene who said he has never felt comfortable in his life unless he has reached a situation in which he was basically very insecure. Then he felt good, so he sought out such situations. And there are many people like that. I think Barney, in my memory of him, always felt best and was most alive when he had to struggle for survival, when he was hanging on by his toenails....

Barney and
Maurice
Girodias in
East Hampton
c.1970

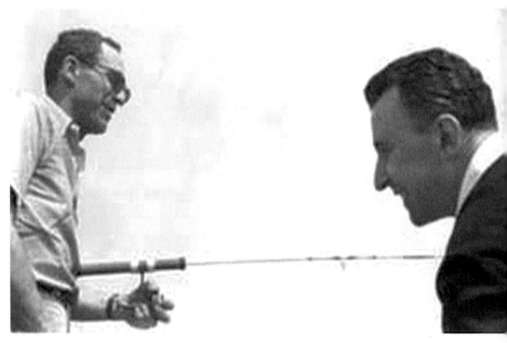

Samuel Beckett Doodle
Harry Ransom Center
The University of Texas
at Austin

Dear Mr. Beckett

[illegible]

Then there was something else that [illegible] would [illegible] been a hearing, for what [illegible] what was going on about him. Not that it was a [illegible] [illegible] [illegible] [illegible] But it [illegible] [illegible] [illegible] changes [illegible] the little [illegible], the little losses, the [illegible] [illegible] the [illegible] the light [illegible], the [illegible] broken, and the [illegible] [illegible] to the [illegible], to [illegible] of all [illegible] [illegible] upon the [illegible] and the [illegible], & the [illegible], [illegible] he [illegible] [illegible] now, the [illegible] [illegible]

Barney Rosset interview
with John Oakes

OAKES: What was the first book you brought to Grove?

ROSSET: The *Golden Bowl of* Henry James. We had to buy the rights to that from Scribner, who for their own reasons had decided to forget about it. This was all in my apartment on Ninth Street. I had all the books there.

OAKES: When you worked out of your apartment, what did that involve?

ROSSET: The actual books were stored in my apartment. I had to carry them up three flights of stairs. It took up so much space . . .

OAKES: The fourth Collyer brother.

ROSSET: That's right, and it began to break the floors. There weren't all that many, a few trunkloads of books, when I had taken over from the other people. They had a few hundred copies left of each book, and I took them and put them into hardcovers. Then I tore those covers off and put them back into paperbacks, but changed the covers. Actually, I was very influenced by New Directions, by [James] Laughlin. The original covers had very pretty kinds of line drawings. I ripped those off and put on plain hardcovers and plain yellow wrappers, just with black type on them. Then I ripped those off and put on plain covers—sort of a cross between French books and New Directions. I was very conscious of New Directions. It was not accidental. They had color, and they had a line of type, but the line went diagonally, which I didn't like. Mine went straight across. From there we began doing more books, one at a time.

OAKES: Who was the first contemporary author you people

ROSSET: At that time there was nobody else. Just me.

OAKES: Well, who was the first contemporary author you published?

ROSSET: I don't know, I don't remember. I'll tell you one thing I did: early on, I became somehow aware that in England there were other publishers who were publishing books that weren't being done here. So I went to England, and I took on a number of British writers. I had read and cataloged various things that interested me, and I went to those few publishers. Faber and Faber, Chatto and Windus, and a few others.

OAKES: This was when you got Beckett.

ROSSET: Right around then. A very little bit later, 1953. He was one of the very first, actually.

OAKES: Whom else did you take on in this early period?

ROSSET: Genet, Robbe-Grillet, Ionesco.

OAKES: These were then names that were comparatively unknown.

ROSSET: In the States, they were. Even in France, Beckett and Ionesco weren't so well known.

OAKES: I read that you have a reputation for driving a hard bargain with authors and other publishers.

ROSSET: Not true. I could say a lot of nasty things about myself, but that happens not to be true. As a matter of fact, it's a fault of mine to be too much the other way. Whenever I get into negotiations or whatever, I let other people do it because I never have been able to make a good bargain with anybody.

OAKES: Why do you think the reporter—it was in The *New York Times*—wrote that?

L'ÉTAT
ENCOUAGE

LA RECHERCHE
LES TIGRES
LES CHAMEAUX CHIMOIS
L'ÉLÉPHANTS

ROSSET: Because, perhaps, we've never had much money to throw around. So if you offer somebody a rather small amount, and they feel they're worth a lot more, they could say he's trying to drive a hard bargain. …

OAKES: I think the comment was made in the context that you publish things that other houses might shy away from, even today—

ROSSET: That's absolutely true.

OAKES: —And because of that, you're in a position where, if you turn down the authors, they have nowhere else to go.

ROSSET: Yeah, so they'll take a smaller amount. But that works both ways. Again, that's all we have. Beckett, for example, gets incredibly small amounts. I've never heard him complain about it. On the other hand, we do something that many publishers don't do: we keep an author's books in print, available. We have over twenty-five volumes of Beckett in print. We have over ten volumes of Pinter, over ten of Stoppard, over ten of Ionesco. We've kept these people in print.

OAKES: Even if they're not profitable.

ROSSET: That's right. We've stayed with them.

OAKES: I understand you just wrote a piece on Robbe-Grillet.

ROSSET: For Grove. It's very important, I mean, not to Robbe-Grillet or the world, but important in terms of Grove Press. I talk about how we first came to publish Robbe-Grillet, and what it means to us. What it meant to me was that it was very connected to Abstract Expressionism.

OAKES: How can a literary work be tied to a visual one?

ROSSET: The attempt to do the same thing, to de-emotionalize content, to make it an observation. Not the old-fashioned romanticism of, say, looking at a rock and saying, that rock reminds me of my grandmother several years ago. She was like a rock. No. You say, the rock is brown and it's six inches wide . . .

OAKES: That sounds more like the stuff of realism. Flaubert or Zola or somebody.

ROSSET: No, it isn't, because even they did that, they put a lot of emotion into things that weren't there. If you read, let's say, *Jalousie* of Robbe-Grillet... Immediately you have a wordplay you can't translate into English, unfortunately. The jalousie is a Venetian blind and it's also a feeling of jealousy. And he's looking through the blinds, and his vision is cut off by that amount of space that he can see through them. The inch and a half between the blinds. So therefore all he can see is his wife's hands going into a drawer. His vision is so restricted. He sees her hand, and a letter coming out of the drawer and he can see some of the writing on it.

OAKES: Not your average omniscient narrator.

ROSSET: No. Only what is literally there. He's a non-establishment writer. He was an engineer, actually an agronomist. And *Jalousie* is about the tropics and a banana plantation. And anything he describes, the leaves of bananas or whatever, is very, very accurate. You can't go out of the frame, is all I'm trying to say. You look at a painting of the same period, a de Kooning or a Pollock, and it's the same thing. You can't go outside of it. Don't go looking for romantic illusions....

Wilhelm de Kooning on cover of Evergreen Gallery Book 8 (Grove Press, 1960)

DE KOONING

by HARRIET JANIS *and* RUDI BLESH

EVERGREEN GALLERY BOOK 8 — E-191 $1.95 (U.K.14/6d.)

OAKES: Were you conscious at the time, when you decided to publish somebody like Beckett or Kerouac, well these authors are setting precedents; they're doing something new? Were you searching out the avant-garde?

ROSSET: Yes, I was, I was absolutely conscious of it. That was the reason I was doing it. We were going after people who had basically failed in a commercial sense, because if they hadn't other publishers would have been involved with them. I, and the rest of us, were looking for new talents, new people who really had something to offer. We were very very aware of the dangers and the possibilities of people like Ginsberg, Beckett, Kerouac, Robbe-Grillet, Ionesco, Genet. They represented something that was going to be very important in the next generation.

OAKES: Why did Grove get so heavily into drama—was that also a conscious decision, or simply a void waiting to be filled?

ROSSET: I'd been very involved in drama, in a personal way, from high school on. In high school, it was the key point of school life—just as I imagine it was for David Mamet, who went to the same school I did. My girlfriend at the time was incredibly talented in acting and directing, which for a woman in those years was unheard of, almost. And in order to be on the right side with her, you had to be involved with the theatre, and that made me very involved with the theatre. We put on such plays as Irwin Shaw's *Bury the Dead*, an early Shaw play about peace and soldiers. We put on Eugene O'Neill and various others. So I was into that. Much later, I became involved with Beckett, and that was a big reintroduction for me to drama, and that led immediately, right away, to Ionesco, and then to people like Harold Pinter, who of course was tremendously influenced by Beckett. There were various openings to why drama was interesting.

OAKES: As the plays came in, did you publish them, or did you seek them out?

ROSSET: We did both. We certainly weren't the first to discover Pinter. I've forgotten how we first decided to do it, but there was no problem in deciding. Same with Ionesco. There were various people at the time who were interested in Ionesco. I went to see some of his plays in Paris. I met him, I thought he had a talent equal but quite different from Beckett.

OAKES: Your fluency in French must have been a big help all this time.

ROSSET: Well, I was never really fluent; although I had lived in France for a year, I'd learned practically nothing. But at the New School, after the war, I learned enough French to be able to appreciate the written word.

OAKES: How'd you come across Robbe-Grillet?

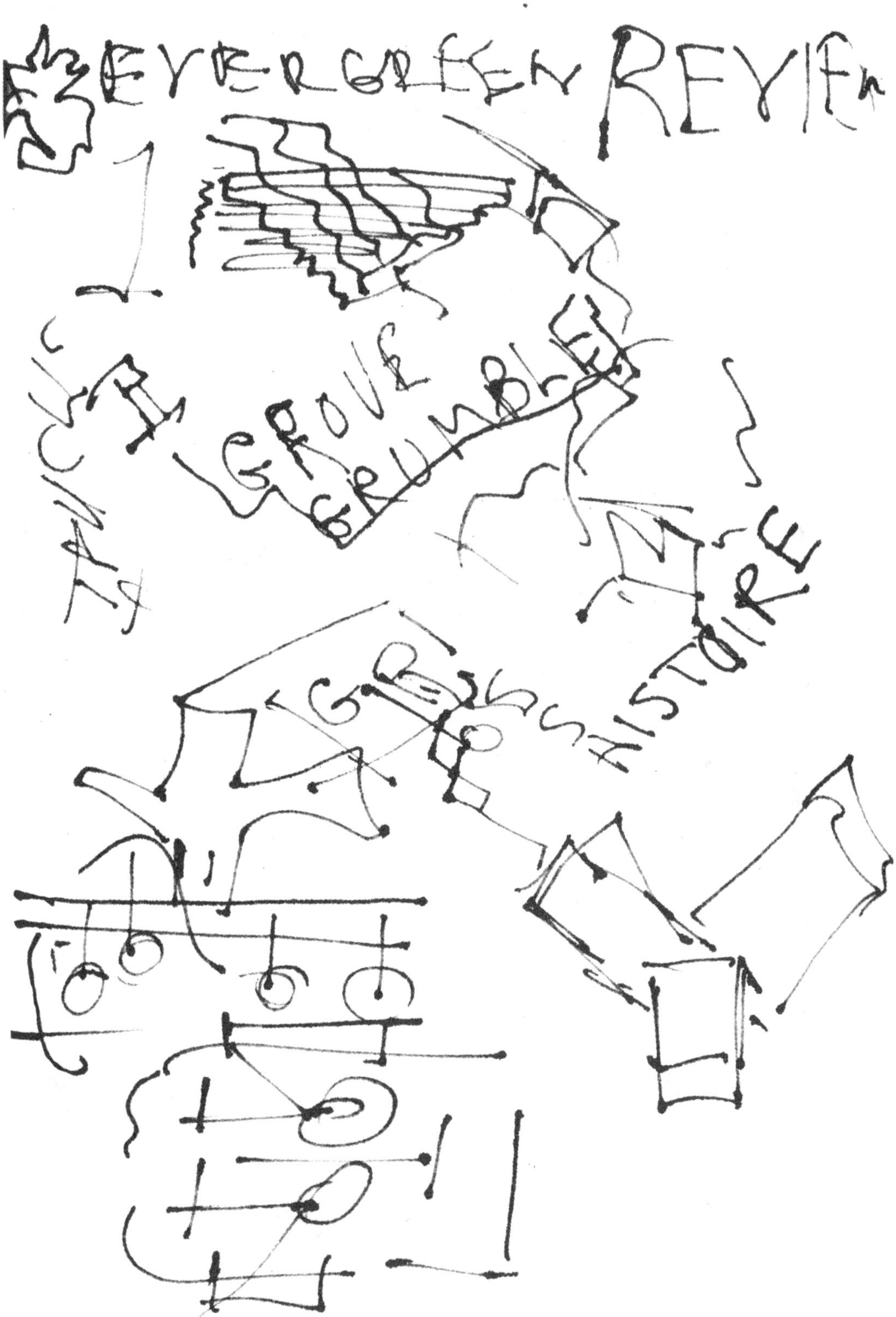

EVERGREEN
GROVE
GRUMBLE
HISTOIRE

ROSSET: He was an editor at Editions de Minuit. I liked his writing very much. It somehow struck a note with my own early attempts at writing in high school and college. Very precise, unemotional statements about very emotional, imprecise situations. Robbe-Grillet says he thought I liked *The Voyeur* because it has a sexy title. I chose that, instead of an earlier book he had done, which we translated into English as *The Erasers*. He was both right and wrong. His style was evolving at that very time, and *The Voyeur*, which I don't think would strike too many people as an erotic novel, although it is one in a sense to me, I thought was the epitome of his style and his precision. Precision which doesn't tell you too much.

OAKES: Reading him, it's as though you're looking through a magnifying glass, you get so close to the action you can't really take in anything. It fills the screen.

ROSSET: Right, a cinematic effect. This can lead to much more exciting thoughts.

(Excerpts from "The Art of Combat Publishing,"
The Review of Contemporary Fiction, Fall 1990)

Café de Paris, Dec. 1985
© John Minihan

quelques parisie

act two

THE FRENCH CONNECTION

"Words are the clothes thoughts wear"

NOV   57

Barney Rosset and
Samuel Beckett, Paris,
1957

Jérôme Lindon interview
with Edward de Grazia

LINDON: I knew about Barney Rosset before I ever met him. I've never been to the United States; I met him through Georges Borchardt, who is a French literary agent in New York, and who suggested to Barney that he ought to publish the works that we had published, of Beckett and Robbe-Grillet. And so that's how I came in contact with Barney, some years back, in the early 50's.

DE GRAZIA: And then Barney came to Paris and met you here?

LINDON: Right. He met Beckett then, and got to know him easier than I did because Beckett spoke English. And then, at that time, he also met Robbe-Grillet—who doesn't speak English either.

DE GRAZIA: What was your impression of Barney Rosset at that time?

LINDON: Very nice. And very enterprising. You know, that was the first time that I had met an American publisher who seemed to me to be on the same footing, the same level, as I was. Because all the publishing houses with which we had had relations, such as Knopf, Simon and Schuster, etc., were a hundred times bigger than we were, while from the financial standpoint and also in his approach to the trade, Barney was a publisher more like us—a little more artisan-like—right from the start. He made one book and then another book, personally concerned each time. He didn't make books by the dozens or hundred, but singly. I felt very close to him as I did to an English publisher, named John Calder, during the same period. They were the two publishers with whom I felt in correlation, in symbiosis. I had the impression we were equals, even if they were already producing more books than I. Calder was also publishing Beckett and Robbe-Grillet, among others, at more-or-less the same time. He was interested in the same sort of books. They had very similar literary and political views, even if there were some disputes between them, at a later date. We all worked with the same type of authors and worked directly on the books, without any middleman. We weren't merely the managers or directors of our companies, supervising the work of others; we read the manuscripts ourselves and decided what to publish, and got involved in publicizing the books to booksellers and others—that's what I mean by "artisans."

DE GRAZIA: What was the first book by Beckett that you published? Lindon: Molloy. In '51.

DE GRAZIA: Did Beckett have difficulty, in the beginning, finding a publisher?

LINDON: Yes, certainly in France. When I published him, he'd already been rejected by five publishers. . . . the three books *Molloy, Malone Dies,* and *The Unnamable* were turned down by five publishers, including Gallimard and Les Editions du Seuil. And Beckett told me that, after that, if Les Editions de Minuit hadn't taken the books, he would have given up looking for a publisher. He would have kept writing, probably, but he would not have tried to be published.

de Grazia: He wrote in French.

LINDON: Not everything. But those three books, yes. He wrote *Watt* and *Murphy in English.* And then, subsequently, he himself translated from the English into French, and he translated what he wrote in French into English. It's a unique case in literature.

*　　*　　*

DE GRAZIA: Can you say anything about Ionesco, compared with Beckett? I believe they both got started at about the same time, and Ionesco has said it was very difficult, at first, to have his plays done. Did you have any interest in him?

LINDON: Yes, yes. I knew of Ionesco through Beckett. It was Beckett who pointed out the production of *The Chairs*, which was Ionesco's first play. And when I saw *The Chairs*, there were ten spectators in the hall, ten in all. And I wrote to the theatre—or it was *The Bald Soprano*, I don't know—yes, *The Bald Soprano*—anyway, I wrote to the theatre because I did not have Ionesco's address, and offered to publish it. And, he has always said to me that he never received my letter. That's possible, but it's also possible that he pretended that he never received my letter. And so he was published by Losfeld, a small publisher, smaller even than me. And then, when he was dissatisfied with Losfeld—oh, I don't know, for financial reasons—and then I proposed again to publish him—but it seems to me Ionesco wanted to be published by a big house like Gallimard. And so he went to Gallimard, and I'm sorry we didn't become Ionesco's publisher because his works, especially the first things he wrote, were extremely important, and they contributed, as did Beckett's works, to a renewal of the contemporary French theatre, that's sure. But you can't have everything—when you are a small house.

But Ionesco is much more attuned to social success than Beckett is. It's not by chance that Ionesco is a member of the French Academy, which would be, for Beckett, unthinkable—absolutely unthinkable. And he is decorated, he has every sort of decoration, and so on; and, to be sure, Beckett has the Nobel Prize, but it's really in spite of himself that he received it.

DE GRAZIA: Would Beckett refuse the French Academy?

LINDON: You have to be French, and Beckett is not French. But it's not even that he would refuse the French Academy: You have to be a candidate; it is required to apply. You are not elected by accident. You have to ask, make visits and so on. But Beckett didn't want the Nobel Prize. He didn't refuse it because you can't refuse it in advance; it is the opposite of the French Academy. You are given the Nobel Prize without asking your opinion.

Beckett told me—because for two years people had been talking about his getting the Nobel Prize—he said, "If anyone contacts you, and asks my position on the Nobel Prize, say I don't want the thing—understand?" But no one contacted me. And when he received the Nobel Prize, he was in Tunis, as I recall, and I called him in Tunis and told him that he had it, and it was as though I told him about somebody's death: It was very bad news. I said to him, "Excuse me, I am going to give you some very bad news..."

Jérôme Lindon and
Samuel Beckett, Paris
Photo by Louis Monier

It got complicated. He was in a place called Nabeul, in Tunis, absolutely surrounded by journalists, and he wouldn't leave his room. He was trapped by all these journalists who wanted to interview him. So I had to take a plane and fly to Nabeul and work out a deal with the journalists, like this: Beckett would leave his room and stay for three minutes somewhere in the hotel—without saying a word—and they would film him for three minutes; and then the journalists would leave the hotel. And that's what was done, just like that, so he was liberated. But he did not say one word. And he was before the cameras for three minutes.

DE GRAZIA: Has Grove had much of an influence in Europe? Because of its censorship cases, or the kinds of books it published?

LINDON: Not really. After all, the battles that Barney fought in New York were, paradoxically, behind France, so far as sexual expression is concerned. Miller and Lady Chatterley were sold here a long time without any problem. France has always been very liberal, in the area of political, as well as sexual, censorship, except for very specific moments such as during the Algerian War. I can't think of any book censored for political reasons recently, for the past ten years, except for a few cases of personal prosecution; but, truly, no official prosecutions have occurred. Those have been suits for defamation—or calumny; there was one recently. But that's not a public, official action.

DE GRAZIA: In the states, the CIA has a very large file—dossier—on Grove Press; and the FBI also. Does this exist in France, also? Is there a dossier on you?

LINDON: Probably. Certainly, during the Algerian War. But that's normal. The police have to do their job, no? It seems normal for the police to have documentation on publications that dare to be considered hostile to the government. That's what they're paid for. And, during the Algerian War, it was effective. Today no one is suffering—no publisher that I know—and not only since Mitterand came to power; it was also true during the time of Giscard d'Estaing or Pompidou or de Gaulle. Except during the Algerian War; that's the sole exception.

Let me add something about a type of censorship—if we can use that word—in France, of which we could be the object, of which we are perhaps already the object—it is much more insidious. It is, in fact, the inverse of censorship. What happens is that many publications in France, especially higher-level books, academic works, translations, and so on, get grants from the Government; and, really, there is no better way, if one wants to impose a policy, than this system. Because it's done openly—no negative measure needs to be taken. There are no book seizures; there are no prosecutions. But if a publisher is never given subventions for any of his books, he can be induced, in effect, to change his policies, and the books he publishes. That can certainly happen: It's invisible, even though everyone can see the lists of what's being aided. Still, you can't prove anything—that a publisher who systematically gets no grants doesn't get them because he has published a book that the powers-that-be don't like. You can never prove that.

DE GRAZIA: Well, the CIA reportedly has done that with some publishers in the States. For example, Praeger, who used to be a friend and a neighbor of Barney Rosset, supposedly received many subventions from the CIA. Also, occasionally, some writers. And I wonder if you have an impression that the CIA, which so as far as American law is concerned, can operate in Europe, has been helping authors or publishers over here?

LINDON: I don't know. I don't think so. ...

DE GRAZIA: I lived in France during the late 50's and for several years, and I had the impression, then, that there was more freedom for homosexuals in France than in the United States. Today I have the reverse feeling: that homosexuals have more freedom in the United States than in France. And it occurs to me that even publishers like Grove Press—which published books by overt homosexuals like Burroughs and Ginsberg and John Rechy, and others—perhaps have had an influence on this new freedom which first developed during the 60's when there was sexual freedom, and license, and the antiwar movement, and all kinds of liberation: liberation for homosexuals, liberation for women, liberation for pot-smokers—and I just wonder if there has been a powerful, free literature for homosexuals in France, too?

LINDON: I think that you're right. At the end of the 50's the USA was behind France, but the USA has caught up and now they've gotten ahead. But I don't think we are any less free in France than we were twenty years ago. The homosexual is freer in France today than he was at the time, but it's just that progress in the States was much more rapid, even spectacular. But it's simply a question of relative progress. ...

I think that there has been a sort of general political demobilization, in France. This is true of the Marxist and other political struggles. It's difficult to imagine today public reactions as great as we had at the time of the Indochina war, and the Algerian War. And, it's the same in the area of homosexuality and feminism. I think these wars have been won, and the people have demobilized, and nobody needs to fight.

DE GRAZIA: Are most of these small houses dominated by a single personality, like you? Like Rosset? ...

LINDON: Yes, in every case. That's why they are still small; that's why they haven't grown big, and that's why they are independent. But that's also why they are fragile, doubly fragile—as regards the question of money and also the question of people. If Barney or I or Calder had an automobile accident, the house would disappear.

DE GRAZIA: I understand. So it's like these houses are like personal organs of expression, of the managing director or the publisher, and the ideology, really, of the publisher is expressed in the books that are published?

LINDON: Exactly. …

DE GRAZIA: In 1970, Grove Press had big difficulties: it had the union strike, it had the women's liberation sit-in, and it had the bomb, a little earlier, the bomb thrown into the building. And Barney—Grove Press—had made a lot of money on this film, *I am Curious Yellow*, and Barney spent a lot of money. But then these things happened and he had to fire people, including women—new women employees—he hired many women and then he had to fire them, and others. And there was a big protest. And I remember that one of the posters, or pamphlets, that the women's group who occupied his office (Barney was in Europe) displayed, said he was a "hip-capitalist," and they complained that the profits he had made on Malcolm X, T*he Autobiography of Malcolm X*, should go to the poor black women who were on welfare, and who were in the prisons, and so on. And even one or two authors of Grove got very angry at Grove and said they wouldn't publish with him anymore—with Barney—because of the firing, really—he had fired these people. And I don't know what he could have done otherwise, and so on, but there was a problem of this kind.

LINDON: Well, I would say that, for me, I have a policy much

more—how should I say it? —well, as a "head of the family."
I have always admired that sense of adventure of Barney's. But
I'm probably less adventurous than he, in management, and in
the books I publish. It's true. I don't want to risk the jobs of my
colleagues, which I consider like my own.

(Paris, July 27, 1983)

Photo by Royal Brown

Dear Mr. Beckett

Alain Robbe-Grillet interview with Edward de Grazia

DE GRAZIA: How did Grove Press publish you?

ROBBE-GRILLET: You know, in the 50's there was really a movement of intellectual fermentation and literary creation, and the literary movement was symbolized in France by Les Editions Minuit. In the States, it was Grove Press. It was a time when the little publishing houses had, overall, a prestige and a fame far greater than their size. I mean, Minuit was much more popular than Gallimard, for example, during that period. And, in the same way, Grove Press was much more popular than, I don't know, Random House, or the other large publishers. And it's to be expected that Barney Rosset got interested in Minuit. I don't remember exactly how it happened. He had already published Samuel Beckett, probably, when he published me. When did Grove first publish Beckett?

DE GRAZIA: I think the first was *Waiting for Godot*, in '54.

ROBBE-GRILLET: Yes? Then, around the same time. But Barney had already published writings by Beckett in *Evergreen*.

DE GRAZIA: In the review, the journal?

ROBBE-GRILLET: Yes. I believe he published writings of mine also in *Evergreen*.

DE GRAZIA: And also, at that time, Allen Ginsberg and Jack Kerouac.

ROBBE-GRILLET: Yes, yes.

DE GRAZIA: Did you know those writers, at that time?

ROBBE-GRILLET: I knew Ginsberg well, yes.

DE GRAZIA: How?

ROBBE-GRILLET: I saw him often. I don't know where—probably at Barney's place.

DE GRAZIA: Did they interest you?

ROBBE-GRILLET: Who?

DE GRAZIA: Ginsberg.

ROBBE-GRILLET: Not at all.

DE GRAZIA: Kerouac neither?

ROBBE-GRILLET: A little. Not very much.

DE GRAZIA: Did you see no connection between the Beatniks and the "New Novel"?

ROBBE-GRILLET: No, I don't think so. What about you?

DE GRAZIA: Me? Well, the Beats in the U.S. were also *le* new movement.

ROBBE-GRILLET: Yes.

DE GRAZIA: Without explicit politics.

ROBBE-GRILLET: Well, you see, I found that those people were completely different from us, especially because of the drugs and from the metaphysical standpoint. But what was funny was how Barney was fascinated by everything that was against the established order, in whatever sense or direction it took. Politically, he was far more Left than most Americans. In literature, for France, it was the "New Novel," but he could get interested in anything else, as long as it was anti-Establishment. It was rather strange; it was an idea he had, to fight against the Establishment, but by every means.

I remember very well, one time, it was in Paris, I can't remember when, at the end of the 50's, or the beginning of the 60's, he pointed out someone sitting on the terrace of La Coupole, and told me, "You see, there, he's a very important American writer." And I said, "Ah, yes? What has he done?" And Barney said, "He put an apple on his wife's head and killed her."

DE GRAZIA: Burroughs.

ROBBE-GRILLET: It was Burroughs, right? Who … who was hardly known, at that time, but it shows the sort of thing that Barney noticed. It wasn't even a book: it was a gesture that interested him. …

DE GRAZIA: … That's kind of interesting, what you say about Rosset. Wouldn't you call that "radical"? Rosset's fascination with all the extremes, against the Establishment?

ROBBE-GRILLET: No, I don't use that word. In French, it makes no sense. Anyway, I'm a friend of Barney Rosset, but I speak English badly, he speaks French badly, and so the contacts between us are necessarily a little limited, you see. It's likely that Barney first got interested in my work because of the sexual stimulation he found in it. That's why he began with *The Voyeur* and not with *The Erasers*. At that time, apparently, people in France who were interested in me, Georges Bataille, for example, were people who were very interested in perversion. And it's very likely that Barney, in the beginning, was interested in me because of sexual perversion. But not any particular perversion. With me it was heterosexual sadism. But it could also have been homosexuals and drugs, that interested him in others. It was the period when he fought the battle over *Lady Chatterley's Lover*, and also over Henry Miller. And, if you look at the final issues of *Evergreen Review* that came out in the 50's, you'll see how it had certain provocative sexual imagery in it.

DE GRAZIA: During the 50's, which was the time in France of the "New Novel" and, in the States, of the Beats, the Beatniks were attacked in the States by the conservative intellectuals, as if they sensed that there was some change, some cultural change, coming, that this was an attack on the Establishment. You see, they were an attack on the Establishment because they were anti-academia, anti-university. They were writers and poets who could be from the streets and not only from the University. Did that exist in France?

ROBBE-GRILLET: Not at all. No, the situation in France was completely different because, first of all, the intellectuals, the upper crust, were Left, and Communist, at that time. And, particularly, that period was the time of Sartre, of Camus, of Left intellectuals who were almost all members of the Communist Party. And what is interesting is that the "New Novel," on the contrary, appeared in the beginning, as a politically disengaged movement. It had no political commitment, and as far as its public reception was concerned, everyone was against it, right across the spectrum, from the Communist newspapers to *Le Figaro* because of our non-engagement. We were accused of making a depoliticized literature.

DE GRAZIA: Ionesco was writing at about that time?

ROBBE-GRILLET: Yes, yes.

DE GRAZIA: And he seems nonpolitical. But Brecht was writing at that time, and he was very political and—well, why was it that Ionesco was not drawn into Minuit?

ROBBE-GRILLET: Actually, when Ionesco was still unpublished, I wanted to publish him here, and it happened that Ionesco, at the same time, was talking to several other publishers, and I have the impression that someone offered him more money—because Minuit has always been a publishing house with very little money. It was not Gallimard who published him then, it was a very small publisher who has since disappeared. I would have published him at Minuit.

I was very friendly with Ionesco at that time although he hated all my friends, rightly, because of Brecht: It was the time

Selection of *Evergreen*
Review covers

when Roland Barthes was "Brechtian," and Ionesco had written a satire of Roland Barthes in which he was called "Doctor Barth-Olomew."

DE GRAZIA: Minuit was a (French) Resistance publisher. Is there some connection between that and writers like Robbe-Grillet coming here?

ROBBE-GRILLET: Certainly. But, then, it's Jérôme Lindon who can tell you about that better than I; since the war it is he who has been its principal owner. The house was begun under the German Occupation to publish books that could not be published. There was German censorship, which prohibited the publication of certain books, and Minuit was started as an underground house to publish banned books. And that's been a tradition of Minuit since its foundation, under occupation, until today.

For example, during the Algerian War, Minuit published books against the French Army and its activities in Algeria. So it's completely normal that this house has, in literature, also published books that the other publishers would not publish. Don't forget that the works of Beckett were almost all written and rejected by all the French publishers when Lindon decided to publish him.

And another thing—rather amusing and not widely known—when the war was over, Lindon published books against the French Resistance. You see, under the German Occupation, he published books that were against Germany, Nazism, and the Occupation, and then, after the war, Jean Paulhan did a book that was a sort of defense of Charles Pétain, and no other French publisher would publish it. Lindon said that Minuit should publish this book because now it is this that one hasn't a right to publish. And he published that book, called *Lettre du lecteur de la Résistance*, which was, in fact, a letter—a book—against the Resistance.

And, also, now Minuit is a publishing house that, after having defended the Jewish cause more than anyone else, published books of the Palestinians. Lindon believes that he ought to publish books that shock, books which do not support the official view or ideology, but which come back just the same.

DE GRAZIA: Isn't that practically the same way you described Barney Rosset's publishing interest?

ROBBE-GRILLET: Yes, a little. Not exactly, but it's a bit the same, all right.

DE GRAZIA: Did you bring Beckett's works to Minuit.

ROBBE-GRILLET: We've published everything of Beckett's here. But Molloy was published in 1950, and I came here in 1952. Actually Molloy was first published in France in 1938, and it was Girodias perhaps who did it, but it wasn't called Olympia; you should ask Lindon; he knows better than I, and the relationship between Beckett and Lindon was already firmly established before I came here. And now, Beckett deals directly with Lindon; it is Lindon himself who takes care of Beckett's affairs. It was Lindon who went to collect the Nobel Prize for him.

It was funny because Beckett had sent a surprising telegram to the King of Sweden, to thank him for the prize and said that he wasn't going to the ceremony in Stockholm because he couldn't cope with it, he didn't have the strength, and he hoped that His Majesty would not be "too shocked" that he wasn't going to be there. And so it was Lindon who went to Stockholm. …

Barney had a house in East Hampton—not the one he has now, but another one, across the street—that was divided into kind of apartments on separate floors, and he would lend a floor to one of us, Beckett or myself, when we went over there. He always was very generous, Barney.

DE GRAZIA: Did he ever bring any black women to France?

ROBBE-GRILLET: One black woman, one time, yes. I don't remember—she was a very beautiful one.

DE GRAZIA: Did it make a scandal?

ROBBE-GRILLET: No, here that wouldn't make a scandal at all—but, at that time, he knew all the night spots of New York, Paris, Frankfurt, Tokyo. And no matter what city on earth it was, with Barney, he knew where there was a spot: you know, at 3 o'clock in the morning, "In that cave there, there's a show," like that. And he knew everyone. All the whores, all the strippers—and he was well known in all those places. I had one impression that he handed out money, as one says in Europe, like Americans at one time did. He had his pockets stuffed with bills, always . . .

DE GRAZIA: . . . there was a time when there were several incidents against Grove Press: a bombing by anti-Castro Cubans, a woman's lib raid—accusing Barney of being a sexist pornographer—and also a union strike against Barney, all of which hurt him and his company.

ROBBE-GRILLET: We had a lot of bombs here also, at the time of the Algerian War. And this place was blown up several times! Yes. All the paint was blown off, and at Lindon's house also. It was a group called O.A.S., which was really an anti-Arab, Right-Wing organization.

DE GRAZIA: There's some question in Barney's mind that perhaps the CIA was behind these actions.

ROBBE-GRILLET: One always thinks it was the CIA. In America, the CIA's behind everything.

DE GRAZIA: What about the Congress for Cultural Freedom, here?

ROBBE-GRILLET: It was a CIA thing, but here it has no point—the CIA hasn't had much success in France—anyway. He's a crazy guy, Barney Rosset. It's a little astonishing because he laughs—for example, he laughs his head off, like this ... and then he tells the most horrible stories: how he has lost many billions, all gone, and then he breaks into that crazy laugh . . .

(Paris, July 26, 1983)

Eugène Ionesco interview
with Edward de Grazia

DE GRAZIA: When was your first play done in France?

IONESCO: Around 1950. *The Bald Soprano.*

DE GRAZIA: Was it difficult for you to get it performed?

IONESCO: I had to find 50,000 francs. When I found it, I gave it to Nicolas Bataille. We lived in a remote quarter near La Porte de Saint Cloud. Bataille only had those 50,000 francs. He didn't have a nickel to buy a metro ticket. But he wouldn't touch that money, which was sacred. He went home on foot and without eating. … Bataille was able to act in the play because he was not professional, didn't ask for union wages, and didn't ask for anything.…

And 50,000 francs was a lot at that time, in '50, but in another way it wasn't a lot. It was barely enough to pay the lighting, the cashier, the upkeep of the theatre for seven or eight days. …. We wrote invitations by hand and got sandwich men into the street, and still it didn't attract an audience, except thirty people. I sent the manuscript to Salacrou and Huitraque, who has since died, and they did a lot of advertising of the play, but they confused it with Dadaist theatre. … *The Bald Soprano* was not a Dadaist play because it had a very ordered construction—very structured—with very ordinary laughter and talking, leading to an explosion of language and a light between sense and sound. …

And still it did not go well. He called people—Queneau—he made propaganda, and what have you, but it didn't work. People are hard to budge.… At the gate, with the famous white wine of Gallimard, he said to the people coming in, the writers, doubtless nice people, "Go see Ionesco's *Bald Soprano*!" Of course, they were bewildered, never having heard talk of that, and so they said, "Ionesco, what has he done, this Ionesco? Who is this soprano of Ionesco?"

Eventually, little by little, they understood, and the play was put on again, in '52, when it was no longer me who put up the money but Louis Malle. But it didn't get going for very long, only for three months. And then in '57, it was talked about, and after '57 the play never stopped being performed. ...

DE GRAZIA: How did Grove Press come to publish your plays?

IONESCO: I don't know the date of my first publication by Grove Press, but I believe it was right after Gallimard, probably in '53.

I'm not sure because *The Bald Soprano* had created a certain stir among the Americans in Paris who spoke of it, to New York. And little theatre groups, in The Village there, put on *The Bald Soprano* and *The Lesson*—and it is *The Lesson* which has always been the best, the best constructed—it's like that, it was the Americans, after France, and then Germany. ...

Eugéne Ionesco on cover of Grove Press edition, © 1958

DE GRAZIA: Have you met Barney Rosset, the head of Grove Press?

IONESCO: Barney? Certainly, I've met him... I met him several times in New York... in Paris and even in ... Scotland ... in that big Scottish City. ...

DE GRAZIA: Edinburgh?

IONESCO: Edinburgh, yes. You know, there was a big meeting of internationally known authors, in '55 or '56, and the English were very serious; they were Brechtians without qualification and . . . they were for Realism and, above all, for Socialist Realism, and they didn't care at all for another sort of freedom, not even that of the Americans. ... And Albee ... organized a show in the midst of all that serious conversation on what theatre should be—Realist, Imaginative, Socialist, ... Educative, whatever—and during that discussion a file of young people came in with wheels—rubber tires—on their backs, and a young woman in mourning, with a child in her arms ... And then, at the very end—that which in '55 or '56 was inconceivable: a naked woman. It made a scandal. I said to Albee, "But what's that supposed to mean?" And Albee replied, "Nothing." But what do you want to prove?" He said, "Nothing." "Well, then, you are an imbecile!" He said, "Yes." And then, afterward, the discussion continued, and there was a very serious Scot who accused all those young people of not being true professionals. That was the worst thing anyone could say. ...

DE GRAZIA: What is your impression of the publishing house Grove Press, and Barney Rosset?

IONESCO: He had a lot of ideas. He had the ideas ... the choice, but it wasn't he who did the work. ...

IONESCO: He published plays and prose-writers. He published Beckett and Genet and me. We were more or less the three authors with which he got going. He had our pictures in New York, in The Village. But he was a very whimsical guy. I liked him a lot because when he came to those conferences, those meetings, and at those meetings people got together—the top publishers got together that way, to find money, but not him— he came because he was a publisher. And it was very funny that he came—every time—with another woman, and one time he came with a superb Negress. And, of course, in '56, '57, that still shocked people. But he doesn't do that any more. He came several times to Paris….

DE GRAZIA: Grove Press has published several important books about sex, which were censored, and they had big legal battles over it. But also they published many political … books. And they published your play, *The Lesson*, in 1958.

IONESCO: I've written books on politics, but they dismay my friends…. And I've written books about sex but in a very round-about way…. But, on the whole, I restrain myself, and my theatre is chaste because I have somebody at home who checks very closely, and that's my wife. And even more closely, there's my daughter, too!

(Paris, July 25, 1983)

De par l'Autorité & le Magistère du Docteur Faustroll inventeur de l'Ordre,

selon les Statuts, Constitutions et Coutumier de l'Ordre, toutes choses égales d'ici et d'ailleurs, en considération de ce que doit être ce qui doit être et de tels féaux et officieux gestes et facultés du sous-dit,

le nommé Barney Rosset, notoire

est par les présentes déclaré, signifié et insignifié, autant qu'il est en nous et pour ce que de droit, proscrit et conscrit sur le Livre Aplanète de l'Ordre au Grade Ubiconorable des Commandeurs (Exquis) Petitzfils Ubus

Pour l'Honneur & Gloire Ethernelle de la Grande Gidouille

Donné à Paris, au Palais de l'Ordre, le 3 palotin 87 E. P.

Le Grand-Conservateur de l'Ordre,

Le Président par Intérim Perpétuel du Conseil Suprême des Grands-Maîtres de l'Ordre,

Le Promoteur Insigne de l'Ordre,

E. ionsco

Le Régistrateur DE L'ORDRE

Par ordre de Sa Magnificence & de leurs Transcendances : LE CONFÉRENT MAJEUR DE L'ORDRE

LE SIGILLIF SUFF.

Pataphysics Award to
Barney Rosset signed
by Ionesco

Publishing the French "New Novel"

Barney Rosset

It started with Samuel Beckett. Through him I encountered Alain Robbe-Grillet. Prior to 1953 or 1952, I had somehow stumbled upon Samuel Beckett's work—bits and pieces of it—at The New School, and had spoken to such people as Wallace Fowlie, who had impressed me tremendously not only with his knowledge, but also with his taste and sensibility. When he assured me that I was correct in thinking that *Waiting for Godot* was a great play and that I should publish it, Grove decided to do so. Then I set off to France to meet the author.

Around that time there were several things that were particularly exciting: what Beckett was doing—and quite soon that meant also what Robbe-Grillet was doing—and earlier, what came to be known as abstract expressionist painting. It was not the kind of painting that Alain had written of in "The Erasers" (*Les Gommes*)—it was Franz Kline, Jackson Pollock, and Joan Mitchell. I saw the breaking up of form, a changing concept of content, of structure, and of the emotional reactions, in order to get down to seeing only what was on the canvas—having its own internal movement. I began to sense a new kind of objectivity which came across in Alain's writing and in Beckett's, as well as in motion pictures. In the latter, I refer to such devices as instant replays from multiple angles which have still not been exploited enough in film (although Alain has explored them in his writing techniques and flashbacks). Instant replay is something that, today, the TV sports people still do the best. But the "creative" people will get to that; we will get over our snobbism and eventually get around to using it under another name. When *Waiting for Godot* was put on and Beckett was asked if it could be made into a film, he said no, he had written the work for the stage. Many people took this response to mean that Beckett did not like film as a medium. But that was not the point at all. He had written *Waiting for Godot* to be seen from the middle of a theatre audience—let's say from the eighth row—and he thought close-ups and other film techniques would make it a different work.

Alain, however, had gone a different way in making a "montage," giving a marvelous sense of visual imagery in his writing. He had objectified the emotional impact of viewing events in the same way instant replay does on television. If, when a baseball player runs from first base to second, the umpire calls him out, you might think it is because the umpire is black and the player white—or vice versa—or that it is because the umpire is from New Orleans and the team from New York. But if you see it from five different camera angles, each of them really trying to be quite objective, the same play will still look different each time and you will begin to get a completely different perception of what has happened.

Our first publication of Robbe-Grillet, in 1957, was an article called "A Fresh Start for Fiction." Despite the fact that Alain is French and that he writes in French, he has always seemed a kind of Midwesterner to me, a non-Eastern Establishment person, more like me, from Chicago. It was very important because to certain others he did seem as though he belonged to the French establishment. After all, Jackson Pollock and Franz Kline never got to France in their lifetimes. I also had the feeling that we shared inferiority-superiority feelings. It is not for nothing that Chicago is called "The Second City," insulted yet bragging, and it is not for nothing that Alain was not first a writer fresh from the Sorbonne, but a botanical engineer from L'Ecole, like coming from MIT rather than Princeton.

In that first article we published, Alain said: "The traditional role of the writer consisted in excavating Nature, in burrowing deeper and deeper to reach some ever more intimate strata, in finally bringing to light some fragment of a disconcerting secret. Having descended into the abyss of human passions, he would send to the seemingly tranquil world (the one on the surface) triumphant messages describing the mysteries he had actually touched with his own hands."

He stated that "This profundity is functional like a trap in which the writer had captured the universe in order to hand it over to society. . . . The revolution which has taken place is in proportion to the power of the old order. Not only do we no longer consider the world as our very own, our private property, designed according to our needs and readily domesticated, but we no longer believe in its depth."

Juxtapose the above to Willem de Kooning's great painting Excavation. Perhaps coincidentally—but only perhaps—the issue of *Evergreen* in which this article appeared also had Jackson Pollock on the cover.

After publishing that article, we then published a novel of Alain's, *The Voyeur*, translated from the Les Editions de Minuit edition. And here Alain adds his own history: he says that we passed over his first book, *Les Gommes*, and published *Le Voyeur* because the title was sexier. It was true—partially. Who could translate *Les Gommes* into English anyway? "The Erasers" is a very unsatisfactory title and "Bum Shoes" would have been equally so. With *La Jalousie* we had the same problem. In fact, the only novel whose title easily translated into English was *Le Voyeur* [*The Voyeur*]. The second reason I can give for our not publishing *The Erasers* first was that I resented the way Alain spoke about painting in the book. His intense visualness is in his words, somehow written as if by a blind person feeling his way by touch.

[W]e at Grove Press were basically publishing something that we simply liked. We are still publishing his work twenty-five years later, just as we are still publishing Beckett, Ionesco, and Pinter—four writers who came to us during the same era.

[*Godot*] was as thoroughly denounced as anything I can ever remember. After a while it was thought of as being rather funny, just as Schoenberg was thought of as an insane person, someone who wrote music without following any rules, and Pollock and his group were thought to be painters who just "smeared" paint. Of this new ferment in artistic freedom and its implicit hopefulness. Alain wrote:

> Today the rule of tragedy encompasses all my feelings and thoughts, it conditions me utterly. My body may be satisfied, my heart happy, but my conscience remains anxious. I claim that this anxiety, this misery, is SITUATED in space and time, like all unhappiness, like everything in the world. I claim that man, some day, will free himself of it. But I have no proof of the future.
>
> For me, also, it is a bet. "Man is a sick animal," wrote Unamuno in *The Tragic Sense of Life*. The bet consists in holding that he can be cured, and that if this is

true it would be folly to shut him up forever in his present sickness and unhappiness. I have nothing to lose. The bet, all things considered, is the only reasonable one.

And I think that is a bet that Beckett has also taken.

Excerpts from Three Decades of the French New Novel, ed. Lois Oppenheim, U. of Illinois Press, 1986

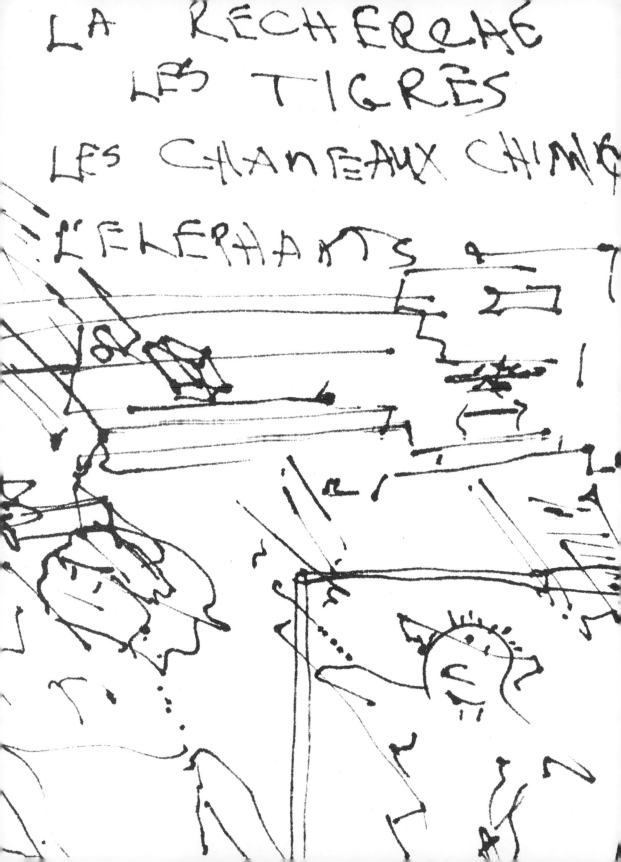

entr' acte

GROVE PRESS ✳

795 BROADWAY, NEW YORK 3, N. Y. ● GRAMERCY 3-7447

May 25, 1962
Memo from Judith Schmidt

Dear Sam,
Do you like these drawings of Moran and
Son? I find them quite charming and thought
you might like to see them. They were done
by William Rice, a painter who lives in
NY. He intended to do a whole series but
thus far there are only two.

Yours,
Judith

P.S. Unless something drastic happens,
I'll arrive in Paris on July 21st. But
I'll write about this again a week or two
before I leave New York.

GROVE PRESS

795 BROADWAY, NEW YORK 3, N.Y. • GRAMERCY 3-7447

June 8, 1962

Dear Sam,

I've just sent the Obie certificate off by first class
sea mail, since Alan won't be going to Paris.

Enclosed are the pages from the Village Voice
dealing with the awards. There really isn't too much to
tell about the meeting. Ruth White made a very sweet
acceptance speech thanking you and Alan. Alan made a very
nice short speech, with a preliminary remark, "I abstain
from stating what I think of Walter Kerr" or some similar
words. There was a kind of shocked silence after the
statement was made that Kerr had abstained. Of course I'm
not surprised that he didn't vote for H.D. since he hasn't
liked a nonmusical play in years (at least, not as far as I
can recollect), but I don't understand the purpose of his
abstaining for the record. The night H.D. opened, we had a
small party, and someone read the Times and Tribune reviews
aloud. At the end of the reading of the Kerr review, Ruth
White said "he just won't let himself be moved," which I
think was a perfect comment.

Six copies of H.D. and six of MURPHY are being
shipped to you. Will also send six of WATT, but they will
come a bit later.

                    Best,

                    Judith

Charlotte Rae in *Happy Days*,
CSC Theater, 1990
Photo © Paula Court

(Vol. VII, No. 32,
May 31, 1962)

A Newspaper of Greenwich Village

the village **Voice** 10c

The 7th Village Voice 'Obie' Awards

Halfway through, Miss Lenya announced an award to Samuel Beckett's "Happy Days" as Best Foreign Play "with judge Walter Kerr wishing to be announced as abstaining." After a moment's hush, there came a scattering of hisses, boos, and some small applause. On the podium co-judge Edward Albee indulged in a brief, dry smile.

GROVE PRESS ✳

April 12, 1963

Dear Sam,
Today a package arrived addressed to you. Since it said
FRAGILE and FOOD we thought we should open it. So we did.
Enclosed were:

> 1 bottle Mustard sauce
> 1 can condensed split pea soup with vegetables &
> smoked pork
> 1 bottle chili sauce
> 1 bottle hot ketchup
> 1 can cheese soup
> 1 can campside beans
> 1 can spaghetti with tomato sauce & cheese
> 1 jar midget gherkins
> and 1 jar Kandied KrinkLChips (pickles!)

All sent with the enclosed card from Heinz 57 varieties on
your 57th birthday. How clever, these Americans!
Peter is coming her to meet Barney this afternoon. He
will choose everything he likes. We will give out the rest
to all interested parties. Barney will take you to dinner in
Paris and duplicate all of the above. (especially the Kandied
KrinkLChips). OK?

> Yours,
> Judith

I was almost tempted to send the package. If I could only have
seen the faces of the French customs officers.

February 4, 1970

Dear Sam,

  Enclosed are letters referring to Anna Sokolow's dance version of ACT WITHOUT WORDS (whether it be I or II is not clear to me).

  I gave her permission to do a couple of performances, pending your return to Paris. Do you want us to allow her to continue to perform her version? Also, if the television question should arise again, should we give permission? She understands that permission was only temporary, so if you want to withdraw it, please do not hesitate.

Yours,
Judith

Judith Schmidt
Grove Press Office
c.1960s

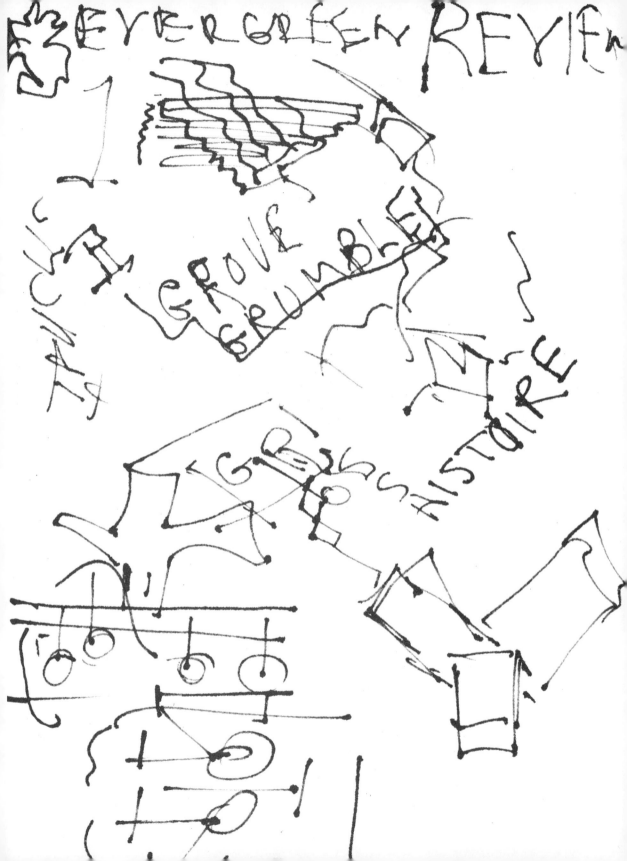

act three

FROM WORD TO IMAGE

"What visions in the dark of light!"

Rosset Recollects

I was visiting Joan in Vétheuil. I was with my wife, Lisa, and I think Tansey and Beckett, my children. Joan and Riopelle were in the process of breaking up, and he wasn't with her that night. We were having a non-dinner with Joan—she didn't cook. She was going around with a candle, and the surroundings were very lugubrious.

While we were trying to eat dinner, I thought I saw a ghost in the window. It was Riopelle staring through the glass, like a ghost with a white face and a beard. It was very mysterious and frightening. He then walked away from the window. I don't know if anyone noticed him. Maybe Lisa did. Riopelle and Joan had been having a fight—a silent one.

Later that night, I got very drunk and walked down a hill—this precipitous hill that Joan lived on. It was a straight up and down approach from the house to the road below, and way below that was the Seine. When you cross the road and go down, at the bottom of the hill is where Monet's house was, and also where Joan's gardens were.

During the early morning hours around 4:00 a.m., I walked down this pathway guided by the moonlight. Dirt and rocks pinched my feet—I had forgotten to put my shoes on, and it bothered me a lot. But, I did it anyway. I got to the road and crossed it. Then I walked from there down into the Seine.

I waded in up to my waist. I could feel my knee hit something. It was a baby carriage. It reminded me of the film "Potamkin"—that great scene where the baby carriage goes down the steps with the baby in it. I dragged the baby carriage, this metal thing, out of the water. It felt like it would hold a big doll. I dragged the carriage all the way back up the hill.

By now it was about 5:00 in the morning. I ran into her gardener caretaker on the way up the hill who looked at me as if I were crazy—which I think I was. But he was very polite and simply said, "Yes, monsieur. Good morning."

I got up to the top, and I dragged that thing right up to the front door. Somewhere along the way, I got a log which I placed inside the carriage, I then went inside and wrote a poem, about two or three pages long, to the two of them, and dedicated the poem to the baby that they (Riopelle and Joan) never had. I put the poem on top of the carriage and went to bed.

Quite some time passed but I never heard a word from Joan. Nor anything about the carriage or the poem. Then a long time later, about a year or two, Joan said, "Oh, Jean-Paul really loved that poem!" I was very, very bitter towards both Joan and

Joan Mitchell's house in Vétheuil

Riopelle, I had written the poem, and never kept a copy of it. I think it was inspired by Samuel Beckett. I was trying to write the kind of poem that I thought he might have written in the same circumstance—a very sad and end-of-the-world kind of thing. Burroughs wrote about a child that died. It's a short story. Joan and Beckett were good friends. Riopelle was very jealous of Joan's relationship with Beckett, and also of my relationship. So, that was probably on my mind. Burroughs' story was called "The Dead Child."

Barney Rosset interview
with Jules Geller

GELLER: A lot of people coming from a political background at that time would look at abstract art and say, it's not political. They wouldn't get it.

ROSSET: I know. We had a big thing about that. I was trying to force Joan to be more political, socialist realist. Then I began to understand that I didn't understand what she was doing. She was very powerful; believe me. And she couldn't stop herself. She could not stop. And when she got back here she immediately got very involved with Franz Kline and de Kooning, Pollock, and so on.

GELLER: And you got involved with them too.

ROSSET: Yeah, all through her. Very inarticulate people. They didn't talk much. Motherwell did, but he couldn't paint so well. He had no passion. He was an academic. But he talked, and published books; he was a good teacher. I bought Motherwell's house in East Hampton after he had moved out. I lived there for 30 years.

There were things in the house he'd left behind—including his family bible. Didn't interest him. But he had left a little cup by Matisse, with a little erotic drawing. I told him that, and he jumped: Where is it? His own family bible for generations didn't interest him. And de Kooning had used his studio as his teaching place, so there were all these rolled up de Koonings. I wish I knew what happened to them.

GELLER: So, in effect, Joan introduced you to the world of modern art?

ROSSET: Totally. That's how I met all those people at the Cedar

Rosset's Quonset Hut in East Hampton: interior (left) and exterior (right), where Beckett visited in 1964 when making FILM

bar and so on. Franz Kline... I liked him the best. He was a nice human being.

GELLER: Then by the time you actually got to something like Beckett, it made sense.

ROSSET: That's right. I could see it for what it was. And then I introduced it to Joan. Now it was in reverse, and she recognized it immediately. And the rapport between Beckett and Joan was fantastic. So it was going in a circle.

GELLER: You mentioned that you had tried to get Joan to paint in a socialist realist manner. Could you speak a little about your involvement with left politics when you were younger?

ROSSET: When I grew up in Chicago, Communism was my idea of personal freedom. Communism meant freedom to me. Especially freedom to make love, right? "Free love" was the huge slogan, which was used against the Communists. I must say that I never heard the Communists use it themselves—but it was implicit in Communism, because Lenin said, "sex should be like having a glass of water."

GELLER: Of course, if you tried to pursue a policy of personal freedom in Russia, you wouldn't have lasted very long.

ROSSET: I know, but it took a long time for me to understand that.

GELLER: And the Communist Party wasn't particularly open to avant-garde art and experiments in personal freedom.

ROSSET: No. But we weren't really in the party; we were on the fringes. We were too young to be in the party. There was the Young Communist League, which we did not join. Oddly enough.

GELLER: You were a fellow traveler, in other words.

ROSSET: A fellow traveler! I suppose we were fellow travelers together, Haskell Wexler, Quentin Young, and myself.

GELLER: Which means that you weren't under party discipline, so you were not told what you can't think, or what you can't say, which would have been the case had you been in the party.

ROSSET: Well, after the war I did join the party in Chicago. It drove me crazy! There was a girl in our group at the University of Chicago, which was a real hotbed. Her name was Elaine, and she did all the party bureaucracy work. I used her name as a generic term to describe a person who only cared about the party line; you could not waver! I'd say, "There's an Elaine."

Each member of the party was supposed to sell fifty copies of the *Daily Worker* a week. I would take mine and throw them in the garbage can! I mean, the idea of going through the South Side of Chicago among all these black families, and selling them the *Daily Worker*, took more courage than I had! So I threw them away. And then I was voted the *Daily Worker*'s best salesman. I had the best record.

GELLER: You would just pay for them yourself, out of your own pocket?

ROSSET: Yeah. They were five cents each. Cheap. Then in 1948 we traveled to Czechoslovakia to show the film I had produced, *Strange Victory*. We were disgusted by what we saw. We got there just after the Communists had taken over. And it was not for the good. It was frightening. You could see the regimentation everywhere. That was the last straw. We didn't say anything; we just got the hell out and went back to France to be decadent, bourgeois slobs. That was the end of it for me.

GELLER: You completely rejected the Communist orthodoxy?

ROSSET: I had never understood the orthodoxy, because in the United States Communists were such a minority—how could you have an orthodoxy? In other words, to say that you were a Communist was already an enormous affirmation of your peculiar self, right? Who else was crazy enough to do that? So you had to think of yourself as very much of an individualist. Only, of course, that wasn't quite true when you got to other countries, where everybody was a Communist just like you! Of course the Communists were antiracism, pro-woman's rights; there were a lot of good positions associated with Communism, and that never changed.

GELLER: The theme of personal freedom, of your trying to extend your own personal freedom, was in effect the thread that runs through all the activities of Grove Press. Grove really was an extension of your personality. And the more you found yourself being free, the freer the company became, in effect.

ROSSET: That's true.

GELLER: Anybody who looks for a programmatic manifesto as to what you wanted the company to be...

ROSSET: ...they'd still be looking. It was self-propelling.

GELLER: It was really the defining of yourself as you published books, right? How did Beckett fit into your political vision, because he's really the opposite of an engaged political activist?

ROSSET: Absolutely. Though you have to remember he was Irish—that was one thing in his favor. And while he may not have been overtly political, he was very liberal. Sometimes it bothered me that he wasn't Left enough.

GELLER: On the other hand, his drama was so radical it really upset the status quo.

ROSSET: They banned him in the Soviet Union. *Waiting for Godot* was not allowed. And neither was Henry Miller. The Soviets condemned them both. Miller especially they would use as an example of decadence. Whereas Miller was actually a very good analyst of how terrible, monstrous American culture was. That they liked, but they wouldn't publish him. I guess it must have been the sex. With Beckett, I guess it must have been the hopelessness.

GELLER: *Godot* certainly wasn't socialist realism.

ROSSET: Though Beckett was published in Poland early on, and successfully. We actually published an edition of *Tropic of Cancer* translated into Russian. A man from Hollywood had spent years translating *Cancer*. George George, a White Russian who had lived in Manchuria. When he came to the States and they asked him what his name was, he'd heard the guy ahead of him say "George." So he said "George George." He worked as a house painter in Hollywood, and got mixed up with all these crazy White Russians and Red Russians—the people around Brecht and other strange, exiled hangers-on, and he became a sort of successful screen-writer. He was the stepfather of Joan Mitchell's closest friend, Zuka. I got to know George, and he did this translation. I've been told that it's fantastic.

GELLER: How did you get the books into Russia?

ROSSET: I never got in that many, though we tried everything we could. Some very strange people came to the office—they were probably CIA, but I was happy to play with them. I'd sell them books, but they never really took enough. I remember asking Herbert Gold to take one with him on a trip to the Soviet Union. He went to the U.S. cultural attaché in Moscow, and the attaché turned up some music and said, "Herbert I've got something to show you"—he already had a copy!

GELLER: Why did you put so much energy into this?

ROSSET: Any country like the Soviet Union where people read this book and like it, changes as a result. We actually published a Russian writer in *Evergreen Review* who told us that he had gotten hold of a copy—it was passed from hand to hand—and it changed his life. He was not particularly anti-Communist, or anti-Soviet. He wanted to be an artist. He said that they sat at home in their little apartments at night, read it aloud and laughed.

GELLER: Would you say that publishing Beckett in the fifties in America had a similar effect on American culture?

ROSSET: Beckett certainly was part of a countercultural movement. *Godot* did not exactly fit in with the rest of what was happening anywhere, France or here.

GELLER: Beckett certainly revolutionized the theatre.

ROSSET: *Godot* was incomprehensible. People thought it was gibberish.

GELLER: When you first read the play, do you remember what it was you responded to?

ROSSET: The strangeness of it. *Godot* has a strangely sad and antireligious feeling; I somehow sympathized with that.

GELLER: How did you first hear of *Waiting for Godot*?

ROSSET: Sylvia Beach, who was Joyce's publisher in Paris and the owner of the Shakespeare & Co. bookstore, called me at Grove Press, in New York. She knew about Grove, one way or another, and she thought maybe we would like to publish it. Actually, I had already read about the play in *The New York Times*. But I admired her very much, I was really struck by her effort, and she bolstered my involvement with the play a great deal. Beckett had already been turned down by Simon & Schuster. An editor there was very interested in Murphy—though I didn't know that until much later.

It's still much the same today. All of the established publishers would have had a much better chance at doing Beckett than Grove, right? They could pay five times as much for him, but nobody wanted to buy it. Nobody was interested.

The same was true of Ionesco. *The Bald Soprano* was put on in Paris and got a lot of attention. Don Allen, who was an important editor at Grove in the beginning—he liked Ionesco very early. Beckett and Ionesco were on the scene together. They liked each other; that I remember. I never heard one say much bad about the other. At a much later date, I think Ionesco became jealous because he never achieved the same level of acclaim as Beckett—and he was a nasty son of a bitch. Ionesco became very reactionary as he got older. But they did admire each other. You have to remember that they both wrote in French, though neither one had French as their native language. They were both not that young when they started to get recognition. They were both struggling to make it in the theatre, and they were very aware of each other. They were really blasting away the existing structure.

GELLER: Did you get in touch with Beckett yourself?

ROSSET: I did. Very quickly, in 1953. Before *Godot* was translated.

In fact, I had somebody else translate it. And I think that aggravated Beckett, which was good because it forced him to do it himself. You know, he looked at that translation and couldn't stand it.

GELLER: This is not so different from what happened with the trilogy.

ROSSET: Dick Seaver's introduction to *I Can't Go On, I'll Go On*, a Beckett reader we did at Grove, is very good about this. He describes how he, Alex Trocchi, and Patrick Bowles are translating Beckett, and Beckett is very sweetly correcting them. Their translation disappears, and without him knowing it, it becomes Beckett's, while all the time he complains, "My God, how can I go on with these people?"

Wallace Fowlie read *Waiting for Godot*, and he liked it, a lot. This was very early on, so that meant something, because Fowlie was not that... wild. That was real confirmation.

Geller: Do you remember when you met Beckett?

ROSSET: I remember the exact moment I met him. It was in the bar of the Pont Royal hotel, which is next door to Gallimard. And at that time Sartre hung out there, as did Camus, and so on. I was with Loly, my wife at the time, and we were to meet Beckett at 6:00 for a drink. And this very handsome gentleman walked in wearing a raincoat, and he said, "Hi, nice to meet you. I've only got 40 minutes." He was all ready to get rid of us! And at four that morning he was buying us champagne.

GELLER: So you hit it off very well.

ROSSET: Right away. He was so gentle and charming. Kind.

GELLER: Then when you came back to the U.S. you continued to correspond with him.

ROSSET: Very early on he wrote me a letter to the effect of "My Dear

Mr. Rosset, I want you to know that there are certain things in my play which, when translated into English, may seem obscene. And you should know, I'm not going to change them." And that was long before I had anything to do with *Lady Chatterley.* Now, listen to this from July 31, 1953. Can you imagine me writing to Beckett: "Dear Mr. Beckett, Your translation of *Godot* did finally arrive…. I like it very much. It seems to me that you have done a fine job. The long speech by Lucky is particularly good. And the whole play reads extremely well. If I were to make any criticism, it would be that one can tell that the translation was done by a person more used to 'English' speech than 'American.' Thus the use of such words as 'bloody,' and a few others, might lead an audience to think the play was originally done by an Englishman in English."

Barney and Loly, 1953, on their honeymoon to meet Beckett

GELLER: He didn't change it though, did he?

ROSSET: Oh, he wrote back about that. The letter goes on, "This is a small point, but in a few places a neutralization of speech away from a specifically English flavor might have the result of enhancing the French origins for an American reader. Beyond that technical point I have little to say, excepting I am now extremely desirous of seeing the play on stage in any language." He originally used the word "skivvy," and so on. And he agreed with me—he said he wanted it to sound like it was first French, not English, and that he did whatever he could to make it that way. And then Lucky he said sounded to him as if it was an American name, so if he had some Americanisms in his speech that would be normal.

GELLER: When you went to see Beckett in Paris, did you see the Roger Blin production of *Godot*? Was it still running?

ROSSET: Yes, I did see it. And it was an amazing night, because I was with Loly. She had been telling me about her life in Paris during the war, which I didn't quite believe. All about how her father, who was a major in the German intelligence, had gotten her a job for the German paper. She was very young, seventeen. She said she became involved with a group of French people, who she didn't realize at first were in the Marquis. It was very romantic and all that, but I didn't quite believe her. But then Roger Blin and all the people in the cast—they knew her! They had been in the Marquis, and they threw their arms around her! Then I had to believe it. That impressed Beckett, that really impressed him. It really impressed me. She told a straight story that was too good to be true. So that moment was very emotional.

GELLER: You became his theatrical agent in America as well.

ROSSET: That just sort of happened. And then later it was solidified in writing.

GELLER: Beckett was extremely loyal to Grove Press, and you became close friends. How did he feel about the other books that Grove published, by writers like the Beats, and Henry Miller?

Allen Ginsberg
on *Evergreen Review*
(no. 42, August
1966)

ROSSET: I took him to lunch with Henry Miller after we won the *Tropic of Cancer* verdict in Chicago. They had known each other from the thirties, and they did not like each other. And, everything that you read about these two would tell you they were not easy people to get along with. They were both quite difficult. But when I brought them together, each of them told me afterwards, "Boy, has he changed! He's so nice now." I don't know what Beckett thought about Miller's writing, but in one of his very early letters he asks if I read *Catcher in the Rye*. He said he really liked it.

William Burroughs was a writer he particularly didn't understand. There is this now famous anecdote about a meeting between Burroughs and Beckett, which took place in Maurice Girodias's restaurant. I brought them together, really, through Girodias. I remember that I was sitting next to Sam, we had a dinner, and Burroughs, who is sort of worshipping Beckett, is explaining to him how you do cut-ups.

And Beckett says to Bill, "That's not writing, that's plumbing." But Allen Ginsberg and Burroughs worshipped him. They were very unusual in the sense that they understood that Beckett was important, at that time. Beckett, though, was out of it with them. They wanted him, almost desperately, to recognize them, and he just didn't seem to connect. I wanted him to like them. It wasn't dislike, it was just ... non-togetherness. He just didn't get it. If he had read anything of Burroughs before the cutups maybe he'd have gotten it. But the Beats didn't impinge upon his consciousness. Trocchi did. Anything of Alex Trocchi's.

GELLER: When you published *Godot* you couldn't have thought of it as a potentially popular title.

ROSSET: We only printed something like a thousand copies, and the first year it sold about 400. It wasn't until the play was

Evergreen Review
(no. 32, April / May
1964)

A Project for Disastrous Success

BRION GYSIN, American poet and painter now living in Paris, has been associated with William Burroughs as one of the apostles of the cut-up method in modern writing.

produced on Broadway a couple of years later—with Bert Lahr playing Estragon—that the book started to sell. The production only lasted six weeks in New York, the audience walked out, and Walter Winchell denounced it as the new Communist propaganda. But that production made it famous.

GELLER: How many copies of *Godot* did Grove end up selling?

Rosset: Well over a million.

GELLER: After *Godot*, you began to publish Beckett's novels.

ROSSET: The first one we did was *Watt*, which was typeset in France. I complained bitterly about that to Sam, because they'd mix up "Watt" with "Not" and so on.

GELLER: Why was it typeset in France?

ROSSET: Because it was first published by Maurice Girodias at Olympia Press, and we offset from that edition. That was a big battle: who really was responsible for publishing that book at Olympia? Was it Alex Trocchi and Dick Seaver, or was it Girodias? Beckett certainly thought it was not Girodias. He did not like Girodias—unfairly, I thought, and I always took Girodias's side in arguments between the two because I felt that Girodias, for better or for worse, was an entrepreneur. He was trying to make a living. And the fact is that there was something about him that was very sympathetic. Only he could go bankrupt in Paris under the Nazis—when you could sell anything! There was a paper shortage, and if you printed something, it sold. The only real question was how many could you get printed. But Girodias managed to go bankrupt. He was a Jew who lived under the Nazis, he went bankrupt but did not go to jail. I still don't understand how he managed that. Nobody knows.

(New York, September 24, 1987)

Barney Rosset interview
with John Oakes

… We sat in the plush bar of L'Hotel and then in a Paris café—"Brigitte Bardot's favorite," according to Rosset. Ignoring the nasty looks of waiters, Rosset pulled out a hip flask of rum and poured it into a glass, claiming French rum wasn't up to snuff. A real connoisseur.

OAKES: You seem to have a close relationship with Samuel Beckett; how did that come about?

ROSSET: Samuel Beckett was available. But it was nothing that happened overnight. I had read various short things by Beckett before Grove Press was started. I had a curiosity about him which wasn't too well satisfied. But I was aware of him. And then *Waiting for Godot* was put on in Paris and published by Editions de Minuit. That was one thing. Also, at the same time, *Merlin* magazine, which was put out in Paris by Alexander Trocchi (Trocchi was later author of Cain's Book) and Richard Seaver, who later worked for Grove Press for many years, and many other people, was publishing some of his stuff. But what really made me aware of him was *Waiting for Godot*. I got a copy of it and liked it very much, and I asked some other people I knew what they thought of it and whether I was just looking for somebody to tell me "yes, it's great," I don't know. But I remember I went to Wallace Fowlie, who was a professor of mine at the New School. He was a person very different from me, a convert to Catholicism, but I valued his sensibilities very much. He said, "I think it's a masterpiece of modem literature"—you have to remember, this was when it was being ridiculed in the rest of the world—and he said

"You must publish it." That gave me the final impetus. Then we made contact, and I came to Paris—1953—and met these people who were already publishing him. That encouraged me even more, and of course meeting Beckett was the best encouragement of all. I was tremendously impressed.

OAKES: Why was that? He has the reputation for being a very quiet man.

ROSSET: I found him an extremely sympathetic person. It's true and it's not true, that he's quiet; he was loquacious enough with me, maybe I was loquacious with him, I don't know. But we became very good friends. I thought that he had something to say about the human condition that was original, really original. Extremely important. It's not that he did something the way that Joyce did it, or the way that Proust did it, but he had something that said to me he was at the same level. It happened to be that he had known Joyce very well, but that never impressed me as being particularly important to him. I mean, last night I asked him if he had ever met Ezra Pound. I don't know why, but I did. I knew he had, but I asked him anyway. He said, yes, he most certainly had, but then he said he really had only met Pound twice. He said once, Pound was very arrogant and sort of contemptuous—that was with Joyce, and Beckett was like the young acolyte to Joyce—and the second was many years later, shortly before Pound died, and he asked to see Beckett. Beckett said sure, and he went to wherever Pound was, he went into a room, just the two of them alone, and he sat there with Pound. Pound didn't say anything. Not a word. So, Beckett said, "I sat there, and I looked at him for a while, and he looked at me, and I got very embarrassed, and finally, I stood up, put my arms around him, hugged him, and left." That was the second meeting. Beckett said he had heard of other people having similar experiences with Pound.

OAKES: You once said that Beckett plots out everything very precisely—

ROSSET: Yes, that's my observation. He uses graph paper! He plots where a character moves, his relationship to everyone else, the lighting. A good example of that is *Waiting for Godot*. Many people have wanted to make a motion picture of it. The last one was a very famous American actor. I can't remember his name—I have a block about this sort of thing—but his agent contacted me from Hollywood, about seven years ago. He said, I represent this superstar, and he wants to put on *Waiting for Godot*. He said, we'll get you Marlon Brando or Laurence Olivier, etc. All of that. And Beckett can have full control, and you can have as much money as you want. So I said, I can't answer you, because I have to talk to Beckett. Then I asked a friend who knew about this sort of thing—because I had no experience in it—how much you should ask. He said the most he had ever heard of being asked for the rights to something, where there was no scenario, was $500,000. So I asked for $500,000. The agent said fine. Later, when he wrote me confirming it, it somehow got down to $400,000, but nevertheless it was incredible. I came to Paris to talk to Beckett about it, and I had the same mental block I have now—I couldn't remember the actor's name. And when I finally remembered his name, I realized I had never seen him in a movie—probably the only person in America who hadn't. Beckett wanted to know what the actor looked like. I thought, well, he must be one of these very large people, like John Wayne, a cowboy actor or something—which happened to be totally untrue—so I told Sam he was sort of like Marlon Brando. Sam asked what Marlon Brando looked like. He's big, isn't he? Sam asked. I said yeah, he's very big and heavy. Finally Sam said, but my characters are ghosts. So we forgot about it. Months later, this agent called back. He said, I know what happened. You're ashamed to call me, because Beckett said no. I really admire that, the agent said. That somebody would turn down all that money. I said, well you're right. You're absolutely right. I'm ashamed. He said, well, would you mind calling my client, because he thinks I'm the one who ruined the deal. I called this client of his, and I got a French maid on the phone in Hollywood, and I gave her the message. Later, I felt guilty, because the man wasn't a cowboy, and when he couldn't get the Beckett thing he went on to do *Enemy of the People*, and then he died. He had cancer and he wanted to do something good before he was finished. And he was also a very thin, slim man.

OAKES: But your film experiences have sometimes been very successful. Didn't you make one film with Beckett?

ROSSET: We made a film called FILM in 1964. I had commissioned several people to write films. I had an idea that, if one went to people like Ionesco, Beckett, Robbe-Grillet, Marguerite Duras and two or three others, and had all of them write film scripts, that somehow one would be able to find backers for all of this. I think I was about ten or twelve years ahead of time, because I think later something like Public Broadcasting would have helped. Actually, I got five scripts done. Beckett, Pinter, Duras, Ionesco, and Robbe-Grillet.

OAKES: What happened to the scripts?

ROSSET: It's sort of tragic. Grove Press went ahead and produced the Beckett one. Ionesco's was never done, though there were several attempts. The Robbe-Grillet was never done, the Marguerite Duras was never done, and the Pinter was done, ultimately by the BBC. I've never seen it, as many times as I've tried to. It was a marvelous script.

OAKES: It's not so tragic. You did the Beckett—

ROSSET: Yes, he came to America, his one and only visit there. We got a wonderful group of people around him. We had somebody who I felt was one of the greatest cinematographers ever, Boris Kaufman, who did the films of Jean Vigo. Vigo did *L'Atalante* and *Zéro de Conduite*. *Zéro de Conduite* takes place in a boarding school, and the children organize a revolution. Marvelous. They take over the school.

OAKES: That appeals to you, as a professional subversive.

ROSSET: It appeals to me totally. I did the same thing at my school. Organized a revolution.

OAKES: You didn't really, did you?

ROSSET: I certainly did.

(Excerpts from "Barney Rosset and the Art of Combat Publishing,"
The Review of Contemporary Fiction, Fall 1990)

Breath

Breath, *a character-less forty-second stage work by Beckett, was given by the playwright to Kenneth Tynan to be used as the Prologue to his erotic revue* Oh! Calcutta!*—with its title a pun on the French "Oh! Quel cul t'as"—first performed in New York City in 1969. According to Beckett biographer James Knowlson, "Beckett intended his sketch to be an ironic comment on what was to follow in the show," "funny simply because of its failure to live up to the audience's expectations." Yet the piece was not used as Beckett had written it: The words "including naked people" were added to the text and the piece appeared, in an illustrated book put out by Grove, with the playwright's name (and a photo of parts of naked bodies!), though it was meant to be anonymous* (Damned to Fame, *Simon & Schuster, pp. 501-2). Beckett's justifiable fury resulted in his withdrawal of the work from the London production of Tynan's revue and ensuing publications—*Gambit *(4:16, 1970),* Breath and Other Short Plays *(Faber & Faber, 1972), and* The Collected Shorter Plays of Samuel Beckett *(Grove Press, 1984)— printed the text as originally written.*

—ED.

BREATH

Black. Then

1. Faint light on stage littered with miscellaneous unidentifiable rubbish. Hold about 5 seconds.

2. Faint brief cry and immediately inspiration and slow increase of light together reaching maximum together in about 10 seconds. Silence and hold about 5 seconds.

3. Expiration and slow decrease of light together reaching minimum together (light as in 1) in about 10 seconds and immediately cry as before. Silence and hold about 5 seconds. Then

Black.

Rubbish: no verticals, all scattered and lying.

Cry: instant of recorded vagitus. Important that two cries be identical, switching on and off strictly synchronized light and breath.

Breath: amplified recording.

Maximum Light: not bright. If 0 = dark and 10 = bright, light should move from about 3 to 6 and back.

—Samuel Beckett

Crosby (2) 35124   Grove Press   Breath   1P   News   5-4-70

2P Repro   5-5-70

WOrth 6-5750—D 10

FILM

BECKETT'S only film, appropriately titled FILM, was written in 1963 and produced in New York the following year. It was directed by Alan Schneider and starred the late Buster Keaton. Beckett's only trip to the United States was for the making of FILM whose "script" was based on Bishop Berkeley's Esse est percipi ("to be is to be perceived"), the notion that self-perception supersedes all external perception. With no dialogue and but one sound—a whispered "sssh!"—FILM was awarded, among others, the Film Critics Prize at the 1965 Venice Film Festival, the Special Jury Prize at the 1966 Tours (France) Festival, and the Special Prize at the Oberhausen (Germany) Festival in 1966.

Alan Schneider and Samuel Beckett, Paris 1957

In his essay, "On Directing Film," Schneider wrote the following:

What was required was not merely a subjective camera and an objective camera, but actually two different "visions" of reality: one, that of the perceiving "eye" (E) constantly observing the object (the script was once titled The Eye), and one, that of the object (O) observing his environment. O was to possess varying degrees of awareness of being perceived by E and make varying attempts to escape from this perception (in addition to all other, or even imagined, perceptions). The story of this highly visual, if highly unusual, film was simply that O's attempt to remove all perception ultimately failed because he could not get rid of self-perception. At the end, we would see that Q = E. Q.E.D.

—ED.

Alan Schneider's award for directing FILM

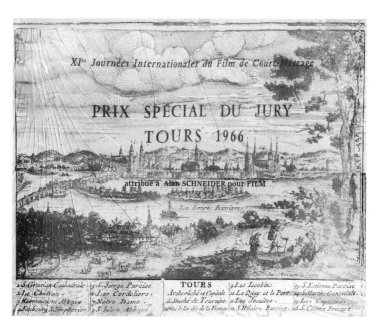

XIe *Journées Internationales du Film de Court Métrage*

PRIX SPÉCIAL DU JURY
TOURS 1966

attribué à **Alan SCHNEIDER** pour **FILM**

Rosset on FILM

Berlin, 2000

This is actually my second trip to Berlin. Both times my mission has involved the film media. When I came in 1963 (or was it '62?) it was to see Günter Grass and to try and persuade him to write a motion picture scenario for us. So, here I am, back with a finished motion picture, but it is not his. It is Samuel Beckett's FILM.

Perhaps the rather fortuitous set of circumstances culminating in my being here could have been predicted back then. Well, almost, maybe.

My own background before Grove Press, which started for me in 1951, had been heavily involved in matters involving motion pictures—it started early, in precollege interest, especially the theatre. My longest-time friend, Haskell Wexler, whom I was close to from about the age of eight, became one of the world's foremost cinematographers, starting with the Academy Motion Picture Award, the Oscar, for *Who's Afraid of Virginia Woolf*. I attended the University of California, LA, where I had gone to study filmmaking just after World War II began; a friendship with another filmmaker started. That was Joe Strick who went on to produce and direct a very special black and white film of Joyce's Ulysses and later of Henry Miller's *Tropic of Cancer*—a book so very important to me. Henry and I were in Paris with Joe during the filming.

During the war I entered the infantry and managed to wiggle into its photographic arm. I briefly attended the army film school outside of Manhattan and was fortunate to have as instructors John Huston and Frank Capra, both in the army themselves. I ended up in China, in charge of a Motion Picture Unit, far out in the hinterlands to begin with, but also having the pleasure of following the retreating Japanese troops to and into Shanghai.

Back as a civilian, I continued my film interests and in 1948 I produced my one feature film, a semi-documentary titled *Strange Victory*, concerning postwar racial discrimination in the U.S.

Then Grove Press stopped all of that, but the film urge remained and about I started a new unit outside of Grove Press—called Evergreen Productions—but with Grove people, specifically Fred Jordan and Dick Seaver, and one outsider, by then a close friend, Alan Schneider, whom I had come to know because of Sam Beckett.

Very ambitiously, I made a list of writers—with the help of my associates—whom we asked to write scripts for us to produce. Those writers were, first and foremost, Samuel Beckett, and then Harold Pinter, Eugene Ionesco, Marguerite Duras, and Alain Robbe-Grillet. We envisaged the Beckett, Ionesco, and Pinter scripts constituting three segments of a trilogy. The Duras and Robbe-Grillet were each full-length films to be.

These five were all Grove Press authors, published in the U.S. in multiple volumes. I asked three more authors to contribute. One Grove author, Jean Genet, was asked. Fred Jordan and I went to London to ask him, but he said no. (Strangely, years later we became the U.S. distributor of the one film he wrote and directed himself—a wonderful, short, silent, b & w film, entitled *Chant d' Amour*.)

Rosset at Beckett
Festival in Berlin, 2000;
with John Calder (top);
photos by Astrid Rosset

Dear Mr. Beckett

The last two, not Grove Press authors, were Ingeborg Bachman and Günter Grass. I trailed Bachman to Zurich (I think) Switzerland to get her number—and I came to Berlin to see Günter Grass. It was a different Berlin—but today I recognized the church on the Kurfürstendamm and the other night it seemed like being at home on the other side of Checkpoint Charlie at Bankstaut. Grass lived in what I recall as being a sort of bombed-out area in a precarious, small building and you reached its second floor, if he wanted you to, via a ladder which he extended down to you in lieu of a staircase.

So, thirty some years later I come back with a film, albeit not the one which I went to obtain in the first place, but a good replacement nevertheless. Fortuitously (but now with a complete lapse of memory concerning the exact circumstances), the head of a TV production company, an Irish American with the Irish underlined, a true student of Beckett's work, came along and financed the production of FILM. Needless to say, he was not reimbursed, and at some early point he totally dropped out of sight. A bit amazing, but there it is.

The project team in its most important roles consisted of Sam—he wrote, he guided, and he kept the ship afloat—Alan Schneider, who had had no previous film experience but a great deal of successful direction including of Pinter, Albee, and especially Beckett—the same for Sam, no film, but there was no doubt in my mind that we could overcome that problem—and the top two remaining people, Sidney Meyers and Boris Kaufman. Sidney Meyers was a veteran and acclaimed filmmaker. In 1960 he was a winner of a British Academy of Film and Television Arts award for *Savage Eye* (which he shared with Joseph Strick and Ben Maddow).

And then there was Boris Kaufman who was the cinematographer for *On the Waterfront* which won the Academy Award for best picture in 1954. He was also the cinematographer for *12 Angry Men, Splendor in the Grass,* and *The Pawnbroker*, which Beckett went to see in preview, and many other American films. And he was the cinematographer for all of Jean Vigo's films, the filmmaker whom I had felt most akin to. Kaufman's brother was one of the most famed of all Soviet filmmakers, Dziga Vertov. A few hours before coming here I found an article by Thomas Hunkeler (who has been here at the conference and is perhaps here tonight), which deals with the possible importance of Vertov on Beckett, and thereby FILM.

But back to New York. Our crew was complete. Judith Schmidt had retyped the script after conferences we held together (and audiotaped) in East Hampton. We went to New York to shoot FILM.

A few years ago Kevin Brownlow and David Gill made a three-part documentary for Thames TV called *Buster Keaton: A Hard Act to Follow*. The following is from an article by Kevin Brownlow on meeting with Beckett in an attempt to persuade him to participate in the documentary:

> I arrived promptly at eleven at the Hotel PLM and spotted his unmistakable figure leaning nonchalantly against a window. He was tall, gray-haired, his face deeply lined, and yet he looked younger than his 80 years, with a charming smile and eyes of light blue. He led me over to the cafe and we sat at a table where he drew out a packet of cigars called Corps Diplomatique, which he lit in the pauses of our

conversation. His voice was distinctly Irish; there was a slightly metallic tinge to it. As for the monosyllables in which he was said to talk, there was no evidence at all. He spoke eloquently, and thoughtfully...

SAMUEL BECKETT: "Buster Keaton was inaccessible. He had a poker mind as well as a poker face. I doubt if he ever read the text. I don't think he approved of it or liked it. But he agreed to do it and he was very competent. He was not our first choice. Alan Schneider wanted Zero Mostel and I wanted Jack MacGowran, but neither was available. It was Schneider's idea to use Keaton, who was available... He had great endurance, he was very tough and, yes, reliable. And when you saw that face at the end—oh." He smiled. "At last."

Buster Keaton and Samuel Beckett on the set for FILM, 1964

I asked if Keaton ever inquired what FILM was about.

Beckett laughed. "No. He wasn't interested."
"Did you ever tell him?"
"I never did, no. I had very little to do with him. He sat in his dressing room, playing cards—patience or something—until he was needed. The only time he came alive was when he described what happened when they were making

Beckett reviewing film clips

films in the old days. That was very enjoy- able.
I remember him saying that they started with a
beginning and an end and improvised the rest as
they went along. Of course, he tried to suggest gags
of his own."

"Did you use any of them?" "No," he laughed, "We
were depriving him of his trump card—his face."
At this point I took a deep breath and asked him
to explain the film to the man in the street. "It's
about a man trying to escape from perception of all
kinds, from all perceivers—even divine perceivers.
There is a picture which he pulls down. But he can't
escape from self-perception. It is an idea from Bishop
Berkeley, the Irish philosopher and idealist, 'To be
is to be perceived'—'Esse est percipi.' The man who
desires to cease to be must cease to be perceived. If
being is being perceived, to cease being is to cease to
be perceived."

*　　*　　*

"I suppose I was in New York three weeks to a month.
I flew to New York and the first thing we did was go to
Long Island, where Barney Rosset had a house at East
Hampton. Sidney Meyers [editor], Boris Kaufman
[cameraman], Joe Coffey [operator]—Keaton wasn't
there—and I talked about the film in the country.
The next phase was the location. When he gets in the
room, that's in the studio. (I don't remember where
the studio was.)"

"Were you pleased with the way he moved—did he give you more than you expected?"

"His movement was excellent—covering up the mirror, putting out the animals—all that was very well done. To cover the mirror, he took his big coat off and he asked me what he was wearing underneath. I hadn't thought of that. I said, 'The same coat.' He liked that.

"The only gag he approved of was the scene where he tries to get rid of the animals. He put out the cat and the dog comes back and he puts out the dog and the cat comes back. That was really the only scene he enjoyed doing.

"There was one big problem we couldn't solve—the two perceptions—the extraneous perception and his own, acute perception. The eye that follows that sees him and his own hazy, reluctant perception of various objects. Boris Kaufman devised a way of distinguishing between them. The extraneous perception was all right, but we didn't solve his own. He tried to use a filter—his view being hazy and ill defined. This worked at a certain distance but for close-ups it was no good. Otherwise it was a good job."

*　　*　　*

"FILM was made by Evergreen productions," said James Karen, who was in it. "Beckett came over, which was the most extraordinary thing about it, and really was in on the direction and production of the film. He was a hard taskmaster, he was very difficult—he had an idea, a picture in mind, and he wanted it that way. I remember him saying, 'Can't you blink five frames less?'

*   *   *

"Buster didn't understand it. Who understood it? I didn't understand it, I mean, I didn't find it very great drama, and yet it is an exciting picture to see and a lot of people think very highly Buster did not."

From *Entrances* by Alan Schneider:

Sidney proceeded to do a very quick very rough cut for Sam to look at before taking off for Paris. And that first cut turned out to be not far off from what we finally used. The editing was painstaking—and painful, Sidney always gently trying to break the mold we had set in the shooting, and Sam and I in our different ways always gently holding him to it. There was no question of sparring over who had the legal first cut or final cut or whatever. We talked, argued, tried various ways, from Moviola to screen and back again, to make it come out as much the film that Sam had first envisioned as we could. Sometimes I loved it, and sometimes I hated it. Remembering all the things I didn't do or did badly. Feeling that the two-vision thing never worked and that people would be puzzled (they were). Seeing all sort of technical bloopers. Laughing—and crying—over that bloody chihuahua. Yet, the film undoubtedly took on an ambiance, a strange snow-soft texture, that gave it depth and richness. Like an abstract painting—or one of Beckett's plays—it grew on the perceiver.

*   *   *

Sam was incredible. People always assume him to be unyielding, but when the chips are down, on specifics—here as well as in all his stage productions—he is completely understanding, flexible, and pragmatic. Far from blaming anything on the limitations and mistakes of those around him, he blamed his own material, himself. He had no recriminations for me or anyone else. He was even prepared to eliminate an important segment of his film. I was ready to quit, kill myself, cry, do it all over again on the sly, anything!

Today it would be so much easier—more possible to achieve the desired efforts. The technology is now on our side. A group of very talented people found a challenge, did the best they could with what was at hand.

Barney Rosset on
The Five Grove Film Scripts

Four Star Television, a TV product company, came to us. It was a very successful company, at least partially owned by Charles Boyer and Dick Powell, who was a famous singer-actor of the time. Like Sinatra. The two had formed a television production company, and they made a highly successful series, *The Rogue*. This was in the early Sixties. Then Powell died and they put an eccentric Irishman, whom we met, in charge of the company. And he liked Beckett. Jason Epstein, then at Random House, introduced us to him. We met him in the Gotham hotel. He financed our Beckett film, but soon thereafter we never saw him again.

And Four Star disappeared, went out of business. Both Boyer and Powell had died, but we already had gotten the money. Each writer received $20,000 for a screenplay. And though Genet didn't do work for us, I got Beckett, Robbe-Grillet, Marguerite Duras, Ionesco and Pinter. They all did it. The only ones who turned us down were Günter Grass and Genet. But it was just at the wrong period. It was a time when we thought that somebody would finance Beckett and Pinter, Ionesco. But this was before PBS. The networks talked to us, but they wouldn't go for it.

We asked Genet if he would write a film for television, and he said, "You can come talk to me if you want." So Fred and I went to London to see if we could get him to write a script. We get there, and... it was extraordinary. He lectured us for a half an hour. "You want to make it for that video? That TV?" He gave this lecture like an orator in front of an audience of a million people, with these huge gestures, all about the nature of television, which he was totally against. He walked behind the television and said, "Where are the people? Like, what's behind the TV? Where are the actors? There are no actors there!" And he was right, of course—I know I didn't argue with him. I was afraid of him. He was a sort of a frightening person when he got angry, and he didn't like this idea one bit. So, no, he wouldn't do it.

Jean-Luc Godard just would have taken the money. He was a different kind of crook. Godard would have said, "$25,000? Okay, I'll do anything you want." He gave you a treatment and then threw it away the minute he got the money. I hung out with him in Paris for a while around that time, and he was a creep. But instead, Genet told us off. Jean Genet was a thief, but he was a real thief. He was a thief from the inside out. Like Sartre said, he was a saintly thief.

I asked Beckett if he wanted to do a script. Nobody had ever asked him before. People wanted to get things from Beckett that he'd already done, but they weren't willing to gamble. They didn't trust him, he was too far out, and they didn't know what he might do next. I think the same was true of Ionesco, as well.

Grove Press went ahead and produced the Beckett one. The Ionesco was never done, though we made several attempts. The Robbe-Grillet was never done, the Marguerite Duras was never done, and the Pinter was done, ultimately by the BBC. I've never seen it, as many times as I've tried to. It was a marvelous script.

We made Beckett's FILM in 1964 from Beckett's script. Beckett came to America for its production. It was to be his one and only visit to the United States. We got a wonderful group of people around him. We had somebody who I felt was one of the greatest cinematographers ever, Boris Kaufman, who did the films of Jean Vigo. Vigo did *L'Atalante* and *Zero de Conduite*. *Zero de Conduite* takes place in a boarding school, and the children organize a revolution. Marvelous. They take over the school.

Boris Kaufman later went to Hollywood and was very successful there. For example he won the cinematography Oscar for shooting *On the Waterfront*. Alan Schneider, who had done everything of Beckett's in this country up to that point, and who had become very close to Beckett, was the director. But we needed a star, a central figure. We left that totally up to Beckett. The first one he suggested was Charlie Chaplin. At the suggestion of Max Shuster, I wrote to Chaplin. All I got out of that was a letter from some secretary who said Mr. Chaplin doesn't read scripts. And I wrote back and said, "I'm sorry, Mr. Chaplin can't read." Then there was an Irish actor who Sam liked, Patrick Magee, and he was going to do it and then he somehow disappeared. So then, we said who do you want, and Beckett said Buster Keaton. We actually found Buster Keaton. It was more or less the last thing he ever did, but he did it, he came to New York… Poor Buster. I didn't get the feeling he understood anything he was doing, but it didn't matter. He was directed. He was almost incoherent, but there was no speaking, not a word, so it was okay. There was one sound in the film: sssh!

FILM was shot right at the foot of the Brooklyn Bridge on the Manhattan Side. We needed a big wall, and we found an abandoned building with a big brick wall, and no windows. Sam liked the texture… The film was black-and-white. We had a catastrophe happening almost immediately. It shows, as Jérôme Lindon, publisher of Editions de Minuit, said, how Beckett will always rise to the occasion. The first shot was a very complicated shot. It cost perhaps $30,000, and it was shot for a film that cost

$80,000, or $90,000, and that ended up being maybe twenty minutes long. The shot was an outdoor scene, and it had about eleven people in it. The people were spread out over an entire block. They were all in couples. It was very difficult technically, to keep everything focused simultaneously. It took a whole day to shoot this one shot, and the shot didn't come out right. There was distorting called stroboscopic reticulation: the image jumped around. There was no way it could be shot again, because of the costs—the costs of the union electricians, et cetera. There were all kinds of people who were totally unneeded, because of the unions. Anyway, that shot occupied about one third of the script. And it was gone. Finished. Zeroed out. And Beckett was magnificent.

A third of his script is gone. And as I've told you, he's extremely careful about what he does. And here a disaster has struck. It didn't seem to bother him at all. Everybody else was bothered. I was. Alan Schneider was bothered. I mean, everybody was hysterical. Except Beckett. He just rearranged things a little, said, All right, if it's gone, it's gone, and we went right on and finished the film. He was marvelous. Lindon is right; he thrived in moments of crisis.

(From 1964 Interview)

SAMUEL BECKETT

May 26, 1964
Paris

Dear Judith,
        Would you inquire of the Oriental Institute
of Chicago, 1155 E. 58 Street, Chicago, about the
possibility of using in my film their photograph
or rather a detail of their photograph No. 24084.
It is of the Mesopotamian sculpture (The God Abu)
discovered in the excavations of the Tell Asmar 1930-
36 and now in the Museum of Bagdad. It figures (Plate
No. xxii) in Andre Parrot's volume entitled Sumer
(Gallimard 1960). I am told the right of reproduction
belongs to the O.I. of Chicago. What we need is an
enlargement of the head, full face. As it has to be
torn from the wall, torn up and stamped on, we would
need at least 10 copies. If the Institute gives
permission, I'll let you know exact detail required
and size of enlargement.

Forgive me and bless you.

        Yours ever

        Sam

Buster Keaton
(a still shot from FILM)

Tell Asmar statue,
Courtesy of The
Oriental
Institute of The
University
of Chicago

On FILM: A Conversation Among Samuel Beckett, Alan Schneider & Boris Kaufman at Rosset's home in East Hampton, N.Y.

BECKETT: And then in the vestibule, he looks at the flower woman.

SCHNEIDER: Why? Are you interested or curious or—

BECKETT: No, in the original version he didn't look at her, and we made him look at her ….

SCHNEIDER: But I mean, from his point of view, why is he looking at her? Not just out of dramatic need, why is he looking at her? Is he scared that she'll see him, or is he examining her to see if she'll do something antagonistic to him, or—

BECKETT: Well, fundamentally, he's surprised. He wasn't expecting this; one stares, and it's the same kind of—

SCHNEIDER: It's an unusual occurrence.

BECKETT: It's the same kind of upsetting thing that possibly makes him look. I mean, I think that psychologically it would be better for him not to look at her at all. Hears somebody coming down the stairs, hides. But technically, for the film, I think it's valuable to have his vision of the flower woman, followed by E's vision of her, so we get a—

KAUFMAN: Yes, I think so. This will be much reinforced by—

SCHNEIDER: We'll just have to find some logical justification for the actor to look at her.

BECKETT: Yes, yes.

SCHNEIDER: He's scared she'll see him; he's scared what she's doing. He doesn't know whether she's noticed him or not.

BECKETT: You could rewrite the passage and have him, have him go up, blindly, up the stairs and run into her, patently run into her coming down. Instead of hearing her, have another collision on the stairs, the way we had a collision in the street with the couple. Goes into the hall, gets to the stairs—

SCHNEIDER: And she's there.

BECKETT: Patently runs into her. She comes down and looks—

SCHNEIDER: He looks at her. Has she seen him? Does she become aware of him?

BECKETT: ... I don't know.

SCHNEIDER: ... Well, he looks at her; if he hides he can see if she's seen him. She's involved with her flowers; your point was that she was so concentrating on straightening out these things, or maybe she's counting the coins that she made upstairs, or l was thinking she was doing something with the flowers. So her concentration was—

BECKETT: I don't think there's any problem with that. I don't think there's anything difficult in explaining to ourselves or to Keaton why he looks at this woman. He hears her coming down and—

SCHNEIDER: Not for Keaton so much as for the audience. Why does he look near her?

BECKETT: To see if she's gone out. Is she going out? I mean, he's hiding —

SCHNEIDER: That's a shot. You're talking about panning from her face to her hands to the flowers to her face, so that takes a certain amount of time.

BECKETT: Mm, yes.

SCHNEIDER: That's all I mean, that to be justified, in terms of the audience; what is he looking at her for? Well, he's looking at her to see if she's become aware of him. That's all, is it not? Just to see if she's become aware of him.

BECKETT: No, that's not the idea.

SCHNEIDER: I know why technically, but dramatically, why is he looking at her?

[long pause]

BECKETT: Well, she's getting in his way, you know, he's inspecting this obstacle, if you like. Just as the people he jostled in the street get in his way, so he looks at them and moves on. Look, I think we're making a problem here where there is no problem.

SCHNEIDER: Only if we pan to her hands, Sam, and then to the flowers and then back to her—

* * *

SCHNEIDER: But I think it's a legitimate question, because it's going to get us into trouble on the set. I'm convinced of that. And, also, from the point of view of the audience, I want to know. Is it just a shot? He looks up and sees a flower woman and the shot, hides, but that's not what you're asking. You're going to pan and see, does she have a... you know, where are the flowers, where are her hands? A fairly elaborate thing.

BECKETT: But nobody's going to ask why does she look first at her face and then at her hands. That's quite a normal thing to do! I mean, one looks, one looks at details of objects—

SCHNEIDER: For a reason.

BECKETT: Were doing this for technical reasons. And, I mean, we can always find a psychological explanation for it. You see, the fundamental function of the two episodes, the one in the street and the one in the vestibule, are the nature. I mean, O is not a man who refuses to look, not at all. He looks very carefully at the room. He wants to get out of all this business, but he does look very carefully at the room.

SCHNEIDER: Because the room offers certain problems to him, which he's trying to eliminate.

BECKETT: Well, just like the couple offers certain problems to him.

SCHNEIDER: Right, right.

BECKETT: And the flower woman offers certain problems to him, too, because—

SCHNEIDER: Because she's in his way going up the stairs.

BECKETT: The two major objects or obstacles on his way to—

KAUFMAN: … She falls down, doesn't she?

BECKETT: Not before—

SCHNEIDER: She faints because she sees E; she sees E.

BECKETT: The function, one of the functions of these episodes, the one in the street, one of its functions is to try and clarify the distinction between the two visual qualities, since the same object is perceived in quick succession, first by O and then by E; so we get in quick succession the two absolutely different kinds of response. That's one function. The other function of the scene is to get a reaction to E's gaze. It's so acute and penetrating that it can't be endured. So you get the first reaction to this in the street. A second and stronger one is when the flower woman collapses before him. And then of course at the end of the film, it's O's reaction.

KAUFMAN: Yes.

BECKETT: And I think that is technically valuable to prepare, or propel, I don't know exactly how we'll do it, but to prepare the quality of O's face at the end of the film, the expression on O's face at the end of the film, by the reaction of the couple to E's gaze and the reaction of the flower woman to it.

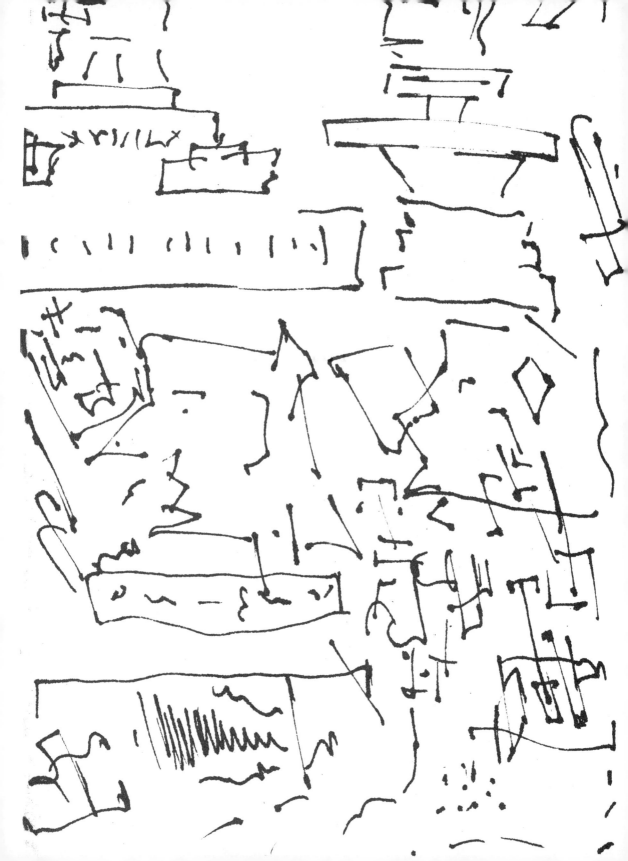

entr'acte

Dear Mr. Beckett,

Shelley Winters and myself are desirous of doing WAITING
FOR GODOT … the play has tempted me often to do some work
on the characters at the Actors Studio here in New York and
now Shelley and I would like to start there and move on to a
production for public consumption.

My lawyer is talking to Grove Press about the rights
to proceed but Shelley and I are more concerned to know of
your opinion on the matter of females essaying same, and
where you may feel the text is uniquely masculine. I will
not bore you here with my opinions but would relish the
opportunity to discuss the matter with you either here or in
France where I will be for a bit of climbing in August.

Hopefully, our work is known to you, having garnered
our share of rewards for both our stage and film work. My
career is of shorter duration than Shelley's and so I will
mention my Academy Award Roles: Blanche in Bonnie and Clyde,
and the lesbian schoolteacher in RACHEL, RACHEL with Joanne
Woodward. Before Broadway went defunct most identifiable might
be my work in Edward Albee's MALCOLM for Alan Schneider,
Myrtle in Tennessee Williams' SEVEN DESCENTS OF MYRTLE and
last year Miss Reardon of Paul Zindel's AND MISS REARDON
DRINKS A LITTLE.

I am thoroughly excited to start work because I think
Shelley and I have the ideal tragicomic mixture in our real
life personalities and work styles to give it a run, but I am
hankering for your feelings. I do hope to hear from you at
your earliest convenience.

Estelle Parsons
505 West End Avenue
New York City, 10024
Phone: 2123621289

Mailed date of letter
is unclear, but there
is a handwritten
notation by Beckett
of July 4, 1973,
beside his response

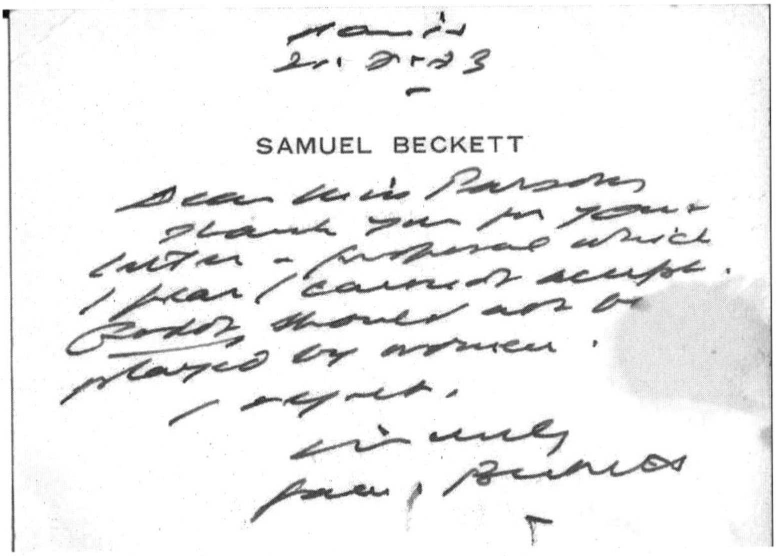

SAMUEL BECKETT

Dear Miss Parsons
Thank you for your letter - proposal which I fear I cannot accept. Godot should not be played by women.
I regret.
Sincerely
Sam Beckett

July 4, 1973

Dear Miss Parsons

Thank you for your letter - proposal which I fear I cannot accept. <u>Godot</u> should not be played by women.

I regret.

Sincerely,
Samuel Beckett

COME AND GO

A Dramaticule

For
John Calder

Characters

FLO
VI
RU

Age
undeterminable

Sitting
center side.
by side
stage right
to left
FLO, VI, and
RU. Very
erect,
facing front,
hands
clasped in
laps.

VI: Ru.
RU: Yes.
VI: Flo.
FLO: Yes.
VI: When did we three last meet?
RU: Let us not speak

> Silence.
> Exit VI right.
> Silence.

FLO: Ru.
RU: Yes.
FLO: What do you think of Vi?
RU: I see little change.
> (FLO moves to center seat,
> whispers in Ru's ear. Appalled.)
> Oh! (They look at each other.
> FLO puts her finger to her lips.)
> Does she not realize?
FLO: God grant not.

Enter VI. FLO and RU
turn back front, resume pose. VI
sits right. Silence.

Silence.

FLO: Just sit toge-
ther as we used
to. in the
playground at
Miss Wade's
RU: On the log.

Silence
Exit FLO left.
Silence.

RU: Vi.
VI: Yes.
RU: How do you find Flo?
VI: She seems much the same.
(RU moves to center seat, whispers in Vi's
ear. Appalled.) Oh! (They look at each other. RU puts
her finger to her lips.) Has she not been told?
RU: God forbid.

> Enter FLO. RU and VI turn back front, resume
> pose. FLO sits left. Silence

RU: Holding hands . . . that way.
FLO: Dreaming of . . love.

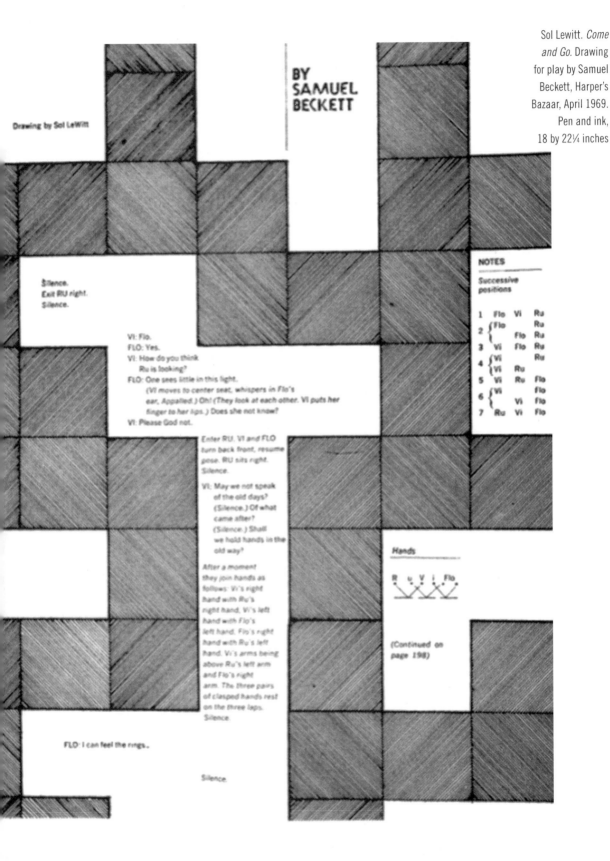

Drawing by Sol LeWitt

BY
SAMUEL
BECKETT

Sol Lewitt. *Come and Go.* Drawing for play by Samuel Beckett, Harper's Bazaar, April 1969. Pen and ink, 18 by 22¼ inches

Silence.
Exit RU right.
Silence.

VI: Flo.
FLO: Yes.
VI: How do you think
   Ru is looking?
FLO: One sees little in this light.
   (VI moves to center seat, whispers in Flo's
   ear, Appalled.) Oh! (They look at each other. VI puts her
   finger to her lips.) Does she not know?
VI: Please God not.

Enter RU. VI and FLO
turn back front, resume
pose. RU sits right.
Silence.

VI: May we not speak
of the old days?
(Silence.) Of what
came after?
(Silence.) Shall
we hold hands in the
old way?

After a moment
they join hands as
follows: Vi's right
hand with Ru's
right hand, Vi's left
hand with Flo's
left hand. Flo's right
hand with Ru's left
hand. Vi's arms being
above Ru's left arm
and Flo's right
arm. The three pairs
of clasped hands rest
on the three laps.
Silence.

FLO: I can feel the rings.

Silence.

NOTES

Successive
positions

1	Flo	Vi	Ru
2	{ Flo		Ru
	{	Flo	Ru
3	Vi	Flo	Ru
4	{ Vi		Ru
	{ Vi	Ru	
5	Vi	Ru	Flo
6	{ Vi		Flo
	{	Vi	Flo
7	Ru	Vi	Flo

Hands

R   u   V   i   Flo

(Continued on page 198)

GROVE PRESS

795 BROADWAY, NEW YORK 3, N.Y. • GRAMERCY 3-7447

August 26, 1969

Dear Sam,

I don't remember whether or not I wrote to you about
this; I can find no carbon copies. At any rate, Harper's Bazaar
asked for permission to print "Come and Go." I thought of
shipping the artwork to you, but there wasn't much time. So
Marilynn looked at the layout; said it was good; and we gave
permission. I do hope that you like it, or, at least, do not
dislike it.

Love,

Barney

GROVE PRESS

795 BROADWAY, NEW YORK 3, N.Y. • GRAMERCY 3-7447

September 6, 2001
WebTV Network
Email message
To: Marek Kedzierski
Subject: Mamet

Dear Marek,
It is difficult, if not impossible, for me to remember exactly what first
attracted me to David Mamet. It certainly was not that we he'd gone to
the same school, even had the same Drama teacher, one John Merrill,
who was old when I had him sort of like a gentle caricature of John
Gielgud. Shakespeare was his man, and that was not all bad. He did try,
mightily, to infuse his students with a feeling of love and reverence
for the theater. American Buffalo was the first play of Mamet that I saw
performed. To me it was a new American theater, very exciting. He took
Beckett, Pinter, his own Mamet background and, importantly, his own
special view of his home grounds, Chicago, and turned these elements
into his genre of playwriting. Pinter and Beckett are most definitely
there, Beckett lurking in the background and Pinter more up front.
However what comes out is Mamet, just as Pinter, writing a generation
closer to Beckett, is still most definitely Pinter. Beckett set the
tone, or perhaps better said, as McLuhan's Medium. A new Medium, a new
stage, a new use of an old language twisted to mean what it does not
say. And did silence ever get put to such great use as by these three?
Another pallette, Pollock's paint perhaps, dripped out with sheer
imprecision. Perhaps as Picasso and Braque learned from each other,
even seeming identical at some junctures, the three writers link up
albeit in a more linear way, separated by age, place, and yes, even
language. Chicago is not Dublin which is not London. By the time that
Glengarry Glen Ross is put up against End Game the family may seem
estranged, but it is not or better, it always was that way.

Mc Luhan could have explained these magic transformations of the medium
better than I can.

              Love,

                      Barney

                                        127 W. 79th St. NYC 10024
                                        15 August, 1978

Mr. B. Rosaceous
GROVE PRESS
196 W. Houston St.
NYC 10014

Dear Mr. R.;
Yrs of the 15th rec.

In answer to your questions:

Sex without racism is like a day without sunshine.
As Voltaire once said, "Une fois, philosophe;
deux fois, recediviste."
And, finally, nothing like a good, free,
book to make one's spirits sore.

Love & Anarchy
Dr. D. Mamet

*S*uch a book as this cannot hope to reveal all there is to tell about Barney and Beckett. In fact, it leaves some glaring blanks unfilled. And it leaves a great deal to the imagination. Imagine, for instance, when Beckett was taken to meet Edward Albee. "I took Sam to the eastern end of Long Island to see [Albee], after Albee's strong request to meet him," Rosset wrote in his autobiography. On that day (as on the subsequent occasions when they met in Paris), they never spoke of Beckett's plays: "You don't do that with people whose work you respect," Albee has said. Listen again to Albee: "When someone as extraordinary as Samuel Beckett, extraordinary both as a novelist and a playwright, comes along, if you are not influenced by it, if you are not aware of it, then you are asleep somewhere. He was the most important playwright of the second half of the 20th century; there's no question." Citing an example of just how "extraordinary" a writer he esteems Beckett to be, Albee has also commented, "In Beckett's late play, A Piece of Monologue, *an extraordinary play, this old guy is looking out a window into a sort of a dark and stormy night. Any other playwright would have written the following line: 'Not much going on out there in the vast black.' That's not a bad line. 'In the vast black'—that's all right. But you know what Beckett wrote? 'Nothing stirring in that black vast.' Now that's the difference between an okay playwright and a great playwright!" And to think, without Rosset, these two titans of the theatre might never have met.*

—ED.

Barney Rosset,
Richard Seaver,
and D. A. Pennebaker
in Conversation

ROSSET: I was in New York and I heard a little about Beckett. I actually read *Godot* and contracted to publish it. I went to France in the fall of '53 to meet Beckett, who greatly intrigued me, but also I read a piece by Dick Seaver in *Merlin* Magazine. When I went to Paris, I hooked up with Seaver and I met him and his wife Jeanette, who he just got married to. And of course, we immediately shared something in common. Specifically, Samuel Beckett. People who liked Beckett did form a bond. That was the beginning.

SEAVER: In Paris in the early '50s we started this magazine, *Merlin*. I lived around the corner from the Editions de Minuit who had become Beckett's publisher a couple of years before after most French publishers had turned down his work. He did not try to sell them, but his wife Suzanne, a lady who became his wife, had taken his work to virtually every French publisher in Paris, several works, including *Molloy* which was then written, *Watt*, I believe the last work he wrote in English. I don't think *Godot* had been written because I don't remember reading a manuscript version, but this young publisher Jérôme Lindon saw it, read it. He thought it was extraordinary and signed it up in my headquarters. Both this magazine itself and a room I lived in above it were in back of an antique dealer, which was a former banana-drying shed. That's where the office was and, as I said, it was a half a block from the Editions de Minuit. I wrote to Lindon and said,

"I hear there's a novel that Beckett wrote in English and we'd like to publish it for the magazine." I never heard back for weeks and weeks, and then one night a mysterious figure appeared at our door (the banana-drying shed) and he handed us a manuscript. He said, "Here... here's the piece you'd asked for."

He turned and disappeared with no more words than that. We spent the next 5 or 6 hours literally reading this book aloud; it was *Watt*. Barney subsequently published it in America. We published, oh no, Beckett dictated a section. I guess he was testing the seriousness of the purpose that it had to be published because we couldn't extract just anything and he picked a very difficult and trying section and we published it. And thereafter, we published a couple of extracts from *Watt*. By then, we had translated two stories, "The End" and "The Expelled." So, in every issue there was something by Beckett.

The rest of the *Merlin* group felt very strongly that he was a major writer. We were also publishing Genet and Ionesco.... But Beckett is really the most important person whose work appeared in every issue.

PENNEBAKER: How did you decide to publish him?

ROSSET: I decided...

PENNEBAKER: He's a far cry from Henry Miller.

ROSSET: Right, but Beckett is also a far cry from Joyce or a far cry from Proust (about whom he wrote a book.) I read *Godot* and I really don't know why or how or what exactly happened. I probably read about the production in Paris, which did cause ripples all the way to New York.

PENNEBAKER: Did you read it in French or English?

ROSSET: In French. Beckett's language in not all that difficult. I mean you take a very limited vocabulary as his was and he manipulates it and changes it and transcends it or whatever. But basically, the language itself is simple. I read it and I remember asking one friend of mine, Wallace Fowley, who was a professor at Bennington, I think, at the time, and teachers at the New School where I was studying (I was still taking the G.I. Bill course all the way into the early 1950s. It took me 12 years to get my B.A.). Anyway, I asked Fowley, who is a very different kind of person from me, but whom I respected. He read it. I had lunch with him specifically to ask him his opinion about it. He said, without hesitation, that this was one of the major works of the 20th century. But Wallace was not an effervescent person; I was stunned! I felt confirmed and signed up the book. I don't know if it was right then or a little bit latter that I began to read *Merlin*. And it went on from there.

PENNEBAKER: How did you deal with the problem of translation? Did you think that was an immediate problem?

ROSSET: It was an immediate problem. The immediate problem was translating *Godot* so it could go on stage. And I, in my infinite lack of knowledge, thought that Beckett would get somebody else or I would get somebody else to translate it. I actually began thinking of people and Beckett kept putting up opposition to whomever I suggested. I actually wrote to him and told him, "There is really one person to translate this and that is you." How much influence I had on him, I don't know, but he did it. He translated it.

PENNEBAKER: When we were doing *Rockaby* the actress Billie Whitelaw would get a phone call from him every morning. He would say to her, "What are they doing? They bothering you?" He had such concern for her: "Are they jumping up and down? Are they hitting you in the head with lights?" I thought that concern for her was very interesting because he seemed so removed, but everyone had this sort of incredible sense of his presence. He hung over everything, constantly.

ROSSET: Once he liked you, it was a kind of affection and loyalty that I don't think I've ever seen in anyone else. The person you mentioned, Billie Whitelaw, was very special and very worried about him.

PENNEBAKER: He picked certain people and then that bond of loyalty was unassailable. Why do you think it was with Billie?

ROSSET: I think he thought she was a very good actress, for one thing. And then, he must have liked her as a person. All I know is that it was there. It was also there with Alan Schneider, the director who directed *Rockaby*. But Alan had a total dedication to the work of Beckett. Beckett really understood that too, because Alan would walk from fire to protect the proper pronunciation of one word of Beckett.

PENNEBAKER: That's true. I was present, I say "present" because it was very hard to have an involved relationship with the first performance of *Godot* in Coconut Grove. Nobody sat down for the first three minutes. People were walking all around complaining to each other, going out and getting drinks, and I was sort of standing in the back watching it and making no sense out of it at all. And later, once on a train, I asked Alan something about what that was like and if he'd ever do it again. He thought and then said, "Certainly!"

And, it must have been a horror for him.

ROSSET: It was, and he was fired, right away, after that, Alan.

PENNEBAKER: He was a kind of Golden Boy of a certain kind of theatre, in New York particularly. That must have been very hard for him.

ROSSET: It was, but it was interesting because Beckett picked up right away on Alan, though he didn't need him for quite a while after that. Schneider was dismissed as the director before the play opened in New York. I had also noticed about Alan—I hadn't met him before either—something drew me to him, the fact that he got fired.

PENNEBAKER: His stock went up?

ROSSET: It did. Beckett felt the same thing.

PENNEBAKER: When those plays opened, you were still involved with Grove Press, right?

SEAVER: I came back to America and I was involved in Grove Press.

PENNEBAKER: Were you involved in those plays at all?

SEAVER: No, not really; the first play I saw was *Waiting for Godot* in the French when it opened because of our involvement with Beckett. I had actually gone to the French radio, about a month or two before it opened on the stage, where they performed it in part.

PENNEBAKER: Who was the actor that was in that?

SEAVER: Roger Blin was the moving force behind it and he played one of the parts, but he also presented it. Beckett was supposed to come to the radio that day, but sent a note saying he could not come. The more he thought about it, he had nothing to offer; there was the play, he had nothing to say about it. Furthermore, I remember the note saying "I know nothing about the theatre." Of course, that was the first thing he'd ever written; there was another play he had written before, but it had never been performed. He knew a great deal about the theatre and one of the things about Beckett, that I know Barney knows even better than I, is that the more he went on, the more involved he was in his work. In France, in Germany, and in England, he very often would go and supervise. There would be a director, but the director would very often confer with him.

PENNEBAKER: Is that because he didn't have confidence? He did seem to have a lot of confidence in Alan. But at the same time, he had such an exact sense about the way he wanted something done.

SEAVER: I think he was there, not to superimpose himself, but to explain. A lot of his work was so new. A lot of it was musical and mathematical and it really required explanation if you really wanted to get it right, get the rhythms right.

PENNEBAKER: You talk about Blin. Blin is an extraordinary example because you could barely have a conversation with him off stage. He stuttered so badly. And then he fell under the spell of Beckett. He was a magical actor. I gather, he was one of the best that ever played that part.

SEAVER: Again, like Alan, he was very, very dedicated to Beckett. He didn't understand fully when he first.. In fact, he hesitated between *Godot* and ...

ROSSET: *Eleutheria.*

SEAVER: *Eleutheria* was an earlier Beckett play out of which, both Barney and I agree, *Godot* came from, from an earlier version of it.

ROSSET: I think there was a split in Beckett: He was a writer and he knew what he wanted to write. He was extremely precise. Everything he did in the theatre, he plotted out on graph paper. On very, very fine, fine lines and actors were maybe a little bit too foreign to him and he didn't quite know what they would do. So he gave them very, very exact instructions. How many seconds to pause, how many feet to walk, which way their head would point. But at the same time, he had utter faith in given people. So I really couldn't quite put those things together.

PENNEBAKER: Well, he got that thing; that fierce... And yet he didn't seem to operate in the sense of the master. Whereas there are people in this role who often assume the regalia of the master and hold court and everybody has to bring a kind of fear with themselves; he was not like that at all.

SEAVER: He was the most unassuming man I ever met. I think to the end of his life he must have had some idea of how important he was and yet he would say, as he read an earlier work, "Ugh, that's so bad, so bad, how could I ever have written this?"

We went to a revival of *Godot* at the Odéon and we met Beckett afterwards. He didn't go; he wasn't involved with that production, as far as I know. But we were saying how wonderful it was and he said, "No, no, I reread the work before the revival and I just found all the bad things in it... it was so terrible." Giacometti had done the set for that and he had come in and kept saying, "No, Sam, it's even better the second time. It's even more wonderful." Beckett would just lower his head. And he was really sincere.

PENNEBAKER: You know, you were talking about the detailed instructions. There is the story at the BBC about the old stagehand who was trying to adjust a door and Beckett went over to him and said, "What are you doing?" The stagehand says, "I'm trying to decide how much the door should open." And Beckett says, "What does it say in the stage instructions? 'The door should be imperceptibly ajar.' That means it's closed!"

ROSSET: Billie used to tell wonderful stories about that too.

I flew over there to see him with Jessica Tandy and Alan Schneider, after Beckett had written *Not I*, which had not been performed. We sat with him for two days and he took out his graph paper and he diagramed every word, action, motion, gesture in the play.

PENNEBAKER: But that image was the only image he had in mind. That's all he ever wanted to do?

ROSSET: As far as I could see it. So we got back on the plane, went back to New York. Alan and Jessica put it on at Lincoln Center.

PENNEBAKER: The idea of having a gigantic mouth totally on the screen, on TV, it works. But to do that on the stage is such an amazing idea.

ROSSET: And terribly difficult for the actors because you had to strap yourself on. In a way, I thought it was Beckett's slight distrust of actors.

PENNEBAKER: He was punishing her.

ROSSET: He was punishing her and you could only see her mouth. But you can hear her.

PENNEBAKER: It's an extraordinary tour de force. It's funny, but I always wondered about the dates. There was a show which began in England, it was called the "Rocky Horror Show." And that had exactly that on the screen in the film. I don't know which came first, but it was interesting. But I can't imagine him having gone to a "Rocky Horror Show."

ROSSET: Nor can I!

PENNEBAKER: On the other hand, he did have strange taste. I mean, towards the last few months or so, the Swedish director Jan Jonson was telling me he had shown a great interest in Bob Dylan. In fact, we had made a transcript with some Dylan of "Don't Look Back." He suddenly got interested in Dylan's poetry. I don't know if that was the music or poetry that Dylan had actually written. I think he had interest in things that people would never imagine he'd be interested in.

SEAVER: He continued to be interested in the productions to his very last days. *Endgame* was put on at the Comédie Française a

Dick Seaver, Barney
Rosset, and D.A.
Pennebaker
Photo by Astrid Rosset

year ago and he didn't get involved in that production, but he received a program and it said on the program "Music by such and such." So he immediately called up his publisher, Lindon, and said, "There's no music in that play, what's that about?" It turned out that the director had taken other liberties with it.

We went to the performance with his French publisher the following week. It was directed by Blin, music by Blin, sets by Blin. Beckett asked us afterwards what we thought. We said it was really quite a good production. One thing that upset him enormously was that in France they had a new kind of automated garbage can and he wanted old tin garbage cans. These were the automatic ones where the lid pops up; they're made out of plastic. He said, "Weren't those plastic garbage cans awful!? The lids pop up. You can't take the lid off it." He was so upset to the point that he would sue the Comédie Française and not let them go on unless they removed them.

PENNEBAKER: He did get upset about things. Why do you think that was? I mean, you bore all the flack for that.

ROSSET: I know.

PENNEBAKER: You had to stand up at NYU and defend yourself against bodily harm.

ROSSET: Right. For the same play. And music, not by Blin, but by Philip Glass.

I was the 'villain', but I was only the conduit of Beckett's anger at the same elements as in the French production. I think it was very important in *Endgame* to understand the stage directions are as important as the text. If he says you move three feet and you're in a certain kind of a room, and that's where you are, you are going to move three feet and there's no music. If you make it into a subway station, underground, with music playing, to him, that is not his play. I must say I agree with him that within his work there is a certain kind of essential, integral feeling to it. If you mess around with the way it looks or sounds, the way people move, you actually destroy whatever it was that he wanted it to mean.

PENNEBAKER: Will that change?

ROSSET: It certainly will change. Beckett was kind of iconoclastic.

PENNEBAKER: But during his lifetime, he didn't want it to change, he wanted to have...

ROSSET: Well, he let people interpret his prose quite freely.

PENNEBAKER: I see. But in theatre, he wanted it exact. Why is that?

ROSSET: I have no idea.

PENNEBAKER: Barney, I want to thank you for taking the trouble of coming in to talk with us, to me, about this and I know that the whole process of watching Sam Beckett die has really been hard on people. The amazing thing is how he kept himself together right up to the end. Jan Jonson was telling me that he was sitting there with a tube out of his nose breathing oxygen and trying to smoke a cigar at the same time. That wonderfully conveys the Irish nature—persistent to the end. And I thank you both for persisting to the end. It was a pleasure.

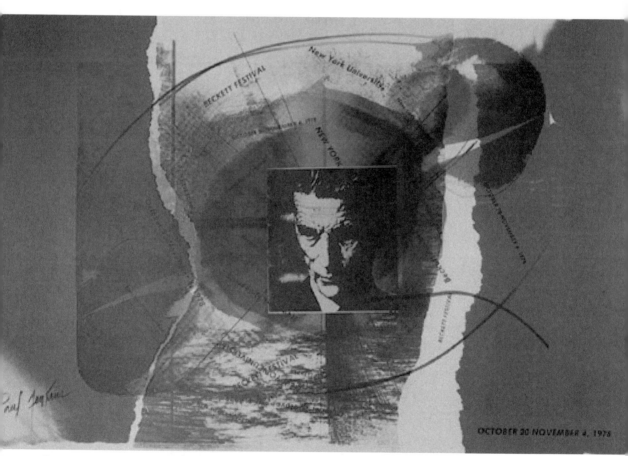

Poster made in 1978 from original collage
by Paul Jenkins for the Beckett Festival,
New York University, New York City

Some years later, Beckett would write his namesake addressing him "Dear Homonym."

4/29 1970
SAMUEL BECKETT
USSY SUR MARNE
SEINE ET MARNE, FRANCE

DEAR SAM,
        YOU HAVE A NEW AND ABSOLUTELY UNAVOIDABLE
HONOR TO BEAR, THAT BEING A NAMESAKE NAMED ' NOW A
YOUNG LAD OF SEVERAL HOURS IN THIS WORLD

LOVE
TANSEY, PETER, CRISTINA AND BARNEY

Cable from Rosset to Beckett

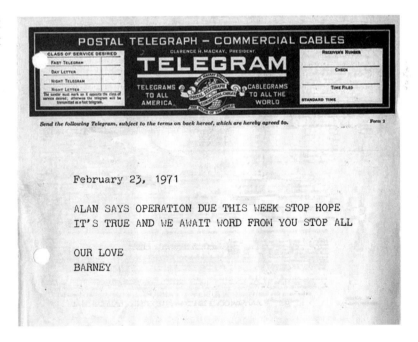

POSTAL TELEGRAPH — COMMERCIAL CABLES
CLARENCE H. MACKAY, PRESIDENT.

TELEGRAM

CLASS OF SERVICE DESIRED
FAST TELEGRAM
DAY LETTER
NIGHT TELEGRAM
NIGHT LETTER
The sender must mark an X opposite the class of service desired; otherwise the telegram will be transmitted as a fast telegram.

TELEGRAMS TO ALL AMERICA

CABLEGRAMS TO ALL THE WORLD

RECEIVER'S NUMBER
CHECK
TIME FILED
STANDARD TIME

Send the following Telegram, subject to the terms on back hereof, which are hereby agreed to.   Form 2

February 23, 1971

ALAN SAYS OPERATION DUE THIS WEEK STOP HOPE
IT'S TRUE AND WE AWAIT WORD FROM YOU STOP ALL

OUR LOVE
BARNEY

April 26, 1971

Dear Sam,

Just had a lovely lunch with Alan. He told me all
seemed beautiful with the eyes and that soon you would be
trundling around in the car. Here we have a fine idea for
Krapp with Alan, MacGowran. Let's hope.

As for the production of the other plays, believe me,
Sam, we have lost no interest whatsoever. Samuel French, because of their better ability to monitor what goes on across
the country, have been asked to handle the details on not only
the amateur productions, which they have been doing anyway,
but also on the professional productions which take place outside of New York. Even those have to be individually approved
by us. Anything for New York we will handle personally from
the beginning as before. This simply gives us the advantage
of their country-wide organization, but leaves final verdict to
us. Don't be worried.

Much love from all,

Barney

NOW AVAILABLE ON FILM

SAMUEL BECKETT'S

Beginning to End

"Brilliance of script, performance and setting are crowded into 58 minutes of as original and probing a piece of theatre as has ever come to film."
—L.A. Herald Examiner

An anthology of the works by
SAMUEL BECKETT
adapted and performed by
JACK MAC GOWRAN

GROVE PRESS

795 BROADWAY, NEW YORK 3, N.Y. • GRAMERCY 3-7447

June 18, 1973

Dear Sam,

Saw Alan last night and he seemed in very good spirits after Moscow. I hope his return trip there works out well. The great Russian leader is here now and nobody seems the slightest bit interested-or perhaps it's only me that feels that way.

The FIRST LOVE translation has long been in my hands and I like it tremendously. I sent Alan off with a copy yesterday.

Following the suggestion in your letter—yes, we would like to publish it together with NOT I. We think the two will make a fine book. It has also occurred to Fred and myself that there are four more prose pieces which we do not have in book form: "From an Abandoned Work," "Imagine Dead Imagine," "Enough," and "Ping."

Would you object to our including any or all of those pieces along with Not I and First Love?

Hope that all goes reasonably well. God Bless.

Yours,

Barney

GROVE PRESS

795 BROADWAY, NEW YORK 3, N.Y. • GRAMERCY 3-7447

July 2, 1973

Dear Sam,

I received your Mss for Moe Gordman and I will want
to hear from Andreas Brown. I am afraid there is confusion
about Andre Gregory. Certainly, as far as we here are
concerned, he has no license to produce Endgame in France
and he is quite aware of the fact. It would seem to me that
only you could grant that permission. Our authority is very
clearly restricted to this country and we have stated that
fact over and over. If anybody says anything to the contrary,
I would certainly like to know about it. Sam, I also hope
you understand this now. Grove Press did not, could not
grant permission to Gregory to perform in France, Poland, or
elsewhere.

Enclosed are two more letters. Going on Nicol
Williamson's word, we did not oppose his performance of
your work here. However, Alan and I feel that a commercial
production, in this case a successful one, should pay
something to the author, simply as a matter of principal if
nothing else. So be it.

The last letter is yet another application for rights
to Godot. This is for you to consider and I would appreciate
hearing from you about it.

Since writing the above I located the contract
between Samuel French, yourself, and Grove Press. It clearly
delineates the territory it can license a production in,
namely, "the United States of America and Canada."

Sam, if you wish to allow Gregory to put on your work
in other countries that is your decision. I just want it very
clearly understood that he gets no such authority from us.

Much love,

Barney

GROVE PRESS ✳

795 BROADWAY, NEW YORK 3, N.Y. • GRAMERCY 3-7447

March 26, 1974

Dear Sam,

Last night an exhibition of Joan's paintings opened
at the Whitney Museum here in New York, a tremendous coup for
Joan, and she, along with Riopelle, was here to enjoy it, if
you can consider whatever it is they do enjoyment. The show was
not the equal of the one of two years ago, but that is because
of the marvelous space provided by a tremendous new museum in
Syracuse, New York.

Your last letter to me, which I was madly searching for,
seemed good indeed, especially the prospects of doing Godot. I
do hope that it works out.

Here we go on, believe it or not, Cristina and I (along
with Beckett and Tansey) spent two most pleasant weeks in Ja-
maica, and looking at the snow and cold here makes me want to
be back there.

Since starting this letter I have seen Deirdre Bair and
had a very nice time with her. She seems bright and perceptive.

Sam, I hope that you are well. Deirdre said that she
thought you were not too well when she was in Paris recently
and that she did not see you. Do let me know. We miss seeing
you very much.
Our love to you and Suzanne.

Barney

RCA Global Telegram

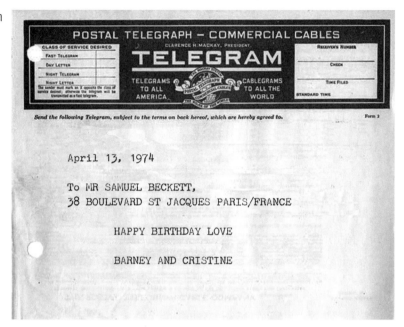

POSTAL TELEGRAPH — COMMERCIAL CABLES

CLARENCE H. MACKAY, PRESIDENT.

TELEGRAM

April 13, 1974

To MR SAMUEL BECKETT,
38 BOULEVARD ST JACQUES PARIS/FRANCE

HAPPY BIRTHDAY LOVE

BARNEY AND CRISTINE

no date; late May,
1974?
RCA Global Telegram

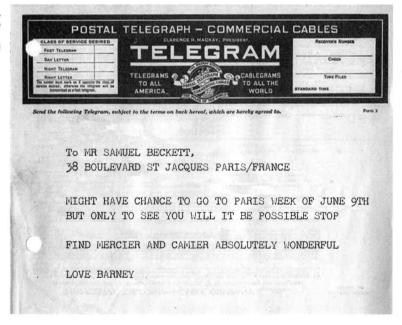

POSTAL TELEGRAPH — COMMERCIAL CABLES

CLARENCE H. MACKAY, PRESIDENT.

TELEGRAM

To MR SAMUEL BECKETT,
38 BOULEVARD ST JACQUES PARIS/FRANCE

MIGHT HAVE CHANCE TO GO TO PARIS WEEK OF JUNE 9TH
BUT ONLY TO SEE YOU WILL IT BE POSSIBLE STOP

FIND MERCIER AND CAMIER ABSOLUTELY WONDERFUL

LOVE BARNEY

GROVE PRESS

795 BROADWAY, NEW YORK 3, N.Y. • GRAMERCY 3-7447

Dec. 3, 1975

Dear Sam,

Just finished reading Dick's introduction to his selection of your work and I found it splendid. It is very human,
personal, and touching and at the same time at what seems to
me a very high level of rationality and intelligence. For me
at least it brings many things together in a very beautiful
and affective way. And so, when I traversed the table of contents and finished by reading the last segment once more, THAT
TIME, which I love most dearly, all seemed arranged in its
proper and good place.

TIME AGAIN and for the first time tempts me to turn
into an Irish Actor, but a pumpkin would be a more likely result of such an effort.

So sorry you will not be in Paris when we will be
there. I had a strong jolt when I read in Dick's piece that in
1932 you were living at the Hotel Taurnon on rue de Vaugirard.
We have planned to stay the Hotel Tournon Palace 1 bis rue
Vaugirard. Can it be the same one? If so it will be a fine tale
to tell Beckett and Tansey R. (incidentally we have a fine mon-
ster of a dog named Oblomov) of some vague wolf-like species
and very lazy tenderness. He is a sort of "a ruin still there"
who decided to come and live with us and refuses to divulge
his past.

Well, we shall think of you often and long as we look
up the rue de Vaugirard toward rue des Favorites. It won't be
the same "never the same after that never quite the same" but
we should try to make do.

All our love to you and Suzanne,

Barney

April 1, 1976

Dear Sam,

It was a delight to see you and to go off with a new
treasure chest of material.

Your titles are so wonderful. ENDS AND ODDS FIZZLES
FOOTFALLS

I wondered if you might not think up something rather
than SELECTED WRITINGS OF SAMUEL BECKETT. Seems a bit flat to
me Do let me know.

I made it home with MURPHY. He's flourishing.

Love,

Barney

GROVE PRESS

795 BROADWAY, NEW YORK 3, N.Y. • GRAMERCY 3-7447

Feb. 7, 1979

Dear Sam,

Delighted to get your note today. I sent you the Avedon book
because he told me that he had sent you his books (via Ed. de
Minuit) over the years and never received any response. He
considers you to be the major influence on his work and he says
it with deep feeling indeed. He recently had an exposition of
his works at the Metropolitan Museum here, which I believe
is a first ever for a photographer. He told me that he would
particularly appreciate it if you would look at the last photos in the book, the ones of his father taken just before his
death. Avedon says his father's last words, seconds before his
death, were "is is isn't." Cristina says you wrote it for him.
Anyway, if you have any word to say about his work I would
pass the note on to him. He's been in a sort of depression
since the Met show feeling like there's nothing left to do and
he is a good person.

     I cannot decipher the dates of your stay in Paris &
Ussy. If you are to be there in April I would like to plan (A
NEW WORD FOR ME—PLAN) to see you the end of the second week in
April. If what you are saying is that you WON'T be there in
April, I will change my PLAN accordingly. Will await further
word about the dates and some little mention from you about
the new work that John says you are doing.

                  Much love from us all,

                      Barney

GROVE PRESS

795 BROADWAY, NEW YORK 3, N.Y. • GRAMERCY 3-7447

Febraury 28, 1979

Dear Dick:

I've just had a note from Sam in which he says, among other things, that he finds your hook "most impressive."
He says that he is leaving for London on April 23, and I remember your saying that you will be in Tokyo until the 11th or 12th of April. Sam's birthday is April 13, and it would be nice if we could be there for that.
Let me know as soon as you can what your schedule permits.

With best regards,

Barney Rosset

Barney Rosset

This and the two following letters are between Barney and Richard Avedon. —ED.

entr' acte   291

April 19, 1979

Dear Barney,

Well, it was an amazing and weird afternoon. I can't wait to have lunch with you and discuss it and give you the picture of Beckett and Beckett. At least that one is lovely. I will be back from Dallas and California around the 6th of May and will call you as soon as I return.

Forever grateful,

Dick

Samuel Beckett and Beckett Rosset, son
of Barney Rosset, Paris, April 11, 1979.
Photograph by Richard Avedon
©The Richard Avedon Foundation

August 7, 1979

Dear Dick,

Thanks for your note. I did receive your photographs of the two Becketts and thought they were
extraordinary. I had them framed, and they really
are striking. As a matter of fact I've been trying for the last two months to tell you how much I
like them, but you have not, apparently, received my
letter and numerous telephone messages. Best of luck
with your project in Texas. I hope we can get together at some point.

              Best,

              Barney

quelques parisien

act four

THE PLAY'S THE THING

"Imagination dead imagine."

DANIEL LABEILLE, *a theatre director and professor of theatre studies at the State University of New York (SUNY), was introduced to Beckett by Alan Schneider in 1978. Labeille's proposal to Beckett that Schneider's creative directorial process be filmed by D. A. Pennebaker and Chris Hegedus, New York documentary filmmakers, met with Beckett's approval and Labeille went so far as to request that Beckett write a play for the project. Beckett, as he was prone to do, had his doubts as to whether he could write a new piece for what was to become a seventy-fifth birthday celebration. The celebrated* Rockaby *nonetheless resulted, with Billie Whitelaw playing the lone woman whose image is reminiscent of a number of well known paintings,* Whistler's Mother *among them. Rosset / Grove published* Rockaby *in* The Collected Shorter Plays of Samuel Beckett *in 1984.*

—ED.

Producing Rockaby

Daniel Labeille

By the time I wrote my first letter to Samuel Beckett, dated October 1, 1979, I had met Sam on two occasions, the first on January 14, 1978, when Alan Schneider introduced us in Paris and then again a year later in January, 1979. In the period between these two meetings, I joined a project to foster artistic collaboration amongst the arts on SUNY campuses, each to be documented on film or video by a noted filmmaker. Eventually six projects were completed, two in music, one in dance, one in the spoken arts, and one in the visual arts. The theatre project would become the world premiere of a new Beckett play, *Rockaby*.

I had originally developed the theatre component to document contrasting methods of directing two or three Beckett plays to be performed at a symposium of Beckett scholars in celebration of Beckett's 75th birthday. By September 1979, I had secured commitments from two major talents: Alan Schneider and Lee Breuer. Lee proposed filming *Waiting for Godot* set in the Bowery. For the film component I approached D.A. Pennebaker and Chris Hegedus whom I'd worked with on a film with Elliot Carter. Alan approached Irene Worth who had recently played Winnie in *Happy Days* for Andrei Serban at the Public Theatre.

Alan Schneider introduced me to Barney in 1978 at the director's production of *Play*, *Footfalls*, and *That Time* at the Manhattan Theatre Club. In late fall of 1979 over lunch at the Minetta Lane Restaurant, Barney encouraged me—based on Sam's October, 7 letter—to select whatever Beckett work Alan was interested in taking up. As for Lee's idea of staging *Waiting for Godot* on the Bowery, he expressed doubt that Sam would agree to it being committed to film.

Barney also suggested that I might ask Sam to write a new play for the event. I was taken aback by the audacity of the request but Barney laughed: "Look, if Sam doesn't want to do it, he'll say no, but it can't hurt to ask." So ask I did. Unfortunately I have lost my letter to Sam of March 7, 1980, which occasioned his response of March 17 where he clarifies his position on our possible use of *Come and Go* and *Footfalls*. He'd had reservations about their appearing on the same program, as I later found out, but consented nonetheless. On my audacious request for a new work, he replied: "A new piece for the occasion if I possibly can. I doubt it."

Almost to the day, two months later Sam sent me a copy of the typescript to *Rockaby* with his note dated May 8, 1980. The opportunity to present the world premiere of a new Beckett play was an outcome nobody, least of all myself, had thought was anything but a fantasy. When it materialized there were many great fantastic repercussions and some pragmatic ones. Because of its impact on our budget, we had to drop the idea of two productions and I had to inform Lee that sadly we could not include him.

Irene Worth wanted to do a film, *Deathtrap*, with Christopher Reeve as she was being offered substantially more than we could offer. She asked us to reschedule but of course we could not reschedule Sam's birthday; instead we released her from her agreement (see telegram from her agent, dated 2/6/81). Sam supported this decision (see his note of 9/10/80). I was on my way to London in January of 1981 to teach for two weeks and scheduled a meeting with Sam to discuss details for *Rockaby* and the need to recast the role. I had also discussed this with Ruby Cohn, a close and long-time friend of mine, and she had suggested Billie Whitelaw as a possible replacement and one that would undoubtedly please Sam. When Sam and I met he welcomed the idea of trying to get Billie to consider doing the play and gave me the relevant contact information. I was scheduled to see her perform at the Aldwych in Peter Nichols' new play, *Passion Play*, but decided to wait for my return to New York to pursue her participation.

When I contacted Billie she did agree to join our project, after a phone conversation with Sam, which pleased him (see his note dated 18.2.81), but her commitment to the Nichols play would require that we rehearse in London during the day while she continued to perform at the Aldwych evenings as *Passion Play* was running until April 3 and the premiere of *Rockaby* was scheduled for Buffalo on April 8. This meant Alan and I, and Pennebaker and Hegedus, had to be in London for a full ten days, all of which raised the cost of the project significantly. However, as the attention was now on presenting the world premiere of Samuel Beckett's latest play, I got approval from SUNY and adjusted the budget accordingly. We were also coordinating dates with Barney as he was rushing to get *Rockaby* published so that it could be released on April 8 as well and be available at the theatre on opening night. In addition, arrangements were now being made for an exhibit at the theatre of Grove Press materials and some of Barney's archival early correspondence with Sam, some of which Barney had donated to the Special Collections Research Library at Syracuse University.

It all came together finally and we played Buffalo as scheduled and then took the production to LaMama Annex in New York the following week as well as to the SUNY campus at Purchase for one performance. Pennebaker/Hegedus completed the film in late 1981 and it was broadcast in the US on Great Performances and in England on the BBC. The Beckett project happened because of the longtime trust and friendship between several key players: Barney's relationship to Sam and Alan dating back to 1953; the friendship and working relationship between Sam and Billie; and finally my friendship with Alan and Ruby which had brought me into the fold.

Samuel Beckett, Alan Schneider, and Billie Whitelaw. Rehearsal at the Cottesloe, National Theatre, 1982. Photo by Daniel Labeille

Samuel Beckett and Daniel Labeille at the home of Billie Whitelaw, 1982. Photo by Alan Schneider

Billie Whitelaw
and Samuel
Beckett.
Rehearsal at the
Cottesloe, National
Theatre, 1982.
Photo by Daniel
Labeille

october 1, 1979

Dear Mr. Beckett,

I hope this letter finds you well, having taken advantage of the
sunny north African climate, and well recuperated from the strain
of your recent productions.
Unfortunately I was not able to see Happy Days in London, as I stayed
in the U.S. all summer, but I did go to see the New York production.
Irene Worth is a very accomplished and technically competent actress
whose control of the language, and use of the voice,hands,face,eyes,etc.
served the play very well, in my opinion.
This year I am on leave from teaching as I have been asked by the
University to produce four programs for television with film and video
documentary makers, working in collaboration with composers, dancers,
musicians, etc. It is a very large endeavor but I am finding it challenging and stimulating. I am also developing tentative project propo-
sals for the next year, as grant application deadlines are fast approaching.

One idea which I've had, and wish to explore at greater length, is
intrinsically linked to your dramatic writing. I have discussed it
at some length with Ruby, Alan, and Lee Breuer. They have all reacted
with great interest and willingness to participate. However I would not
want to pursue the matter further without first presenting it to you
for your consideration and, if there are no objections, for your approval.
I would look forward to working again on a project that was related
to your writing and I would make every effort to see that the project
was carried through to completion in complete observance to your
concerns. However I would not want approval, if granted, to come as
a favor to Alan or to Ruby as I would not want to take advantage of their
long and close association with you.

That being stated, I proceed.

We would arrange for Alan and Lee to come to the campus of the State
University of New York at Buffalo and reside there for four weeks.
During that time they would rehearse, with their respective casts of
professional actors, two of your shorter plays for eventual presentation
on the campus. Their very different approaches to the work would be
observed by both interested students and staff. Once or twice a week
the directors would meet informally with the observers to discuss the
process, the problems, the solutions, etc. Also sharing in these discussions would be Raymond Federman, a faculty member at that particular
campus, Ruby and, hopefully, Martin Esslin. The work would form a base
for a unique teaching and learning experience and the participants would
have access to two very different processes and the work of several
very capable artists. All of this (rehearsal, discussion, performance)
would be recorded on film by a noted documentary maker, D.A. Pennebaker,
and would eventually be edited to form several hours of programming
which would be intended for distribution on the public educational
television system.

Lee has expressed the desire to do That Time. Alan is very interested
in working on either Theatre I or II but, as these are not currently
available, he has asked that I officially request your permission for
one of these to be done on this special project. Should you not want
either of them done at this time, or under these particular circumstanc
Alan would then want to do Come and Go, pending your approval.

1 shall not proceed with the application for public and private grants
until 1 hear from you regarding this proposal. I should mention that
there are certain deadlines which 1 am expected to comply with, if we
agree in principle, and 1 would therefore look forward to hearing
from you at your earliest convenience.

Should the project materialize and receive appropriate funding from the
various agencies, we would then follow through with the matter of right
and royalties.

Very cordially,

Daniel Labeille
P.O. Box 259
Skaneateles, New York
13152
USA

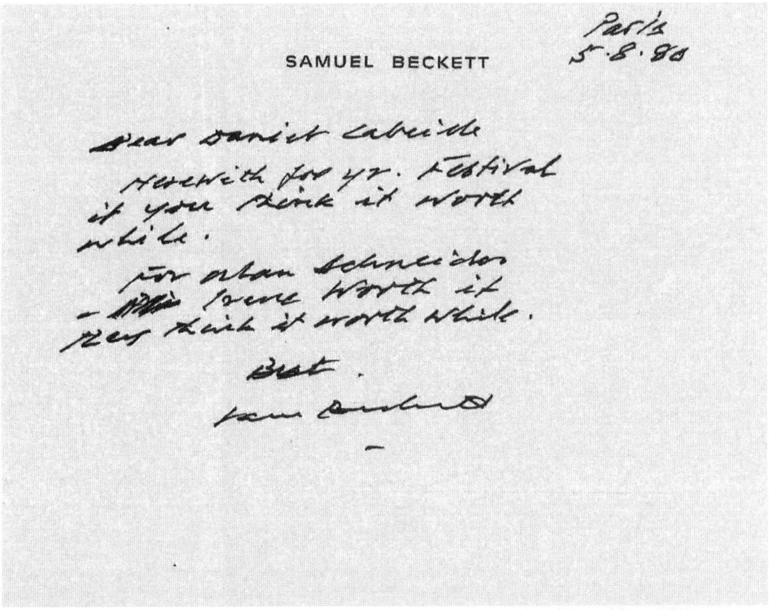

SAMUEL BECKETT

Paris
5.8.80

Dear Daniel Labeille

Herewith for yr. Festival
if you think it worth
while.

For Alan Schneider
& Irene Worth if
they think it worth while.

Best.
Sam Beckett

Paris
5.8.80

Dear Daniel Labeille

Herewith for yr. Festival
if you think it worth
while.
For Alan Schneider
& Irene Worth if
they think it worth while.

Best
Sam Beckett

12/8/80

Dear Sam Beckett,

Have received your new piece, Rockaby, and am very moved by your kindness
and generosity. It is a very powerful piece and I am grateful that you are
allowing me the opportunity to include it in our project. It will contribute greatly to making it a very special event. I thank you, and on
behalf of the State University of New York, I want to express our deep
appreciation to you for having written a piece specifically for this
program.
Although we were not granted all of the funding we initially set out to
raise, we did receive substantial moneys and, as a result, will follow
through with plans to produce and premiere Rockaby, to be directed by
Alan, in Buffalo during April of '81. It will hopefully play with a companion piece of yours, to be directed by Alan as well. We are still negotiating with Lee about his doing a short piece also.
I called Alan yesterday, when I received the script, and he asked that I
read it to him over the phone, which I did. I am sending him a copy today.
He liked a great deal and is looking forward to doing it. We are trying
to contact Irene Worth and hope to meet with her next week.
I am also writing to Barney so that he is aware of the University's intention to proceed. I spoke with him yesterday and he mentioned having received his copy. He sounded very pleased about it. I will meet with him
within the next few weeks to discuss pertinent details. I will keep you
informed of our progress on all these fronts.
On a different matter, I want to share with you the fact that I have been
invited to direct Endgame, by the same company for which I directed
Come and Go two years ago. I am very much looking forward to doing the
play a second time, particularly as we talked about it in some detail
last January. It is a play That I could work on time and time again,
encouraged and fascinated by its richness and what it yields. I know that
you recently directed it in London and am interested to know if you made
any changes in the sript and, if so, whether or not you would wish to have
them incorporated in this production. If you recall, I had, with your permission, incorporated those crucial changes in Come and Go.
In closing, let me again mention what I said in Paris. If you feel the
urge, or the curiosity, to travel to the U.S., either next spring for
rehearsals and/or performance, or at a time more convenient to you, you
have only to let me know and I can arrange for you to come as a guest of
the University. I assure you that I would work to keep such a trip as
private as you would wish.

Ben
Daniel

1/10/80

Dear Sam,

Have just talked to Alan re:<u>Rockaby</u> and he shared with me your very
real concerns about Irene's expressed intentions of doing the piece
in a most inappropriate manner. Both he and I are agreed that it will
not be done in any way that violates your intentions and I trust Alan
implicitly, as I think you do, to serve the play and you in this
matter most faithfully. I am somewhat surprised and disappointed that
Irene took it upon herself to presume a style or an interpretation of
<u>Rockaby</u> outside of a rehearsal situation and without discussing it
in depth with Alan first, particularly as she has not yet definitely
committed herself to the project, as yet. Negotiations between her
agent and me are still going on. As you already know I am very grateful
to you for your cooperation and generosity in this project, and I
want to emphasize that nothing will be done which goes against your
intentions, or without your prior consent.
This brings me to the point of a companion piece, if you permit it,
to be done with <u>Rockaby</u>. You may remember that we were initially going
to do at least two pieces, Alan directing one and Lee Breuer the other,
with a documentary film being made of the rehearsal process, the
scholars' discussions, and the performance of one play. Budgetary cut-
backs have obliged us to limit the evening to the work of one director
and I chose to have Alan continue with the project, for many reasons.
Lee and I have recently discussed the change in plan and he was very
understanding and accomodating. He has offered to be available should
the opportunity present itself again. In any case, the first evening
of <u>Rockaby</u> will still include a symposium and Martin, Ruby, Ray Federman
and Eric Bentley have all agreed to participate in that part of it.
However, as the play will be presented for four nights running, Alan
and I thought that it might play with one or two companion pieces of
yours so as to make it an "evening". Although <u>Footfalls</u> had been mentioned as a possibility, no decision had been made, nor were we about
to make one without first clearing it with you. As Alan, Barney, and I
discussed it, we had every intention of approaching you for your suggestions as to what you might want to see appear on the same programme
with <u>Rockaby</u> if, indeed, you consented to have it play with another
piece to begin with.
Regarding our previous communication re:<u>Endgame</u> I thank you for your
permission to use cuts and additions from your recent production, as
I deem appropriate. Ruby had mentioned my interest in these changes to
Marty F., and I recently received a copy of the script from Marty with
all notations, along with a very kind note.
I think I will be in London January 5 through 17, and will come over to
Paris on the 11th or 12th. I would very much look forward to meeting
with you again, if possible. Please let me know so that I can work my
London schedule around those two days.
In closing, I want to appologize for any misunderstandings that have arise
regarding the project, and I assure you that my first and foremost con-
cern in these matters is to see to it that your intentions are respected.
That was my position from the start and that is the only way in which
I would want to continue to produce this project. Best, David Salmento

Paris
9.10.80

Dear Daniel
Thank you for your letter.
Rockaby was written for yr. ~~Xxxxxxx~~ Project
& must have its first performance
on this occasion. If Irene Worth is
not available another actress should
be found.
I suggest as companion piece
Krapp's Last Tape with Rick
Cluchey (San Quentin Drama Workshop),
directed by me in Berlin some
years ago & at present playing in
Chicago after runs in the Abbey
Theatre, Dublin, the Oxford Playhouse,
the Young Vic & Arts Theatre in London.
Rick's present address: c/o Goodman
Theatre, 200 South Columbus Drive,
Chicago.
I should be happy to see you in
Paris in January. But I shall

probably be in Morocco at that
time. I won't know definitely
before mid-December. I'll let
you know then one way or the
other.
Best.
Sam

310   Dear Mr. Beckett

Paris
9.10.80

Dear Daniel

Thank you for your letter.
Rockaby was written for yr. Project
& must have its first performance
on this occasion. If Irene Worth is
not available another actress should
be found.

I suggest a companion piece
Krapp's Last Tape with Rick
Cluchey (San Quentin Drama Workshop),
directed by me in Berlin some
years ago & at present playing in
Chicago after runs at the Abbey
Theatre, Dublin, the Oxford Playhouse,
the Young Vic and Arts Theatre in London.
Rick's present address: c/o Goodman
Theatre, 200 South Columbus Drive,
Chicago.
I should be happy to see you in
Paris in January. But I shall

(verso)
probably be in Morocco at that
time. I won't know definitely
before mid-December. I'll let
you know then one way or the
other.

Best,
Sam

2/11/80

Dear Sam,

I thank you for yours of the 9th. Although the University would look forward to bringing Rick, directed by you as Krapp, to Buffalo it does present two very major problems within the context of this particular event:
1) The scope of the festival had to be cut back as money from
   foundations was less than originally requested, hence our
   having to release Lee Breuer from the project, and
2) as the documentary film which is to be made for television
   will focus on rehearsals and performance, as well as on discussions
   between Ruby, Martin, Ray, Alan, etc., to bring in a piece
   already completed would reduce the material available to the
   documentary maker and to the students and faculty who are to
   have access to the development of the pieces.
I have, however, suggested to the University at Buffalo that they bring
in the San Quentin Workshop at another time, if they can, under the auspices of their cultural programs office.
We have finally completed negotiations with Irene's agent and she has
agreed to commit four weeks to the project. She is looking forward to
doing Rockaby, and Alan seems pleased to have her do it and I'm certain
that once they work together he shall bring her around.
Our problem remains to select, either at your suggestion or with your
approval a second piece for Irene to do, as directed by Alan, which
would play on the same bill with Rockaby. This second piece could be
a dramatic reading, rather than a staged performance, and along these
lines the suggestion was made that Enough might be appropriate. I defer
to you for your reaction and/or suggestions.
Regarding my trip to England I will send you the name and phone number
of my hotel in London, within a few weeks. Should your plans change re:
your trip to Morocco, I hope we can meet in Paris.
Have begun rehearsals for Endgame and am pleased with the cast. It's their
first time working on a piece of yours and they are both eager and very
manageable. I do not anticipate too great a problem in getting them away
from the American tendency toward naturalistic acting, and into the
rapid and stylized theatricality of the piece, as you and I discussed last
January. I keep reminding them that they should deal with the play's
structure and rhythms in terms of music.
I look forward to hearing from you at your earliest convenience so that
I can finalize the Buffalo plans and I thank you for your help in this
matter.
Have recently finished reading Company, which Barney generously sent to
me. It is stunning. Keep well,

Best,

[signature]

via Graphnet

99 WEST SHEFFIELD AVENUE ■ ENGLEWOOD, NEW JERSEY 07631   201-569-7707

\:
DVDP

B914 317-2 0702 ZZ 02/07/81 02:52 TM

3A 02/06 21:46 B094 6-1 B914 317 02/07/81 02:50 13152   GOLDMAN

DANIEL LABEILLE
EXECUTIVE PRODUCER
SUNY/THE ARTS ON TELEVISION
P.O. BOX 259
SKANEATELES, N.Y. 13152

DEAR DANIEL LABEILLE: I DEEPLY REGRET THE NECESSITY OF
INFORMING YOU THAT IRENE WORTH HAS BEEN OFFERED A MAJOR
ROLE IN A MAJOR MOTION PICTURE WHICH IS IN DIRECT CONFLICT
WITH YOUR DATES FOR "ROCKABYE". THE FILM WILL TAKE HER FROM
MARCH 16TH THROUGH MAY 23RD. CAN YOU RE-SCHEDULE THE BECKETT
TO SOME TIME AFTER THIS DATE. SINCERELY, MILTON GOLDMAN ICM-NY NNNN
DVDP

SAMUEL BECKETT

Paris
18.2.80

Dear Daniel
    Thanks for yrs. of Feb. 12.
very pleased at switch to Billie. I am
to phone her next Sunday Feb. 22, at her
request.
    End of section 3 (l. 4) second "time"
she stopped & shd. be underlined, i.e.
spoken live. Faintly.
    It would help me to know as soon as
possible when Alan will be in Paris.
Have appointment with Tom March 2.
            as best.
                Sam

Paris
18.2.81

Dear Daniel

Thanks for yrs. of Feb. 12.
Very pleased at switch to Billie. I am
to phone her next Sunday Feb. 22 at her
request.
End of section 3 (p.4) second "Time
she stopped" shd. be underlined, .i.e.
spoken line. Faintly.
It would help me to know as soon as
possible when Alan will be in Paris.
Have appointment with Tom March 2.

All best,
Sam

SAMUEL BECKETT'S

rockaby

AND A DRAMATIC READING OF ENOUGH

CENTER THEATRE   APRIL 8, 9, 10 & 11

Skaneateles 28/4/81

Dear Sam,

Please forgive my not writing sooner to give you some of the details re:the
Rockaby production. In spite of the pressures of time everything came together
very well and the production was received with interest and praise - Alan
and Billie appeared pleased with the results, and I am pleased in so far as
everyone worked diligently toward a common goal, namely to give R. a precise,
meticulously detailed, and very moving first mounting. Perhaps you have
already heard from Billie and Alan who will have shared their reactions with
you.
I was particularly honored and pleased to work with Billie. She is an extraordinar
warm and generous person, of great talent, so unselfish and giving of herself that
it made the entire project very rewarding, from my point of view. I want to thank
for suggesting that we approach her about it, and for all the support and trust yo
friendship brought to our endeavor. Alan was a meticulous task master, as well
he should be, and the results justify the means, or something along those lines.
As his producer, his assistant, and his stagemanager, not to mention his roomate
for two weeks, I shared all his anxieties, his fears, his excitement, etc.
Have just received "Mal Vu Mal Dit" from a friend and am eager to start in -
the end of classes, exams,and all the other crap that burdens an academic position
will soon be done with, and I can immerse myself in what appears, at a glance,
to be a major undertaking.
Am enclosing a cassette of Rockaby, the track used for the performance, some
photographs of Billie in Enough and Rockaby, and a few photos from the Endgame
I did in January. Also included are a few clippings from the newspapers.
The whole thing was a unique experience for all of us and I want to again thank
you for your trust and generosity in allowing me to bring it to the stage this
first time.
I hope this letter finds you in good health and enjoying the warmth of spring
in Paris. I look forward to seeing you again.

All the best,

*A*S James Knowlson notes in his biography, *D*amned to Fame: The Life of Samuel Beckett *(Simon & Schuster, 1996), Beckett gained "something of a reputation" late in his life for being an "arch-controller of his work, ready to unleash fiery thunderbolts onto the head of any bold, innovative director unwilling to follow his text and stage directions to the last counted dot and precisely timed pause." This idea of Beckett's tyranny was ill-founded, the result of "almost saturation coverage in the international press of two or three cases" (p. 607). One such case, and arguably the most celebrated, was that of The American Repertory Theater Company's 1984 production of* Endgame *in Cambridge, Massachusetts. The play, first performed in 1957 and the one he preferred—or, as he once said, "the one I dislike the least"—was set by director Joanne Akalaitis in a subway station and included other changes that veered significantly from the playwright's specifications. To avoid the legal action that had been threatened, a program insert was agreed upon in which Beckett proclaimed the ART production was not the play he had written and the artistic director of the company, Robert Brustein, defended directorial freedom.*

—ED.

First
Endgame
production.
Paris, 1957
Photo by
Barney Rosset

Reception After *Endgame* Performance

Photos by Barney Rosset

Samuel
Beckett
and Alan
Schneider

Suzanne
Deschevaux-
Dumesnil

Barbara Bray
and Samuel Beckett

```
CONFIRMATION COPY OF TELEPHONED MESSAGE VIA RCA
        NEWYORK NY
                      51/50 04 1308
        SAMUEL BECKETT

38 BLVD. ST. JACQUES
        PARIS14
AM INFORMED THAT BRUSTEIN WITH BOSTON REP. COMPANY
PLANS PRODUCING END GAME AS TAKEN PLACE IN SUBWAY
STATION AND COSTUMING HAMM AND CLOV AS BLACK
RASTAFARIAN AND NARCOTICS DEALER. IF THIS IS TRUE
WHAT DO YOU WISH ME TO DO. AWAIT WORD.
LOVE
BARNEY
```

```
CONFIRMATION COPY OF TELEPHONED MESSAGE VIA RCA

NEWYORKNY
          31 07 1659
          ROBERT BRUSTEIN
                                        AMERICAN
REPERTORY THEATER
          64 BRATTLE STREET
          CAMBRIDGE, MASS.
SAMUEL BECKETT REFUSES PERMISSION FOR PRODUCTION
OF END GAME WITH ANY CHANGES IN SCENERY COSTUME OR
SOUND NOT DESCRIBED IN TEXT
BARNEY ROSSET
GROVE PRESS
196 WEST HOUSTON STREET
NEW YORK NEW YORK 10014
```

Synopsis of Harvard *Endgame*

Fred Jordan, December 1984
Sent to Samuel Beckett

The set is a cavernous underground subway depot, a bombed-out, vandalized subway car extends from stage left more than half way across, its doors missing and its windows broken. In the rear a wall rises the full height of the stage, with long, narrow, iron ladders climbing to the top in two places where the windows might be, except that they are obscured (if they exist) by a huge iron girder traversing the top of the stage. At the rear is a doorway with an old air raid shelter sign. Left stage are five beat-up oil drums, two of which turn out to harbor Nagg and Nell. Hamm, once the plastic sheet covering him is removed, sits on a chair placed on a cart of the kind to be found in railroad depots, in front of the burned-out subway car center stage. A large puddle of water spreads before him to stage right. Clov, scantily dressed in rags and showing scabs and open wounds on his bare back and legs, often tramps noisily through the puddles as he scurries back and forth across the stage, darting in and out of the subway car. Hamm, a black actor (Nagg is black as well), is dressed in a rumpled dressing gown, wearing a wig of long, black, tightly curled hair which might be taken for the "dreadlocks" of a Rastifarian. The dialogue follows the script faithfully except that at least 14 lines are missing in two scenes for no apparent reason and that on one occasion three lines are rapidly repeated three times in violation of the text where they are without repetition. One departure from the script is a scene in which Hamm and Clove freeze onstage as the lights dim and their dialogue continues on tape over a loudspeaker from the rear of the audience. The lines are usually spoken with great rapidity, disregarding the instructions to "pause" as noted in the script. The Philip Glass music begins as an overture when the house lights are still up and the audience is being seated and continues after the curtain rises during Clov's frenetic climbing of the steel ladders. It is mostly percussive with a bass background, rising to a crescendo after the curtain has risen. Later, during one of Hamm's short soliloquies, the music resumes to underscore his words.

Barney Rosset
and Fred Jordan
Grove Office c. 1970

American Repertory Theater production of *Endgame*, 1984, Hamm and Clov: Ben Halley, Jr., John Bottoms Photo by Richard Feldman

American Repertory Theater production of *Endgame*, 1984, Nagg and Nell: Shirley Wilber, Rodney Scott Hudson Photo by Richard Feldman

Grove Press
196 West Houston Street
New York, NY 100149983
December 10, 1984

Robert Brustein
Cambridge, MA 02138

Dear Mr. Brustein,

       Many years ago the late Alan Schneider, regarded by Samuel Beckett as the foremost American director of his works, spent some intense hours of searching on the Left Bank in Paris preparatory to our much anticipated afternoon with Samuel Beckett. Having pulled me along, Alan was finally successful in his quest. He had found a battered, secondhand copy of volume entitled something like 1,001 *End Games*. It was the perfect gift for the master of chess and the state of the human psyche. Naturally, we were meeting to discuss no other project than the American production of *End Game*. Samuel Beckett had little success in teaching me the finer nuances and maneuvers of chess, although he tried with great patience. He did, however, let me know the importance of the *End Game* – to chess and to himself.

His great play *End Game* merges the concept of infinite myriads of possibilities, moves, countermoves, evasions, attacks, and desperate defenses of the endgame in chess with its counterparts in our own human lives. The same calculations and ambivalences go on within us as we try to avoid or implement our final moves. The setting is sparse for *End Game*, both on the chessboard and on Beckett's stage. Just as the chessboard has its absolute stringency of space and permutations of movement, so has Mr. Beckett's drama and settings. It is all detailed in his stage directions. We are given the parameters of its world, its movement, its actors, and its scenery. Everything is set in place for total concentration. There are no extraordinary props, costumes, or sounds. This drama has a crystal purity, providing its own insights, posing its own questions. It allows us to create our own personal vision of what is happening to the actors and to ourselves. There is no straight message.

And so, Mr. Brustein, you took this exquisite work, absolutely mapped out by its author (whom you say you "revere") to be a spare, integrated whole, and you tore it apart to embellish it with your own ideas. Where there were supposed to be two bins to hold Nell and Nagg, you put five, and later moved Nagg to a chair. Where the set was to be a small, bare room punctuated by two tiny curtained windows and a picture turned to face the wall, you grandly gave us an underground subway depot of some sort housing a wrecked subway car, and even more – a large puddle of water across the stage. Two of the actors are purposefully black. Where silence was intended you added music – to precede the play, open the play, and enter once again later. At one point in your *End Game*, the actors freeze into position and have their words spoken, as recorded, by an amplified sound system emanating from the rear of the theater. Of course, none of these elements were meant to be in the *End Game* which Mr. Beckett wrote.

But Mr. Brustein, you want to tell us something. You are going to clarify Mr. Beckett's message and bring it up to date. You want us to know about homeless people – in Boston no less (the program points it out to us) – and about miscegenation. Perhaps you have underrated the public's knowledge – the public you are so anxious to educate and impress with your control over big things, like the big set, the sound amplification, and all the other showmanship techniques you would probably say poor Beckett lacks. Yet all this tumult and glitter, this insensitivity resulting in bowdlerization and puerile oversimplification gets us nothing but a pile of fool's gold, where there had originally been that thing so rare, a work of integrity. It occurs to me that you in your effort to rehabilitate Mr. Beckett in this gross way may really be only concealing your contempt for what you profess to admire.

Mr. Brustein, you tell me that you are shocked that a publisher with my experience of censorship would attempt to interfere with your interpretation of the play Your concept of censorship and mine are very different. I fought for the complete, original version of Lady Chatterley's Lover to be published. It made me ill to read the truncated version published here. How could we ever know from that what Lawrence was really all about? And how will we ever know from your grandiose, tormented, and twisted production of *End Game*. What Mr. Beckett had in mind, for better or worse. Mr. Beckett's play is of a piece. You have distorted it, added one artifice after another, and, worst of all, you have violated the prerogative of Mr. Beckett as an artist – to have his work performed the way he intended. That, Mr. Brustein, is what I call censorship. And just as it did with Lady Chatterley's Lover it makes me ill to think that the audiences which see your unfortunate production of *End Game* will leave thinking that they have seen and heard the words of Samuel Beckett as he created them.

Mr. Brustein, we have long thought of you as a very important, creative, and innovative voice in the American Theater. Your collaborators are equally regarded. Perhaps that is what makes our anguish deeper. Why can't you attend to all the rich avenues in the theater which are open to you and need you. Turn to other playwrights of ability and let Samuel Beckett remain untouched "old hat" if that is the way you persist in viewing him.

Sincerely,

Barney Rosset

STATEMENT BY BARNEY ROSSET, DECEMBER 11, 1984

Samuel Beckett, whom I have been keeping informed about the American Repertory Theater staging of his play *Endgame*, called me from Paris this morning at about 9 a.m. to ask what I had been able to find out about this production. I told him that Fred Jordan of Grove Press had gone to Cambridge on December 9, 1984, to see a preview of the play and, upon his return, had submitted to me a written report describing the stage set, the costumes, the music and some other aspects of the staging that differ from the play's written text (Appendix A). I began to read this report to Beckett over the telephone. I had come about half-way through when Beckett interrupted me in an agitated tone: "I've heard enough. This cannot be done." Then he added, "This has nothing to do with my play. They have no permission to do this. They cannot do this." I might add that this was the angriest I had ever heard Beckett in the more than thirty years I have known him.

[Inserted into the American Repertory Theater's program as part of the legal settlement]

STATEMENT BY SAMUEL BECKETT
ABOUT THIS A.R.T. PRODUCTION

"Any production of *Endgame* which ignores my stage directions is completely unacceptable to me. My play requires an empty room and two small windows. The American Repertory Production which dismisses my directions is a complete parody of the play as conceived by me. Anybody who cares for the work couldn't fail to be disgusted by this. — Samuel Beckett"

As personal friend and publisher of Samuel Beckett, Grove Press is charged with the obligation of protecting the integrity of Samuel Beckett's work in the United States. The Audience of the American Repertory Theater can judge for itself how the stage before you differs from Beckett's directions as they are reproduced here from the printed text. In Beckett's plays, the sets, the movements of the actors, the silences specified in the text, the lighting and the costumes are as important as the words spoken by the actors. In the author's judgment—and ours—this production makes a travesty of his conception. A living author of Beckett's stature should have the right to protect himself from what he perceives to be a gross distortion of his work. We deplore the refusal of the American Repertory Theater to accede to Beckett's wishes to remove his name from this production, indicate in some way that this staging is merely an adaptation, or stop it entirely.

Grove Press, Inc. [1986]

Dear Sam,

Am writing this on the plane home from New York—if you can call New York home.

It pleased me tremendously to see you—seeming in far better shape than I had anticipated. That is the best kind of surprise. Having you see the San Quentin tape meant a good deal to me. I remember your note to me to encourage and help Jan [Jonson] in any way possible and I tried to do just that. Included in the effort was getting [John] Reilly interested, resulting in his going to San Quentin himself and recording the production and the life going on around it. So, bringing the tape for you to see sort of completed the circle. At least it was a mission, albeit a small one, accomplished. And the same held true for the Lincoln Center GODOT—photos, reviews, and letter.

As for what you said about Reilly, I forwarded what I believe was your message immediately after leaving you—and that was for him not to press himself upon people by saying that he had your blessing—thereby making them feel that they had to deal with him as if he were you. I told him to rely on himself for any cooperation from others— and not to use you for leverage.

Sam, as I told you, I am not in his film, at least as of now, although I suppose I might be interviewed. Actually I was brought together with Joe Coffey for a talk about the shooting of film, but I have not seen it or heard further.

If I am questioned about or asked to help on any matter concerning you, I have done so. That is equally true of [Gregory] Mosher and Lincoln Center, Jonson at San Quentin, and Reilly in the making of his documentary. I am an observer and adviser to the degree asked of me, but I am not an active participant in any of these things.

As I told you, I would be delighted to assist Reilly in any way possible and I will write telling him so within the next few days. If Reilly wants to lend me the tapes of his new production for me to show you—I will do so without delay. That would more than equal my pleasure of having been able to show you Reilly's tape of Jonson's and the San Quentin inmates' work.

Do keep walking Sam; think more about your friend BRAK'S doing some helpful things for you. That sounded like a wonderful idea to me, maybe a bit of a godsend.

I remain available Sam at any time.

All my best and my love,

Barney

Lincoln Center production, *Waiting for Godot*

Robin Williams, Steve Martin, Bill Irwin, and F. Murray Abraham
Director Mike Nichols

Photos by Brigitte Lacombe, 1988

Photos by Brigitte Lacombe, 1988

Photos by Brigitte Lacombe, 1988

Photos by Brigitte Lacombe, 1988

Photos by Brigitte Lacombe, 1988

BLUE MOON

BLUE MOON BOOKS INC.

61 Fourth Avenue, New York, NY 10003, Phone (212) 505-6880, Fax (212) 673-1039

23 November 1992

Mr. Robin Williams
c/o Michael Menchell
CAA
9830 Wilshire Blvd.
Beverly Hills, Ca. 90212

Dear Robin Williams:

When I saw you in Waiting For Godot at Lincoln Center I felt, both as a private theatergoer and as Samuel Beckett's theatrical agent in this country, that I had never seen a better performance in Godot by an actor than yours, nor a better ensemble effort. You and Steve Martin, without in any way slighting Bill Irwin or F. Murray Abraham or Mike Nichols, were simply superb. For me, at least, whole new nuances of feeling and ideas seeped through. I so informed Samuel Beckett shortly before he died.

My qualifications as agent for Samuel Beckett were and are almost non-existent, but as the founder of Grove Press and its publisher for 30 years, I became close to Beckett. He was my friend and thus my perks.

During the Lincoln Center run I received four tickets to every performance, which allowed me to see you in the role many times. As a matter of fact and fantasy I had the pleasure of being jarred awake by your elbow one evening as I sat, or rather dozed, in the front row, which only increased my respect for you. Since then I have continued to admire you in different roles, and I fell that your range is enormous and brilliant.

And to the point of this letter. I have a manuscript which I deeply believe would make a wonderful film, and it seemed to both the author and me that you would be ideal for the protagonist. Although I have no publishing interest in this book (a former colleague of mine, Dick Seaver of Arcade Publishing, will be publishing it in the Spring of 1993), I did want to make contact with you to see if you would have some interest in the project, which personally so grips me.

My one and only attempt heretofore to interest an actor was many years ago when, at Beckett's request, I sent a Beckett script to Charlie Chaplin to look at, only to be told that "Mr. Chaplin does not read." So goes it. Anyway, Buster Keaton took the part.

I have enclosed a copy of Beam Me Up, Scotty. If you are interested, please contact me or through Michael Menchell at the above address, or the author at the following:
Michael Guinzburg, 334 Mulberry St. NY NY, 10012 #5a (212 334-5062).

Sincerely,

Barney Rosset

September 22, 1986

Dear Sam,

Thanks to dear old Krapp I have managed to keep my dear old head attached
to a living body these past two weeks. On my first trip to the theater to see
Rick I took my own little video camera, and with Rick's and Jack's permission
I attempted to tape it from the tiny balcony; attempt is the word because I got
a blank tape and the camera fell off the balcony. But I liked the performance.
And coincidentally had just met a John Reilly who is a longtime videotape
professional and a splendid person.

I brought him back to the theater with his helpers and they did it again the
following night. The results of that were so promising that he got Rick and Jack
to let him re-tape for a full afternoon under more controlled conditions. I have
just come now Monday afternoon from Reilly's little video studio where I looked
at what they had accomplished. It looked very good to me. The sound quality of
Krapp on the old tape comes across especially well.

When the full piece is put together, and it is about done now, I would very
much like to show it to you. I am sure we could see it in a room at the P.L.M.,
just getting a TV set and a player. I would take care of all that. It means a great
deal to Rick [Cluchey] who is at Notre Dame this week, and to me too, and
others. The saving part for me has been being able to occupy my time with Rick,
Jack, and John Reilly.

Outside of that the whole situation has been impossible but now I am Krapp
and that helps a lot.

Dear Sam, I hope all is well as can be and that I will hear from you shortly.

Love,
Barney

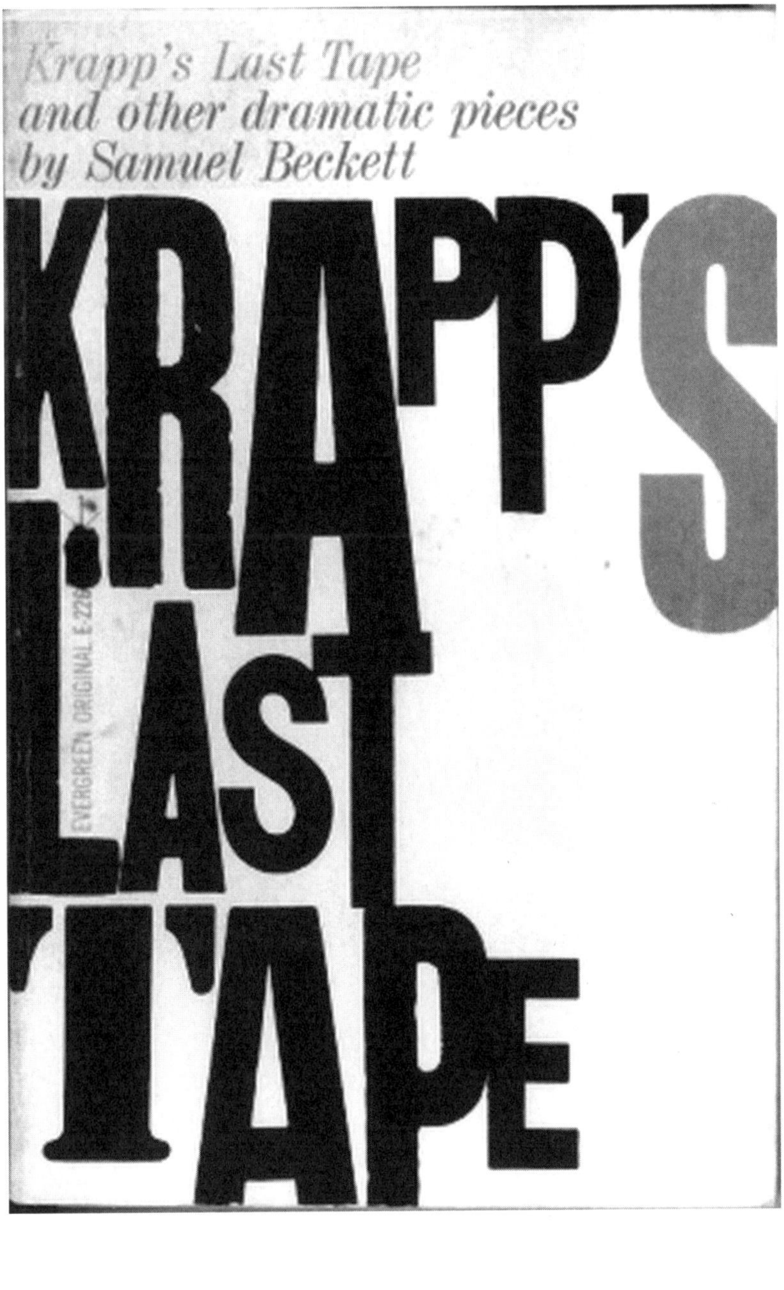

Krapp's Last Tape
and other dramatic pieces
by Samuel Beckett

KRAPP'S
LAST
TAPE

EVERGREEN ORIGINAL E-226

Evergreen
Original
E-226

March 16, 1987

Dear Sam,

Safely back from Paris and in possession of a typewriter once again—bear with me if you can.

Today I had lunch with Bernard Gersten who is second in command to Gregory Mosher at the Vivian Beaumont-Lincoln Center Theater complex. You will recall that I gave you Mosher's letter, which indicated that he wished to do *Godot* with Mike Nichols as director. As far as I know that is still his wish and, if I understood correctly, you will be hearing from him (Mosher) shortly. Now, while I welcome warmly the idea of *Godot* being put on at Lincoln Center, I am worried about Mike Nichols (and now it appears Dustin Hoffman, Nichols' sidekick) having something else when he is needed. I tried to emphasize that fear to Mosher and I strongly suggested that he have a backup director in mind just in case. In fact, I suggested to Mosher that he think of being the director himself. That idea did not seem to displease him. In addition, I would very much like to cling to the videotaping rights and it seems to me that with two celebrities like Nichols and Hoffman that that might be very difficult indeed. Anyway Sam, please do let me know about any contact you may have with Mosher—I wish him the best of luck. I do want, if at all possible, to hold the video rights, just as Rick is doing for his hoped-for production—and so it goes.

As soon as I got back I called the person who notified you about the Commonwealth Award. He told me that he had received your letter. As for the award ceremony itself, and the payment of the money, he was very vague—something about June or July, and I did not want to press him too closely.

Then I called Rick Cluchey and he naturally seemed very pleased indeed. First, I forewarned him about the frustration involved in being told you are going to get something and then not knowing when it will actually happen. For his sake I hope it will not be too long— and I am writing a letter of enquiry about it.

So with my heart hoping that a third third is incubating, and that other things are survivable, that's it for now.

Love,
Barney

Rick Cluchey, while a San Quentin inmate, formed a theater group at the prison and staged *Godot* and other Beckett works as well. Upon his release, Cluchey created the San Quentin Drama Workshop and, at Beckett's invitation, became second production assistant to the playwright on the 1975 Berlin production of *Godot*. That friendship developed to the point of Cluchey's becoming like a son to Beckett. Beckett's support of Cluchey (financial, professional, and paternal) was in no way surprising. As Knowlson relates of Beckett, "Prison was a world that he did not know at all but one that made him shudder because of his fear of enclosure and claustration, his hatred of violence and degradation, and his horror at a penal system in which for so many there was no hope of either rehabilitation or release" (*Damned to Fame*, p. 542). Here, too, as in the myriad ways articulated in the introduction to this book, Rosset, that life-long fighter for freedom and reform, was akin to Beckett knowing full well that "hatred" and "horror" of injustice himself.

—ED.

NO. ....

DATE ....

Friday, Feb. 5, 1988

Dear Sam,

    I am so sorry I was not here when you called, came in five minutes later. Please don't worry too much about seeing us, much more important is how you feel. Please tell me more.

    Sam, we had reservations to come from 18th Feb to 20th. If we cannot see you then we will simply not come. If there is a good chance we might see you, we will come; if there is no chance, we will not. If you say yes, and then cannot see us, no big problem. Paris is not so bad a place to be for three days, but if we are to come we must know in the next few days.

    All this aside, Sam, I am terribly worried about you and I would very much like to hear your voice if only on the phone.

Much love,

Barney

Sam, this letter is sent through the FAX system.

Hope it saves some time.

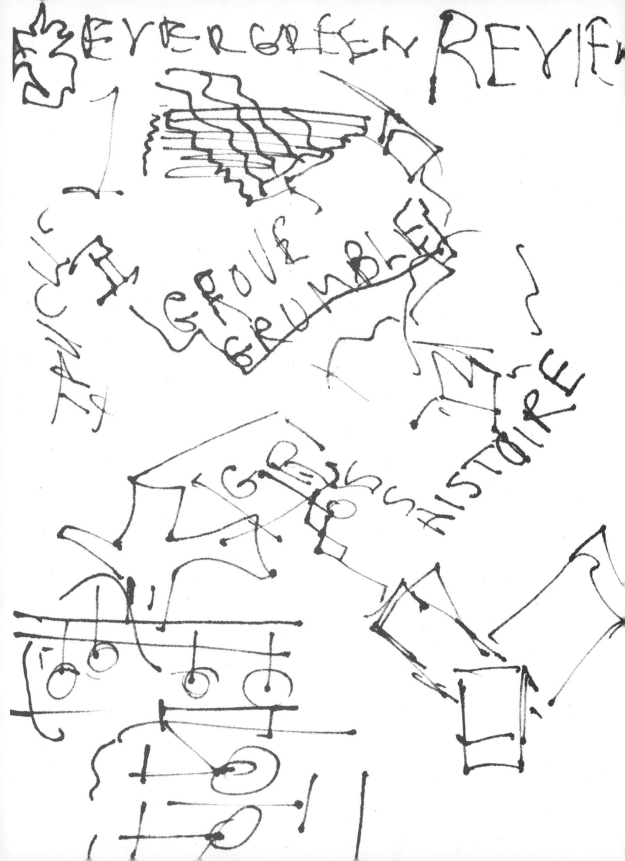

act five

APRÈS (BARNEY'S) GROVE

"The end is in the beginning and yet you go on."

"One of the last things Beckett said to me while he was alive was 'Be good to Barney, he's been through a rough time at Grove Press.'"

—Robert Scanlan

February 1, 1986

Dear Barney,

    This is to confirm that I have appointed you as my sole theatrical agent for North America. This agreement shall remain in effect until such time as either one of us decides to terminate it.

    Yours sincerely,

Sam

Samuel Beckett

Tom Bishop's introduction of Barney Rosset

Centre Pompidou Paris, 1986

I now have the pleasure of introducing Barney Rosset, who is as closely associated with the works of Samuel Beckett as anyone. Barney Rosset has been linked throughout his whole professional career with Grove Press. He has been Grove Press and, as you may know—there were echoes in the press here—as recently as two weeks ago Mr. Rosset was ousted from Grove Press in a scandalous affair that has the New York publishing world up in arms.

Barney Rosset took over the young Grove Press in 1951, and made it. He brought to Grove Press Samuel Beckett's *Waiting for Godot* in 1955, I believe, and most of the major authors whom many of us are interested in. Whether Duras or Pinter, Genet, Ionesco, one finds them all, or most of them, in the United States at Grove Press. Grove Press has also published a number of American authors, among whom are Selby, Berne, Malcolm X, just to name a few. Barney Rosset's work at Grove Press has also been famous for the civil liberties and anti-obscenity battles that he has fought and won—the most notable being the *Lady Chatterley's Lover* case, in addition to *Tropic of Cancer* and Selby's *Last Exit to Brooklyn*. For a period of time Grove Press was heavily involved in films and at that time again a famous case was fought on the banning of *I Am Curious Yellow*.

Grove Press and Barney Rosset have become synonymous with the battle against censorship of all forms. It's ironic that he himself is now being censored. One can only recognize and applaud the work that he has done all these years and express solidarity with him and hope that the way will be found for him to carry on his work in a productive form. I'm sure you will, Barney Rosset.

Opening to address
by Barney Rosset
Centre Pompidou (Paris, 1986)

Thirty-three years ago this fall, I came here to Paris with my then wife, Hannelore [Loly], for the express purpose of meeting Samuel Beckett. Now, thirty-three years and many such voyages later, I am back again for the same purpose. Although since 1953 we have published some thirty volumes of Beckett, *Waiting for Godot* rests ensconced as the crown jewel of our publishing house. It is in our *Evergreen* series, and, naturally, it is *Evergreen* number thirty-three. In the *Waiting for Godot* numbers game the game was fixed. Number thirty-three it was going to be, had to be, and is. We departed from New York at gate thirty-three; my high school football number was thirty-three. And so in this year of the thirty-threes, and having nothing new to add to the Beckett canon, I thought my contribution to this colloquy might be to read some fragments of the correspondence that took place between Sam, Loly and me thirty-three years ago, starting before we all met in Paris, which meeting took place downstairs at the end of the bar in the Hotel Pont Royal. Perhaps the fragments to follow point out that the problems of translating, of creating, of living—in short, of going on, or as Beckett would say, "I can't go on, I'll go on"—have not changed that much in the meantime.

Statement by Barney Rosset

1986—I was abruptly discharged from Grove Press by its new owners. It was a very traumatic period for me. At that time a member of the "new" Grove Press went to speak to Beckett in Paris. He is reported to have said to that emissary "You will get no blood from this stone."

I and others with me, notably Richard Seaver and Fred Jordan, had worked increasingly for more than 30 years to make his work known, read and studied in this country. *Waiting for Godot* became a part of our American language and a powerful metaphor for modern life. His work was and is circulated far more widely in this country than in any other, including France.

And, in 1986, after he so harshly dismissed the new leaders of Grove, he came to me and he offered the most valuable and important gift which he possessed—something for me to publish, to reestablish my life as a publisher.

It was then that he gave me a typed manuscript of *Eleutheria* and told me that it was mine to publish. I say "a" manuscript. The latter was in an envelope marked, in Beckett's handwriting, "The original manuscript of *Eleutheria* for Barney Rosset."

As it is what appears to me to be a "thermofaxed" copy of an earlier manuscript it obviously cannot be the original. However that fact hardly changes the intent. In fact, it strengthens it because he most certainly did not give it to me to sell, as the original, to some library. There are other copies in other libraries but this one was given to me to publish, not to treasure as a souvenir. I am not a collector of manuscripts. I publish them.

It is impossible for me to say how important that gift of *Eleutheria* was to me.

And then the realization must have hit Beckett that *Eleutheria* was written in French.

Since the mid 1960's Beckett had been again writing in English and I am proud to say that I had strongly urged him to do so.

Now he had to face a terrible task, namely to translate a play longer than *Godot* from French to English, a play which had brought him nothing but failure and as was his wont, a work which he had dismissed as being unworthy.

He simply could not bring himself to do it. He would be dead three years later and I deeply believe he knew it. It was much better from his point of view to say to me that he simply could not bring himself to translate it, that after all it was not any good and if I would only agree, he would write something new.

How could I say no, I was still at one of the lowest points in my life, how could I turn down a request from someone whom I considered to be the greatest living writer in the world, how could I refuse his request to write something for me.

Patrick Stewart visits Barney to discuss future performance in *Godot*.
Photo Astrid Rosset

We the undersigned strongly endorse Barney Rosset's continued leadership
of Grove Press. Together, Grove and Rosset are major forces in American
publishing. In the second half of this century, there has been no one
and no company as daring, as controversial, as imaginative in publishing
and we are all the better for it.

Now we learn that, despite assurances to the contrary, outside interests
are coming between Barney Rosset and Grove Press, intent on separating
them. We object. And we ask Ann Getty and the Wheatland Corporation,
owners of Grove Press, to either give Grove a chance to exist autonomously,
under Rosset's leadership, or to allow the company to be bought by more
sympathetic owners.

Samuel Beckett

Petition signed by
many authors in
addition to Beckett.
Courtesy of
John Oakes

"BARNEY *Rosset, fin de partie" [Barney Rosset, Endgame]: So reads the sardonic title of an article published in the weekend edition of the French newspaper Libération, October 18-19, 1986. One year prior, the article's authors Dmitri Savitski and J. Lahana explain, Ann Getty, wife of an heir to the Getty Oil fortune, and her British associate, publisher and philanthropist Lord George Weidenfeld, made a visit to Rosset widely known to be in financial difficulty. A spectacular offer to Barney resulted: Getty would buy Grove Press but Rosset would remain at the helm. Thrilled that his financial problems were resolved, Rosset set out to sign up new authors only to be shown, in April 1986, the door. No longer was he to run the show, but to be given a title that carried no real authority. Rosset refused. Wheatland Corporation, of which the publishing house of Lord Weidenfeld and Ann Getty was a division, "swallowed" Grove Press, reported Savitski and Lahana who wanted to know why. According to Getty, Rosset was very independent, his interests favoring above all else "ce qui lui plaît personnellement" [what personally pleased him]. Proposing to buy back for 4.5 million dollars the press that he had sold for 2 million, he received the following response: "une maison d'édition ne se vend pas" [a publishing house can't be sold].*

Interviewing Rosset, Savitski and Lahana learn of the early years of Grove Press; the publication of Lady Chatterley's Lover, which produced in 1957 an enormous scandal and an even greater success; and the several years wait that finally resulted in Henry Miller's letting Rosset publish Tropic of Cancer. Rosset was significantly aided in that effort by French publisher, writer, and founder of Olympia Press

Maurice Girodias (along with German publisher Heinrich Ledig-Rowohlt) who, despite Miller's categorical "no" to Rosset's request, persisted on his behalf and elicited Miller's agreement. Girodias telegrammed Rosset from Germany: "Henri est ici. Venez sans délai." [Henry is here. Come immediately.] And Rosset was on the next plane to Hamburg. "Miller et moi avons joué au ping-pong et, à la fin de la partie, il a signé le contrat," Rosset related to his interviewers. [Miller and I played ping-pong and at the end of the game, he signed the contract.] How did he manage, starting with nothing, to sign the likes of Beckett and Miller? Beckett, for one, was advanced the grand sum of $500. That was for Godot. Other Beckett titles appeared in English under the Merlin imprint of Girodias' Olympia Press: Watt as well as Molloy, Malone Dies, and The Unnamable, a fact consistently overlooked, as Girodias rightfully reminded both Beckett and Serge July, co-founder of Libération. In fact, Olympia Press brought out Beckett's trilogy in a single volume in October 1959, followed but a month later by Rosset's edition at Grove.

Rosset sympathizers were many when Getty and Weidenfeld forced him out, as a petition signed by Beckett, among numerous others, reveals. And then there is the immeasurable gift of a work made to Barney by Sam.

A final question was posed to Barney Rosset for the interview cited here: "Vous avez consacré trente-cinq ans de votre vie à Grove Press. Qu'allez-vous faire maintenant?" [You have dedicated thirty-five years of your life to Grove Press. What are you going to do now?] His reply: "Je crois que je vais ouvrir une autre maison d'édition." [I think I'm going to open another publishing house.] He did. In fact, three.

—ED.

September 17, 1986
Mr. Samuel Beckett
Paris

Dear Sam,

This letter "out of the blue" will speak for itself. As I am now working on a second volume of memoirs dealing with the years 1942-1974, centering on the Olympia Press story, I find that this effort implies an honest re-examination of my rapport with the authors I published in those days.

But I don't want to bother you with astringent questions that you might not like to answer. I prefer to describe in what follows my difficulties with certain aspects of my story which relate to you, more or less directly, and find out whether you would agree, or not, to speak or write to me on the subject, however briefly. But that is, of course, entirely up to you.

The only general biographical source I have is Deirdre Bair's book, whose shortcomings I appreciate because in their own way they are so illuminating. The Beckett paradox comes out in it more clearly, perhaps, than it would have in a more abstract treatment; and I must say that I was moved and impressed, in particular, by the account she gives of your struggle for self-definition in relation to the struggle for publication. One senses that the urge to deliver a certain message preceded and indeed guided the definition of the said message; just as if the writer had to live and suffer through that endless, terrible ordeal of creation and rejection by any number of moron publishers in order to discover the nature of his own art.

It may well be that the publisher's mental passivity is a

necessary ingredient of the creative process, since he symbolizes a cross-section of the general public. But it seems equally important that the rule should suffer occasional exceptions, and that some individualistic publishers should come up from time to time with a certain gift of intuition and a sense of adventure since, without them, no "new" authors would ever be set into print. My old daddy, Jack Kahane, was one such publisher, and so was Sylvia Beach who gave her whole life to one book, and was so poorly recompensed by her hero... Forgive me for stating here that I boldly situate myself within that rare category (since no one else will take the trouble of doing it), and that I am proud to share the honor with Herbert Read of having launched one of your two novels in English. I do not discount in the least the role played in this by Alex Trocchi and Austryn Wainhouse, Patrick Bowles and the rest of their *Merlin* entourage, in the set of circumstances which led to my publishing *Watt* in 1954 (that is, ten years after the manuscript had been completed, and after it had been rejected by every other publisher under the sun, including Herbert Read himself); and I am, and always will be, grateful to them for bringing your book to me.

This being said, I am miffed by the way this episode is continuously being misrepresented as it is in the Deirdre Bair biography, in particular, which no [longer] seems to be considered as the standard, official account of your life and career. I am presented as a sort of brain-damaged pornographer, son of another pornographer, who bought the rights to *Watt* under the belief that it was "just another dirty book." The truth of the matter is that I took a costly chance with this book, only one year after having started The Olympia Press (on the proverbial shoestring), with a program of four books by

Bataille, Miller, Apollinaire and de Sade — not such a shameful selection for a start. It is also true that I took that chance on the recommendation of Alex and Austryn (certainly not Dick Seaver) who had helped me set up the initial Olympia program as editors, translators, and anonymous "dirty books" writers. Seaver's function within the Merlin structure was definitely menial, but that did not stop him from claiming later that he ran the show at *Merlin* — a small magazine that never printed more than four issues all told — and that he founded Olympia. Obviously he needed those fabricated credentials in order to impress New York publishers to whom he offered his services, and I find it remarkable that your biographer concocted her story on the basis of such loaded misrepresentations.

In the six years of its active existence Olympia had published, besides *Watt*, major books by Miller, Nabokov, Durrell, Genet, Queneau, Burroughs, Bataille, de Sade, Donleavy. It would be idle for me to ignore my reputation as a pornographer since I myself coined the term "dirty books" (dbs for short) to describe that meat & potatoes part of my production: much needed since I lost money on all of my more glorious authors (including yourself, Miller, Genet, Burroughs), and made some only Nabokov's *Lolita* — that book being the only one that was actually *bought* from me by a New York publisher instead of being, like all the others, merely stolen. In order to survive I did create a line of so-called dirty books, but all of them were the work of pretty good people — such as Alex Trochhi, Iris Owens, Terry Southern, Mason Hoffenberg, Georges Bataille, John Glassco, Pauline Réage (Story of O), Frank Harris, Christopher Logue, Chester Himes, Frank Harris, Norman Rubington, etc. I did turn down George Plimpton's application because he really didn't make the grade... The Olympia 'dbs' were indeed a parody of pornography, rather than the real thing (witness such books as *Candy* or *Story of O*), but done convincingly enough to satisfy the sex-obsessed whose sense of humor is notoriously blunted. My motto was that "no four-letter word ever killed a reader," and my long-range plan was to heap ridicule over the Anglo-Saxon censors and so destroy their power. In this I think that I did succeed, at least to a large extent; and it is my misfortune that at the same time, through a strange twist of fate, a new race of imitative French censors was emerging out of the woodwork just as the British-American brand were gasping their last. And, although they were unable to read what I published, they sent me down for the count; and no one came up then to cry over my dead bones.

We're all part of the same story; we were all engaged in this long-winded battle against censorship, Joyce and yourself, my father and myself, Rosset, Calder, and a few more of that ilk dispersed in various countries — Miller, Bataille, Nabokov, writers and artist who were concerned not so much about sexual freedom as about intellectual freedom. It seems hard to explain to the younger generations that Samuel Beckett's work might have been affected by the existence of censorship in those days; but it is a fact that it was. Not just the bans in Ireland and the minor quibbles with censors over words; but the overall ostracism dictated by the "spirit of censorship" which prevailed in the middle class public, and which therefore caused so many publishers to reject it. You made the good choice when you gave me *Watt* to publish simply because Olympia was fighting at the forefront in that battle, and victory was in sight; you knew it then, and I hope you have not quite forgotten the nature of the struggle... And would it be impertinent to suggest that you owe your next publishers, Rosset and Calder, to the fact that I had published you in the first place?

One thing that struck me in Deirdre Bair's book is the manner in which she omits the fact that, beyond *Watt*, Olympia did publish the three major novels which followed, *Molloy*, *Malone Dies*, and T*he Unnamable* in their original English version. In Chapter 19 she describes the manner in which I was led to sign a contract for Watt with Samuel Beckett despite his revulsion for "any publishing venture the least bit immoral or unsavory," and then proceeds to heap more sneaky derogatory remarks on my father and myself. Two pages later, with no transition to speak of, we see the great white hero come to the rescue: "Barney Rosset wanted to introduce Americans to the newest and most exciting writings in Europe. Beckett was one of the first authors he signed for Grove Press. Ionesco and Genet soon followed and, before long, most of the new French novelists published by Lindon in France were under contract to Rosset in America." (P. 437). In this manner she telescopes a few years and simplifies a complex situation so as to make it obvious that you only signed a contract for *Watt* with me with the greatest reluctance, and only because I didn't know what I was doing; that Rosset published all your other works in English; and that Rosset's moment of glory in the sixties came from the Nouveau Roman authors he got through Lindon — simply ignoring all the Olympia authors he pumped away from my list such as, besides Beckett, Miller, Genet, Burroughs, etc.

I know that you warned Deirdre Bair that you would "neither help nor hinder" her in the elaboration of her biography of you, but she also states that she had a number of conversations with you about it. I do agree that the skillful misrepresentations I pointed out to all bear the mark of those who inspired them (for obvious self-serving reasons): Barney Rosset and his minions. But since I am about to write my own version of this degrading affair, I feel compelled to submit this debate to your arbitration. You may of course decide, once again, to "neither help nor hinder," but even your silence, following this letter, would have a clear enough meaning for me.

I must still replace this episode, however, in a broader context to make the picture complete, and therefore more understandable. I met Rosset and Calder in the late fifties, at a time when Olympia had already reached international fame; this thanks, in particular, to our publication of *Lolita*, which had just obtained a triumph when it was reprinted in New York, in the summer of 1958. We became good friends, and they seemed to share my militant attitudes with respect to censorship, and to freedom of expression. They were both making their debut as publishers at the time, and I had made my own (the hard way) nearly twenty years earlier. Up to that point Grove Press had specialized in campus-oriented publication, all very dull and respectable, but the *Lolita* miracle had dazzled him: the first "immoral" book to break the U.S. censorship barrier thanks to its "literary merit." In fact, at least one year before we met, Barney had written to us to enquire about the American rights of Lolita, but he had dropped out of the competition when he found the price to be too high for his purse... In other words, I appeared then to Barney not just as an undemanding friend, but as a potential source of fabulous material thanks to which he should be able to change his orientation, and make his fortune. In 1959, he made his maiden try in that direction by launching the first American edition of *Lady Chatterley's Lover*, all long-suppressed symbol of sexual freedom as well as literary, which a recent decision by the British courts made reasonably safe in America; and furthermore a book for which he did not feel compelled to pay any royalties... That last detail should have alerted me to Barney's vision of business, had I been aware of this side aspect of his exploit at the time; but I was not, and I felt that the *Lady Chatterley* precedent made Barney my natural ally for the years to come. I already envisioned the time when censorship would definitely break down in the United States, and then gradually in the rest of the English-speaking world, an event that I had worked to prepare in the fifties just as my father had done in the thirties, and in the same spirit.

The mounting pressure the police and the courts were exercising on me in Paris had put my business in jeopardy, and my only hope of avoiding bankruptcy was to transfer my enterprise to America; and this meant getting rid of my scandalous image, and finding a partner with whom I could make a fresh start in the U.S. by launching an American edition of my best authors. Each time I saw Barney we discussed this partnership project, and he seemed even more eager about it than I was; such a plan would allow me to play my creative role directly in America while Barney would take care of the business side of the venture. We were perfectly complementary and this made good sense.

And, in order to show my good will, I took it upon myself to talk Henry Miller into signing a contract allowing Grove to publish *Tropic of Cancer* in America. After *Lady Chatterley* this appeared as the logical next step, but it was not easy to get Miller to agree since he distrusted Barney, and it took me two years, or close to that, to achieve my purpose. Barney was overjoyed to get the contract, he immediately rushed into print with his edition of *Cancer*, and this was the occasion for the last great book censorship battle in America. Barney won in the end, and this remarkable victory took a lot of wit and courage to get; he certainly deserves the title of "hero" you bestowed on him (according to the New York Tabloids) for what he did *then*.

Our projected association, however, never materialized. It is during that period that all my great authors vanished one by one, in the manner of a classical Agatha Christie novel, only to pop up again on Grove's list. Being now bankrupt, with royalties still owed to some of the said authors, I was in no position to prevent the hemorrhage; Grove having given the example, dozens of mafia-type entrepreneurs set up publishing businesses whose only activity was to pilfer my backlist; and by mid-67 about one hundred Olympia Press titles, good or bad, had already been pirated. Meanwhile Dick Seaver, who had strictly no experience in publishing, had been made senior editor of Grove, presumably because he knew personally most of the authors, translators and editors who had been connected with my firm in Paris, and this qualified him as "the Olympia specialist."

And yet my trust in Barney's friendship was such that I continued to ignore for a long time the systematic nature of his strategy. On each occasion I was confronted with a fait accompli, and a good, respectable explanation as to why it had gone that way... It is John Calder, for instance, who explained to me that it was my moral duty to share the English-language rights to the four novels I had acquired from you, with Barney for the U.S., and with his own firm for the British market, and to do so without any financial compensations since we were such good friends, and since we were only concerned, all three of us, to serve the great writer we all admired, Samuel Beckett. I bowed to his reasons, and thus I lost even the right to call myself, albeit retroactively, your publisher... To be fair, however, I should add that John was not fully aware of the part he was made to play by Barney. He had been hesitating to duplicate Grove's program in Britain where censorship was still active. Indeed his timidity bothered me so much that we had a serious argument over his reluctance to publish *Tropic of Cancer* in England even after Grove's victory at the Supreme Court. Later he thanked me many times for having virtually forced him to take that chance, since this is what made him "a real publisher" in the eyes of his peers. (But I had already helped George Weidenfeld in the same manner, when he was still a fledgling, struggling publisher, by getting him to publish *Lolita* in Britain — which made him suddenly rich and famous...)

Twenty years later: Barney, having drained Olympia's backlist to the dregs, has been aimlessly floundering about, being quite unable to find all by himself the author, the book, the idea required to save his neck, and is finally being swallowed up by this other alumnus of mine, the victorious Lord Weidenfeld. Dick Seaver was quick to leave the boat as it started to sink, and quick to use his accumulated credentials in order to secure new fatuous jobs for himself. John Calder is deploying a lot of energy [...] struggling to survive. Samuel Beckett is now a Nobelized legend, and celebrates his 80th birthday after a life struggle with literary death. As to myself, Maurice Girodias, having nothing else left to do, I devote my efforts to putting those events back in their true perspective for the doubtful benefit of the 21st century school children. My book is tentatively titled *The Real Story*, and I hope that it will show that the creative passion can be as authentic and respectable with *certain* publishers at least — if not all of them — as it is with yourselves, sublime writers and artists.

But of course, as you know so well (and so did Arjuna), all this is an exercise in futility; the worms and the cockroaches will have the last word on us all. Our epitaph could even go further, as those words of hobo wisdom I once deciphered on a Lower Manhattan palisade: "Anti-Matter Doesn't Matter."

Maurice Girodias

Cc: Lord Weidenfeld
    John Calder
    Barney Rosset
    Georges Belmont
    Jerome Lindon
    Deirdre Bair
        . . . et al.

October 27 1986
Mr. Serge July, LIBERATION
9 rue Christiani
75018 Paris

Dear Sir,

I have just learned with some amazement of the Barney Rosset article, "Fin de Partie" (Libé, October 18/19) appearing under the joint signature of Dmitri Savitski and J. Lahana. This text, presented in the form of an interview, contains more untruths and shrewd gaps per line than one would expect to find in the French press, which seems literally dizzy when it comes to dealing with American literary life.

Barney Rosset, who so bitterly complains that one "took" his publishing house when he himself sold it, attempts to render credible by any way possible a fantastical and very flattering version of his place as a publisher. Now the authors of this article together spread this packet of lies without even taking care to check what anyone has said to them. Is this by ill will, or plain ignorance? The principal authors who made the reputation of Grove Press were published ten years earlier in Paris, and in English, by myself under the imprint of Olympia Press: Miller, Beckett, Burroughs, Genet were launched by me, and this fact is clearly left out of this article.

I certainly do not deny the merits of Barney who fought the legal battle in the United States that allowed the publication of Tropic of Cancer, a significant phase of the evolution which resulted in 1967 in the abolition of the puritan censorship exercised in this country from the start. I note however the cunning and audacity evidenced in this battle; I was systematically stripped of my discoveries used to create his own publishing venture. I was at the time (at the end of the 50s) the friend, the ally and the role model for Barney, and yet my role is reduced to the minimum in this text where my name is cited only in an untrue and unfavorable context.

I can't enter here into a detailed analysis of the fibs, but as I am currently working on a book intended to restore the historical truth, I can't ignore an article that is so seriously prejudicial against me. It is in this spirit that I recently sent to Samuel Beckett the letter a copy of which I send you here; and it is also for this reason that I ask reparation from you. It's up to you to decide the form that your rectification is to take, and I hope that you will judge it desirable that it be done in a friendly way.

I await therefore your reply to this letter.

Sincerely yours,

Maurice Girodias

Barney Rosset Fights for His Right to Publish

An Interview with Michael Coffey

*I*N APRIL 1985 *a company headed by Ann Getty (wife of one of the heirs to the Getty fortune) and British publisher Lord George Weidenfeld bought Grove Press for $2 million. Rosset was assured he would remain in control as president. A year later he was forced out.*

Grove Press may not be a small press by some standards but under the direction of Rosset it certainly has been by any standard an independent one. Literary and social culture in America would be greatly different were it not for Rosset's taste for what is challenging in world writing and his willingness to bring such works to print fighting censorship and mainstream opinion along the way. The issue of independence in publishing, which is fast becoming the hallmark of small publishers, seems to be at the heart of the recent events surrounding Grove.

—M.C.

BARNEY ROSSET: What I was led to believe very, very strongly was that I was to be the head of the company for the next five years. I was told so explicitly *just* before I signed the agreement, because it had occurred to me, very intuitively and at the right moment, that they didn't mean that, and I said so and said, "maybe it's better to call the whole thing off." And I was told "No, no, absolutely no… we're only doing this [buying Grove] because we want you and you're going to run it for five years and everything's going to be as it has been." And so it went ahead.

MICHAEL COFFEY: There was some clause in your contract that gave them the right to demote you from president to senior editor, was there not?

BR: Yes. They had a clause whereby they could replace me and leave me as something called the senior editor which still carried a great deal of power. But they haven't given me those powers. The first thing that happened after I was thrown out as president was that I was told I couldn't go to an editorial meeting, that I could not acquire a book. I couldn't sign a check, and later, even attend the ABA [American Booksellers Association] for Grove.

MC: Did something particular happen that caused a change of thinking on their part or do you think all this was the culmination of a plan?

BR: Marc Leland, who is a financial something or other in charge of the Getty money, was so strong on the point that I should be there and stay in it and I would run it [Grove Press]. When I was informed that I no longer had a job he said, "Well, you knew that from the moment you signed this [contract] that we were going to get rid of you as soon as possible," which I took to mean that *he* knew that, but I didn't. And there have been no complaints whatsoever — f - far from it. We have given them a plan and the plan was succeeding. The company was making money and everything was going along beautifully.

MC: Are they letting Grove backlist titles go out of print?

BR: The last list I made up of books to be reprinted, let's say of about 60 titles, they reprinted about four.

MC: Haven't you offered to buy Grove Press back from them?

BR: I did. I gave them a more than fair offer and they told me, "We don't want to hawk it around." I offered all the money they had put into the press plus the money they were supposed to spend this year plus what they paid for it.

MC: Why do you think Ann Getty ended up buying Grove Press, of all the presses out there?

BR: Well, there weren't so many out there our size and with our literary list, first of all. Second of all, I had known George Weidenfeld for 30 years, *known* him, as to differentiate it from being a "friend." But I had known him and we were quite . . . amicable.

Weidenfeld came to New York in September of '84, I mean [laughing] he probably came every two weeks but this time he called me, and I went to see him. He said he was involved with this wonderful person, Ann Getty, who had absolutely limitless funds, which I saw no reason to doubt, then or now. She had told him that she wanted to be involved in American publishing. I don't know if he thought of Grove or she thought of it, but I would guess that he did and she approved.

I imagine that her main goal was a certain kind of prestige, and that becoming the publisher of Samuel Beckett and Stoppard and Pinter and Ionesco and David Mamet and so on appealed to her. I in no way think that Grove Press was their only objective. It just so happened that when Weidenfeld told me that she would buy the company and put limitless amounts of money into it, we were the first that acquiesced.

MC: How did you see Grove benefiting from the sale to Getty?

BR: I thought it was going to take a lot of anxiety off my mind as to how to stay afloat financially and proceed in a fashion that would enable us to build upon what we already had. And it would give us money for new projects. It worked beautifully for one year. It worked absolutely perfectly and with money that was peanuts compared to what they were pouring into Weidenfeld & Nicolson, which is bringing out its first series of books in the fall, starting with *How to Decorate Your Christmas Tree and How to Make Miniature Desserts* . . . [laughing]. I'm picking the most vulnerable, of course.

MC: Dan Green is now president of Grove Press, since your demotion.

BR: Dan Green had already been hired by Getty and Weidenfeld. He was the CEO at Wheatland. It is an incredible anomaly — Dan Green the president of Grove Press. If there could be a worse combination imaginable I wouldn't know what it would be. They kept me in close contact about who they were thinking of hiring for the overall company that was to oversee Grove and Weidenfeld & Nicolson. I'd say they went through nine different people, all of whom I thought would have been wonderful. Some were too good to be true. But all of them fell through. Suddenly, they told me that Dan Green had been hired. He was the only one they never told me they were considering. I think it was in their minds to get me out.

MC: Have the people at Wheatland given you problems about publishing specific titles?

BR: That's never the way things like that are done. I've had a long experience with censorship and I brought it up right in the beginning: The first time I met Ann Getty I brought her a book, from our series on Latin America edited by my wife, Lisa Rosset, called *The Other Side of Paradise*, which deals with the domination of American conglomerates in Bermuda, Haiti, and the whole Caribbean. I said to her, "Do you know what you're getting into?" She said, " Oh yes, it doesn't bother me. We've sold all our oil to Texaco." Well, I liked that remark. And Texaco was not favorably displayed in the book!

At the same meeting, I gave her an order form, which included the Victorian Library. She picked up on one title and said, "Oh my god. It says *Lashed into Lust*. I better not show this to my children, they'll all go out and buy it." I liked both those remarks. I thought they were genuine and friendly and that she understood the two things that Grove has always stood for — a mixture of politics and a fight against the fear of eroticism, a celebration of it, if you will.

And I said to George Weidenfeld, "What can't we publish? And he said, "You can publish anything, my boy, but I'd appreciate it if you wouldn't publish anything too anti-Israel or too pro-Arab." So I said, "OK, I'll live with that," since we had no such books anyway. And we held to it … almost. One of the books cut from the fall list was an Israeli novel, *The Road to Ein Harod*, that is quite critical of the government there.

MC: Your lawyer was quoted in *Publishers Weekly* as saying that two titles, a book on South Africa and one on Cuba, were canceled as part of what he called the "emasculation" of your proposed fall list.

BR: You must remember that Dan Green comes from Simon & Schuster, which has the bottom-line thinking that anything you're going to publish must be ready a year ahead of time and they've used that as an excuse for cutting the list. And it's a poor excuse because, first of all, it's a bad one publishing-wise, and second, many of the books they postponed were ready to print — many were in fact reprints that were just going to be photo-offset. Consider anyway the kind of company Grove was — how could we not take books that came up suddenly? A recent example is *The Freedom Fighter's Manual*, which centered on the handbook for guerrilla tactics distributed by the CIA to the Contras in Nicaragua. My son Peter, who lives in Nicaragua, found it and sent it to us, and my wife said, "My god we've got to publish this," and in a few weeks we did. And it *sold*. Now this could not be done under Dan Green's new program. And it would be ruled out *technically*. They wouldn't say it was political. They'd say we didn't get it in enough ahead of time.

MC: Let's look at the fall catalog that just came out. How much of what you proposed was actually cut?

BR: Cut in half, just about. …

MC: What will your removal do to the continuation of the many Grove series, the Latin American series, for example?

BR: I don't know. What are they going to do? So far we've done a book on Nicaragua, one on El Salvador and another on Guatemala — and we've sold these books! We've just done one called *Outlaws in the Promised Land*, which deals with Mexican migration to the U. S. Now that book, we kept delaying it and delaying it because things happened, changes in the law, in policies. Just suppose you were doing a book on Grenada and the Americans invaded; would you think it was worth waiting three months to redo it? Of course. On the Mexican book, we tried to reincorporate what was happening in an on-going situation.

MC: One can see that the larger houses, with all their planning, don't want to touch volatile dynamic topics. Their decision-making structures are too rigid to respond effectively to a changing scene.

BR: Absolutely. And also maybe they don't want to respond. Gulf & Western owned the biggest sugar mills in the world in the Dominican Republic. On *60 Minutes* they did a very good documentary on how they were exploiting the sugar workers, practically keeping them imprisoned. Can you imagine Simon & Schuster, which is owned by Gulf & Western, ever publishing a book about that?

You may remember Abbie Hoffman wrote a book called *Steal This Book!* just as Grove had gone to Random House for distribution. Hoffman was *their* author. They almost exploded when he brought them that manuscript. And there we were, distributed by Random House, so we took the book anyway. But we had to invent a way to distribute it. Random House wouldn't touch it! And we sold a quarter-million copies.

MC: Of the many possible consequences of this ordeal with the new owners of Grove, the most damaging would seem to be the prospect of Barney Rosset no longer publishing the books he wants.

BR: Yes; surely for me this is *the* problem. But let me tell you a story: Samuel Beckett was very annoyed, to put it mildly, about this whole situation with Getty and Weidenfeld. And when I saw him in Paris in April, he did something extraordinary. Around 1946 he wrote two plays, *Waiting for Godot* and one called *Eleutheria*. He put that last one away. It has never been published, and it's a full-length play. Well, he gave it to me. He said, "All writers should give you something; here's my contribution." The play is in French, and it's already wonderful.

I asked him who should translate it. Sam said, "Oh that's a detail. I'll do it." And now, he's not only going to translate it, he's going to "adapt" it, a word I'd never heard him use before. That is, he's going to make the play more like he now would see it. I ask you now, who is going to publish it? I'm not allowed to publish a

Grove author for four years. And Beckett's not going to give it to *them* — that's the whole point. To register his protest. I think this puts Ann Getty in a moral bind that is quite incredible. Are they going to prevent a new work by Beckett from being published? It would take a lot of courage for them to let me publish, but they could do it. This is really the ultimate challenge for them. Are they, of Grove Press, going to say "no" to Beckett?

[Rosset did eventually publish *Eleutheria*, in 1995, in partnership with John Oakes at Foxrock Inc.]

Excerpts from Small Press, 1986

Barney Rosset interview with Jerome Gold

…And when I was thrown out at Grove by the Gettys, Beckett stood forth—as did John Oakes—stood up and said, "What can authors do for their publisher?" And one thing an author can do is give him a book.

And he wrote something. Well, first, he gave me a play. It's called *Eleutheria*. He wrote it before *Waiting for Godot*. It's the only three-act, full-stage play he ever wrote. It hasn't been put on to this day. He wrote it in 1943 or thereabouts. Then he wrote *Waiting for Godot*, and he couldn't get it produced. He wanted either one to be put on the stage, and *Godot*, which had one set and three major characters, was a lot cheaper and easier for Paris, and they put that on. It's also better. And so *Eleutheria* went into his suitcase. It was never done. It was written in French. So when I was thrown out at Grove, he brought that to me in Paris. He gave me the manuscript and then realized that it had to be translated. So he started to translate it.

Beckett himself did?

Yes. And he came back to me very shortly thereafter and said he couldn't do it. Little did I know he was going to be dead within about three years. And he said that it was too late, he was too tired, but that if I would forgive him, "if I would forgive my unforgivable Sam," he would write something new for me. And he did. He wrote a very short little book called *Stirrings Still*. And I published it.

(*Obscure in the Shade of the Giants: Publishing Lives Volume II*, Seattle: Black Heron Press, 2001, p. 231.)

BECKETT'S *radio play* Embers *(1959) and his short narrative* Stirrings Still *(1988) were both, at some point, to contain art by Joan Mitchell. Rosset told interviewer Patsy Southgate the following:*

> *It probably was the last time Joan ever saw Beckett. It was on her birthday, February 12th. I'd gone to Paris to see Beckett; he already was well into this slow change where he didn't go any place, except into that damn hotel. He was already in that era. But he liked Joan very much and he hadn't seen her in a long time and I told him that it was Joan's birthday and could he possibly come and see her. And he said he would which amazed me. I had the worst case of jet lag that I'd ever had. I fell asleep one night with the phone on, off the hook, speaking to New York and got a bill for $5,000 the next morning. It took me several days to convince them that it was their fault and not mine, which of course wasn't true. But he said he would come and I got Joan to go there, without telling her the reason, and the place was so quiet and calm we were the only people in this rather large lounge bar in the Montalembert. Totally deserted. He came, and we spent several hours together. He seemed very pleased and Joan seemed very pleased. What they talked about at great, great length was the use of color. Beckett had written a radio play called* Embers *and*

Joan had agreed long before to try to illustrate a special edition of it. And she had actually done dozens of what I thought were watercolors. I saw them on a wall in her studio outside of Paris. I thought they were beautiful abstractions. And they were all lined up on the wall on a hinge so that one could get an idea of how they might appear in a book. Then I never saw them again. God knows if she destroyed them or put them away. But that day she said to Beckett that it was really impossible to illustrate the play because the play was the color itself. His use of language obviated the need for any kind of decoration. But they talked specifically about the use of reds and browns, and yellows, and all in harmony with the title of the play, Embers. *I was very busy photographing the two of them with the camera I brought and I remember at the end of the day I went upstairs and I was still sort of groggy, sleepy, and I started taking the film out of the camera and I destroyed it.*

Yet Rosset said this to John Reilly, producer of the documentary Waiting for Beckett:

I had asked Joan to take one of his radio plays, Embers, *and paint illustrations for it, and she did so. I saw twenty or thirty beautiful small paintings; then she said to me, "I can't do it." I never saw them again.*

But I do remember during those hours when we had no company, we were talking over and over and over again about the use of color and language and how they interchanged, but ultimately, Joan admitted she just couldn't produce what she felt would be equal to his level.

It should be noted that Mitchell would not have "painted" images to illustrate Beckett's work, as paintings cannot be reproduced by printing. Mitchell did collaborate with several poets, but these collaborations for publication were prints (lithographs, screen prints, etchings). Moreover, in the archives of the Joan Mitchell Foundation in New York, there is a typescript of Embers *that has been cut and annotated. Whether a group of drawings may be related to that portfolio is under investigation, but remains purely speculative at this time.*

With regard to Stirrings Still, *Beckett's English publisher, John Calder, proposed to Mitchell that she create six lithographs and, conceivably, "some additional smaller illustrations to go with the text" (letter of December 15, 1987). This illustrated volume never appeared either. Originally titled "Fragments," it was to be a 48 page limited edition. One can only wonder why the offer was extended to Francis Bacon (in a letter dated March 3, 1988) and then, when Bacon turned it down, to Louis le Brocquy. What caused Mitchell to withdraw from this project as she had from the illustrated* Embers? *Perhaps, as Dirk Van Hulle has suggested based on the Calder correspondence, it was the sense of urgency arising from the difficult financial situation of both Rosset and Calder who were putting out the edition together and the reality of Beckett's advancing age given that he was to sign all the copies. Perhaps, as with* Embers *(according to Rosset), Mitchell felt she somehow wasn't "equal to [Beckett's] level." Whatever the reason, it is indeed curious that she never saw through to completion the plan for either* Embers *or* Stirrings Still.

—ED.

JOHN CALDER (Publishers) LTD
18 Brewer Street London W1R 4AS
Telephone 01-734 3786/7 Cables·Bookdom London

Joan Mitchell
12 Avenue Claude Monet
Veteuil
FRANCE

15th December 1987

Dear Joan

First of all thank you again for a wonderful lunch and a memorable day. I think
we have after all this time got to know each other very much better.

I will not repeat everything I told you on the telephone, but I now see an
attractive 48 page limited edition, which I think we will bind in calf and
heavy cloth. and put in a cloth slip case. I think that six lithographs
would be perfect and if you wish to do some additional smaller illustrations
to go with the text that would work out within the 48 page frame work. If
you wish to do one or two more lithos we would then add sub-titles and bring
it up to probably 60 pages. The enclosed is the design of the book as I see
it at present, with 12 lines to the page but without separate half titles
between each of the three sections. If you felt like doing an additional,
larger litho this could be on a seperate sheet across two pages and inserted
between page 24 and 25. It would be a seperate centrefold.

The question remains as to whether the book should be bound or left as loose
pages, but we can think about this later.

I shall be in New York in a weeks time and will talk to Ben Sthiff, who does
very fine additions for a specialist book club, about the typography. I will
get this set, probably in Febuary or March. If then you wish to go to Lille
or work in Paris, I can be around in either place if that would be any help.

The reasons for not letting this delay any longer are basically three. The
most serious is perhaps that Sam is not immortal and it is essential that he
signs. the copies; there is also a considerable need of money on the part of
both Barney and myself which this will do much to relieve, and there is no
doubt that sooner or later some academic is going to put these texts into some
other publication without permission in order to steal a march and it is
essential that ours should be the first edition.

Lovely seeing you again.

Yours

Director: JOHN CALDER
Registered Office: Northway House, High Road, London N20 9LP   Registration 1227 392
Whilst every care is taken of MSS in our charge, we accept no responsibility for their accidental loss or damage

Barney and
Samuel
Beckett at
Joan Mitchell
show in Paris

 **riverrun press**, inc.

Suite ~~8th Avenue, New York, 10010~~
Te~~lephone 212-228-0390~~
Suite 807, 1170 Broadway, New York, N.Y. 100~~~
Telephone: 212-889-6850

December 23, 1987

Ms. Joan Mitchell
12 Av. Claude Monet
95510 Vetheuil
FRANCE

Dear Joan:

Enclosed specifications for STIRRINGS STILL, but size must
ultimately be up to you. I will phone the first week of
February.

Happy New Year.

Yours,

John Calder

JC:cm
Encl.

Affiliated company: John Calder (Publishers) Ltd, 18 Brewer Street, London WIR 4AS

Dear Mr. Beckett

STIRRINGS STILL

De Luxe Edition

Samuel Beckett	Three Fragments (inedit)
Joan Mitchell	Six Original Lithographs

Page 1	Half title
2-3	blank
4	First Litho
5	Title page
6	Copyright page
7	blank
8	Second litho
9	Fragment 1 begins
9-14	Text (12 lines for page)
15	blank
16	Third Litho
17-20	Text continues
21	blank
22	Fourth Litho
23-28	Fragment 2 begins
29	blank
30	Fifth Litho
31-36	Text continues
37	blank
38	Sixth Litho
39-43	Fragment 3
44	Samuel Beckett. Photo with Biography.
45	Joan Mitchell. Photo with Biography.
46	blank
47	Specification of book. Number. Two signatures.
48	blank

Affix size 303 x 225 mm

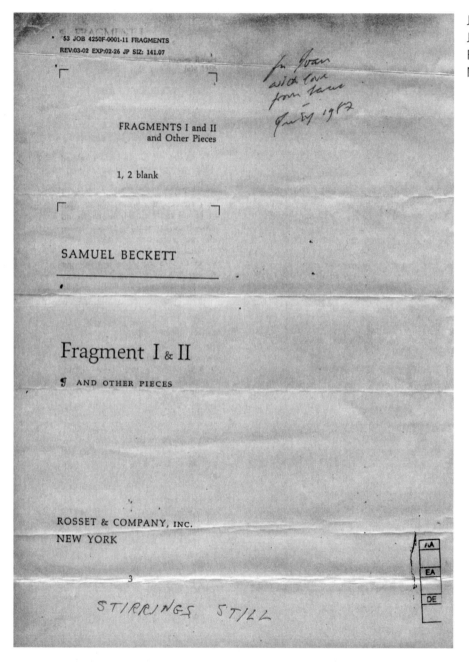

FRAGMENT

For Barney Rosset
July 1986

One night as he sat at his table head on hands he saw himself rise and go.
One night or day. For when his own light went out he was not left in the dark.
Light of a kind came then from the one high window. Under it still the stool
on which till he could or would no more he used to mount to see the sky. Why
he did not crane out to see what lay beneath was perhaps because the window was
not made to open or because he could or would not open it. Perhaps he knew only
too well what lay beneath and did not wish to see it again. So he would simply
stand there high above the earth and see through the clouded pane the cloudless
sky. Its faint unchanging light unlike any light he could remember from the days
and nights when day followed hard on night and night on day. This outer light
then when his own went out became his only light till it in its turn went out and
left him in the dark. Till it in its turn went out.

One night or day then as he sat at his table head on hands he saw himself rise
and go. First rise and stand clinging to the table. Then sit again. Then rise
again and stand clinging to the table again. Then go. Start to go. On unseen feet
start to go. So slow that only change of place to show he went. As when he disappeared
only to reappear later at another place. Then disappeared again only to reappear
again/at another place again. So again and again disappeared again only to reappear
again later at another place again. Another place in the place where he sat at his
table head on hands. The same place and table as when Darly/died and left him. As
when others too in their turn before and since. As when others would too in their
turn and leave him till he too in his turn. Head on hands half hoping when he disappeared again that he would not reappear again and half fearing that he would not.
Or merely wondering. Or merely waiting. Waiting to see if he would or would not.
Leave him or not alone again waiting for nothing again.

later /

for example /

Seen always from behind whithersoever he went. Same hat and coat as of old when he
walked the roads. The back roads. Now as one in a strange place seeking the way out.
In the dark. In a strange place blindly in the dark of night or day seeking the way
out. A way out. To the roads. The back roads.

A clock afar struck the hours and half-hours. The same as when among others Darly
once died and left him. Strokes now clear as if carried by a wind now faint on the
still air. Cries afar now faint now clear. Head on hands half hoping when the hour
struck that the half-hour would not and half fearing that it would not. Similarly
when the half-hour struck. Similarly when the cries a moment ceased. Or merely
wondering. Or merely waiting. Waiting to hear.

There had been a time he would sometimes lift his head enough to see his hands.
What of them was to be seen. One laid on the table and the other on the one. At rest
after all they did. Lift his past head a moment to see his past hands. Then lay it
back on them to rest it too. After all it did.

The same place as when left day after day for the roads. The back roads. Returned
to night after night. Paced from wall to wall in the dark. The then fleeting dark of
night. Now as if strange to him seen to rise and go. Disappear and reappear at another
place. Disappear again and reappear again at another place again. Or at the same.
Nothing to show not the same. No wall toward which or from. No table back toward which
or further from. In the same place as when paced from wall to wall all places as the
same. Or in another. Nothing to show not another. Where never. Rise and go in the same
place as ever. Disappear and reappear in another where never. Nothing to show
not another where never. Nothing but the strokes. The cries. The same as ever.

Till so many strokes and cries since he was last seen that perhaps he would not be seen again. Then so many cries since the strokes were last heard that perhaps they would not be heard again. Then such silence since the cries were last heard that perhaps even they would not be heard again. Perhaps thus the end. Unless no more than a mere lull. Then all as before. The strokes and cries as before and he as before now there now gone now there again now gone again. Then the lull again. Then all as before again. So again and again. And patience till the one true end to time and grief and self and second self his own.

Samuel Beckett

STIRRINGS STILL

Harvard Book Review, Winter/Spring 1989
Robert Scanlan

Stirrings Still
Samuel Beckett, illustrated by Louis le Brocquy. Blue Moon
Books, $1,500 (Collector's Edition) ISBN 0714541427

On April 13, 1989, Samuel Beckett's eighty-third birthday, a
limited edition of a new prose work, *Stirrings Still*, was published
in America. The slim text is dedicated to Beckett's American
publisher, Barney Rosset, and this $1,500 collector's edition,
complete with original brush drawings by Louis le Brocquy and
the signatures of both author and illustrator, is launching a new
imprint, Blue Moon Books, New York. A more affordable trade
edition will be issued when the collector's edition of 226 runs
out.

Beckett had not expected to publish any more now that he
has reached his eighth decade. He had written to friends that "the
writing is over" and stated candidly in conversation that there
would be no more. But a powerful fragment of prose was sent
to his publishers in 1986, and it proved to be the first of the
three parts which would eventually be *Stirrings Still*. The new
work is written in the lean, spare, lapped-rhythm prose which
is Beckett's latest style, both in prose and in dramatic texts. It
carefully records a consciousness reporting on itself, on its perceptions of a Self (perhaps itself, perhaps a fictional second self,
the perennial unsolved, insoluble problem of Beckett's prose).

The text builds up in haunting, ghost-ridden rhythms an

image of a figure at first found leaning wearily over a table, seeking rest with its head on its hands, hearing the striking of a clock and, at recurring intervals, indeterminate cries. A space "indoors" which is the figure's habitual space is highly reminiscent of the setting of *Endgame*, written over thirty years ago. It has obvious affinities too with the vision recorded in the 1983 video composition Nacht und Träume. In parts 2 and 3, an outdoor setting alternates with the more familiar interior, and clearly wearies and confuses the perceiver, who cannot evade a wish for the end of it all, even as he half-guesses the end has come.

A consciousness wondering to itself what its true condition might be is familiar territory for Beckett's prose, but this latest text is full of a sense of farewell, puzzled by a persistent inability to tell what is going on, even on this last verge, haunted by a felt proximity to what Hamlet, brooding on being and not being, called "that bourne from which no traveler returns." Here is Beckett's quiet allusion to the undiscovered country:

> … he could recall no field of grass from even the very heart of which no limit of any kind was to be discovered but always in some quarter or another some end in sight such as a fence or other manner of bourne from which to return.

The brooding voice generating *Stirrings Still* finds its focal figure (itself but not itself) in a limitless field of bleached white grass, not knowing whether this is the "end" or not, unable to puzzle it out, tormented by the fact that the puzzling goes on. The grimly punning title can be found buried in a passage from *Company*, an earlier text published in 1980.

... the mind closes as it were. As the window might close of a dark empty room. The single window giving on outer dark . Then nothing more. No. Unhappily no. Pangs of faint light and stirrings still. Unformuable gropings of the mind. Unstillable.

The internal action of this voice is our surest guide through *Stirrings Still*. There is a stilled dignity and a clarity of diction which is far more accessible than the impacted and abrupt style of *Worstward Ho*, which appeared in 1983. Battered by recurring cycles of disappearance and reappearance, by the endless strokes of a clock marking the hours and half hours, and by unceasing recurrence of distant cries, the seat of this consciousness sees itself rise and go, acting out a final retreat. Patience, however, is the only available recourse against time, which cannot be made to cease. *Stirrings Still* is the last or just the latest testimony of Beckett's creative vitality, his unmatched power of endurance still masquerading as nothing at all.

Dear Harold,

       As I write this I am sitting in flight 8-TWA en route
to Paris from New York to visit Sam-and also looking at a
handsome photo of you-or handsome you photographed.

       Anyway Mel Gussow's article concerning you is under
this yellow paper N.Y. Times Dec. 6, 1988. I am on my way
to see Sam-not at the Olde English Pub but at some sort of
nursing home. -And along the way I stumbled on you-and the
"politicization of Harold Pinter-which is making itself
increasingly evident in his art" (excuse handwriting, but the
seat belt sign is for good reason).

       I am sorry that the above noted Pinter trend has led
to his "growing dismay over world affairs." That is indeed
a predicament. Which is "minimalist" now-the art or the
politicization or both. If I sound slightly bitter perhaps
it is because I am. I guess that one is dropped once the
Weidenfelds and Gettys have dropped off one's boat-or one has
been dropped off their plane.

       Anyway, thanks much for the minimalist support.
But we do still have some mutual interests. I have been to
Nicaragua several times in the past few years-my son Peter
coedited two fine volumes on that country, besides becoming a
resident of it himself-he is now in Costa Rica where I will
shortly spend my second Christmas with him. Won't run into
George or Ann in those climes.

       It was somewhat fitting that you referred to Stoppard-
his political enthusiasm analogous to your penchant for
acting-Does your fellow cricketeer, Uncle Tom, view your June
20th movement with "scorn and derision" as does the press-
here we chuckle followed by Pinteresque silence. That's the
real thing, isn't it?

       Am enclosing-if this missile makes it to Paris-my
citation from PEN. Sent a copy to George but somehow forgot
you-never too late to make amends. He who amends well stays
suitable.

       Harold, I am pleased to have known you (the you you).

       May your politicization flourish. May you shine from
the strokes of 3 hundred brushes-may we meet again, perhaps
in the midst of an ever burgeoning June 20th movement-may you
do the scenario for it later-may Warren Beatty play you- etc.
or you play him.

       So, adding "a dash of minimalist-jazz-New Age spice

(see N.Y. Times below Pinter 12/6/88)" Keep the ball in play.
Love,
Barney

P.S.   2 Plays

(1) [illustration]   (2) [illustration]
SHORT   SHORTER
AND   AND
BRUTAL   EVEN
                              MORE BRUTAL

Ah, not even three hundred brushes could make me a Pinter.
POLITICIZATION
Please write that 100 times on the blackboard.

Q. What did one Turkish dissident say to another Turk.
A. We have seen Pinter and now they will have us for
Thanksgiving (très American, n'est-ce pas) - I'm
hallucinating.
Q He who is more brutal will be what?
A Shorter.
Q Shorter than what
A More brutal
Q Is that a tall story
A No, it's a short story
Q But is it a play
A No, it is a play
Q Will you play with me
A No
              [There is a Pinteresque silence]

P.P.S.
        Now Sunday in Dec—and I am back on the plane headed
for New York—the Sunday Times (London) says "Britain Buys
America. About time. It will put us into the common market
in 1992 - 500 years to the day. But I thought that Japan had
already made us part of East Asia.
        Anyway I saw Sam and seemed better than one might have
hoped for.
        He told me that Barbara Bray had informed him that

you had seen the New York Godot and liked it—but that you
doubted that Sam would feel likewise. I am not so sure of
that—No GODOT can be all things to all people, but any given
one—maybe this one especially could give a great deal of
pleasure—and even insight—to many, including Sam. Why don't
you tell him directly what you felt. I think that that would
please him,

                    Again, my best,

                    Barney

Beckett's nursing home in Paris. Photo by Barney Rosset

BLUE MOON BOOKS INC.
61 Fourth Avenue,
New York, NY 10003
Phone (212) 5056680, Fax (212) 6731039
Nov. 25, 1989

Dear Sam,

Somehow changing address makes it more difficult to communicate and we have both changed rooms since last I wrote. Both changes for the better.

I am back to just about where I started from—9th St. in Greenwich Village—and it feels much better. But not easier.

Constantly word comes drifting through about you from John C. or Jon J. or Tom B. [John Calder, Jon Jonson, Tom Bishop] or others and it makes me feel as though I am in contact with you. Not easy, but nevertheless.

And now I think that I have an adequate reason to go to Paris. It is long enough that I have not seen you and that is the reason.

So, to be Beckett precise, Thursday, Dec. 7th, you name the time, and then, Friday, Saturday, when or if you wish. I plan to return here on Sunday, the tenth. I will actually get to Paris on the 6th, hopefully staying at the Crystal Hotel on rue St. Benoit, but I will cable you as soon as I know for sure.

I do hope to see you and look forward to it very much indeed.

Love Barney

P.S. Enclosed is another 5 Gs.

P.S. again

Have you noticed the emergence of Vaclav Havel from his Czech cocoon? It all seems quite wonderful. Very strangely I stumbled on a copy of the LORD JOHN (?) limited edition of *Catastrophe* (copyright Samuel Beckett 1983) and this copy signed and with good wishes from you to Havel is imprinted as being Havel's copy. Somehow I ended up with it, probably because I did not know how to get it to him (in jail ?). I will bring it with me and, if you feel like it, you could add another note and we could send it on to Prague.

Dear Mr. Beckett

Samuel Beckett

CATASTROPHE

FOR VÁCLAV HAVEL

DIRECTOR (D)

HIS FEMALE ASSISTANT (A)

PROTAGONIST (P)

LUKE, IN CHARGE OF THE LIGHTING, OFFSTAGE (L)

Rehearsal. Final touches to the last scene. Bare stage. A and L have just set the lighting. D has just arrived.

D in an armchair downstage audience left. Fur coat. Fur toque to match. Age and physique unimportant.

A standing beside him. White coverall. Bare head. Pencil on ear. Age and physique unimportant.

P midstage standing on a black block 18″ high. Black wide-brimmed hat. Black dressing gown to ankles. Barefoot. Head bowed. Hands in pockets. Age and physique unimportant.

D and A contemplate P.

Long pause.

A (*finally*): Like the look of him?
D: So-so. (*Pause.*) Why the plinth?
A: To let the stalls see the feet.
(*Pause.*)
D: Why the hat?
A: To help hide the face.
(*Pause.*)
D: Why the gown?
A: To have him all black.
(*Pause.*)
D: What has he on underneath? (*A moves toward P.*) Say it.
(*A halts.*)

A: His night attire.
D: Color?
A: Ash.
(*D takes out a cigar.*)
D: Light.
(*A returns, lights the cigar, stands still. D smokes.*)
D: How's the skull?
A: You've seen it.
D: I forget. (*A moves toward P.*) Say it.
(*A halts.*)
A: Molting. A few tufts.
D: Color?
A: Ash.
(*Pause.*)
D: Why hands in pockets?
A: To help have him all black.
D: They mustn't.
A: I make a note. (*She takes out a pad, takes pencil, notes.*) Hands exposed. (*She puts back pad and pencil.*)
D: How are they?
(*A at a loss.*)
D (*irritably*): The hands, how are the hands?
A: You've seen them.
D: I forget.
A: Crippled. Fibrous degeneration.
D: Clawlike?
A: If you like.
D: Two claws?
A: Unless he clench his fists.
D: He mustn't.
A: I make a note. (*She takes out pad, takes pencil, notes.*) Hands limp. (*She puts back pad and pencil.*)
D: Light.
(*A returns, relights the cigar, stands still. D smokes.*)
D: Good. Now let's have a look.
(*A at a loss.*)
D (*irritably*): Get going. Lose that gown. (*He consults his chronometer.*) Step on it. I have a caucus.
(*A goes to P, takes off the gown. P submits, inert. A steps back, the gown over her arm. P in old gray pajamas, head bowed, fists clenched. Pause.*)
A: Like him better without? (*Pause.*) He's shivering.
D: Not all that. Hat.
(*A advances, takes off hat, steps back, hat in hand. Pause.*)
A: Like that cranium?
D: Needs whitening.
A: I make a note. (*She drops hat and gown, takes out pad, takes pencil, notes.*) Whiten cranium. (*She puts back pad and pencil.*)
D: The hands.
(*A at a loss.*)
D (*irritably*): The fists. Get going.
(*A advances, unclenches fists, steps back.*)
D: And whiten.
A: I make a note. (*She takes out pad, takes pencil, notes.*) Whiten hands. (*She puts back pad and pencil. They contemplate P.*)
D (*finally*): Something wrong. (*Distraught*) What is it?
A (*timidly*): What if we were to…were to… join them?
D: No harm trying. (*A advances, joins the hands, steps back.*) Higher. (*A advances, raises waist-high the joined hands, steps back.*) A touch more. (*A advances, raises breast-high the joined hands.*) Stop! (*A steps back.*) Better. It's coming. Light.
(*A returns, relights the cigar, stands still. D smokes.*)
A: He's shivering.
D: Bless his heart.
(*Pause.*)
A (*timidly*): What about a little…a little…gag?
D: For God's sake! This craze for explicitation! Every *i* dotted to death! Little gag! For God's sake!

A: Sure he won't utter?
D: Not a squeak. (*He consults his chronometer.*) Just time. I'll go and see how it looks from the house.
(*Exit D, not to appear again. A subsides in the armchair, springs to her feet no sooner seated, takes out a rag, wipes vigorously back and seat of chair, discards rag, sits again. Pause.*)
D (*off, plaintive*): I can't see the toes. (*Irritably*) I'm sitting in the front row of the stalls and can't see the toes.
A (*rising*): I make a note. (*She takes out pad, takes pencil, notes.*) Raise pedestal.
D: There's a trace of face.
A: I make a note. (*She takes out pad, takes pencil, makes to note.*)
D: Down the head.
(*A at a loss.*)
D (*Irritably*): Get going. Down his head. (*A puts back pad and pencil, goes to P, bows his head further, steps back.*) A shade more. (*A advances, bows the head further.*) Stop! (*A steps back.*) Fine. It's coming. (*Pause.*) Could do with more nudity.
A: I make a note. (*She takes out pad, makes to take pencil.*)
D: Get going! Get going! (*A puts back the pad, goes to P, stands irresolute.*) Bare the neck. (*A undoes top buttons, parts the flaps, steps back.*) The legs. The shins. (*A advances, rolls up to below knee one trouser leg, steps back.*) The other. (*Same for other leg, steps back.*) Higher. The knees. (*A advances, rolls up to above knees both trouser legs, steps back.*) And whiten.
A: I make a note. (*She takes out pad, takes pencil, notes.*) Whiten all flesh.
D: It's coming. Is Luke around?
A (*calling*): Luke! (*Pause. Louder.*) Luke!
L (*off, distant*): I hear you. (*Pause. Nearer.*) What's the trouble now?
A: Luke's around.
D: Black out stage.
L: What?
(*A transmits in technical terms. Fadeout of general light. Light on P alone. A in shadow.*)
D: Just the head.
L: What?
(*A transmits in technical terms. Fadeout of light on P's body. Light on head alone. Long pause.*)
D: Lovely.
(*Pause.*)
A (*timidly*): What if he were to…were to… raise his head…an instant…show his face… just an instant?
D: For God's sake! What next? Raise his head! Where do you think we are? In Patagonia? Raise his head! For God's sake! (*Pause.*) Good. There's our catastrophe. In the bag. Once more and I'm off.
A (*to L*): Once more and he's off.
(*Fadeup of light on P's body. Pause. Fadeup of general light.*)
D: Stop! (*Pause.*) Now…let 'em have it. (*Fadeout of general light. Pause. Fadeout of light on body. Light on head alone. Long pause.*) Terrific! He'll have them on their feet. I can hear it from here.
(*Pause. Distant storm of applause. P raises his head, fixes the audience. The applause falters, dies.*)

Long pause.

Fadeout of light on face.)

Samuel Beckett [signature]

SAMUEL BECKETT

PRESENTATION COPY

Barney Rosset interview with Patsy Southgate

ROSSET: I don't remember Beckett being... I never even heard him being very strong about the Irish-England thing. But, on the other hand, he certainly was... his propensity would have been to be what we would certainly call liberal. Liberal left. Left centrist. But more interested, I think, in people than in political parties as such. As Havel said ... the time has come for political parties—to wither away—to be like Lenin, that individuals are more important. What you are and what you do is more important than allowing a political party to be important, because a political party enables people to be important without you knowing who they are.

SOUTHGATE: Yes. Yes.

ROSSET: But if you remain yourself, that's better. And I think that's Beckett. He sympathized with Sean O'Casey, as a person. I don't even think they were friends. And probably they couldn't have been friends because Casey had very strong political positions, like Brecht let's say. Beckett was not like that at all but that doesn't mean that he couldn't admire—and he did, 'cause I heard him admire Casey and thereby—like O'Casey's daughter, Shivaun. But there—he would put that on a personal liking, not on a particularly specific political thing. But his play *Catastrophe*...

SOUTHGATE: This is what I was going to ask you about.

ROSSET: Yes. Yes. No, that play is the only—there are only two things that I know of Beckett that are specifically political. And Lindon and Paris think of them as only one, but I, maybe because the other was done for television, I'm not sure Lindon ever looked at television—*Catastrophe* is a play written for

Havel; inspired directly by him, it says so. It was put on in 1983 at Avignon as specifically with a political connotation. It's about a dissident who refuses to be … whatever. A short, 15-minute play, most of that dialogue. Of course it doesn't name any political parties, but it gives a very strong idea. If he said it's for Havel, who's in Czechoslovakia, in prison, you could, without too much effort, say that he disapproved of the government of Czechoslovakia … And then there is a TV … well, it was also put on the stage and TV, I forgot where. A very short thing, which is also about prison. I think it was a direct inspiration for a recent play of Harold Pinter.

SOUTHGATE: Which one?

ROSSET: It also deals with torture, political. So there was that political undertone there, but I know that never came to the surface like it did in *Catastrophe,* which was hardly the major work of Beckett's life.

SOUTHGATE: It's a wonderful work.

ROSSET: It's a wonderful short thing, which he did, you know, for a purpose. It's mentioned in the *Village Voice* this week. This woman went to Czechoslovakia and in Havel's office said there were two interesting things. One of them was this thing.

SOUTHGATE: Which?

ROSSET: *Catastrophe.* He had it there, but Garbus brought it.

SOUTHGATE: In manuscript form?

ROSSET: Yes. Yeah, I had this limited edition I discovered here…

ROSSET: A few weeks ago, well, before Beckett died…

SOUTHGATE: Let me interrupt you a minute. You never got around to telling the story about Ann Getty, so let's try and work that in.

ROSSET: So, I discovered out here in East Hampton, rummaging through some old papers, a rolled up scroll, you might say, about 20 inches by 24. And it was one copy of a limited edition of *Catastrophe* published by Lord John Press. I don't know who they are. Must be somebody we gave permission to do this little one page, but big one page, beautifully printed, embossed, whatever, limited edition of *Catastrophe*—it says—and then I unrolled this particular copy and up at the top it said, "For Vaclav Havel, *Catastrophe*" and then down below signed, personally signed by Beckett, best wishes or something. And then, below, "Samuel Beckett," and his name was imprinted, and below that is imprinted "this is Vaclav Havel's copy." Here I'd been sitting with it for six years and he's about to become the president of Czechoslovakia…

SOUTHGATE: Do you know how you happened to get it?

ROSSET: No. I had three of them. One was for Havel and the other two say "Presentation Copy." I don't know what that means. All three, though, signed by Beckett. So I thought, you know, what an interesting thing if we could take this to Beckett now, right now, and Havel is out of prison, he's about to come to power, then maybe Beckett would have something more to say. And then it would be great fun to take it to Havel. And that would be an event, a happening, a serendipity, whatever. I called Fred Jordan at Grove Press and said, "Look, I've got an idea for Ann Getty. It seems to me she bought Grove Press to get good publicity for herself and create a nice image and perhaps some real sort of excitement in her life. Why don't I give this to her, or you give it to her, and let her take it to Havel?" Also, Grove Press is Havel's publisher. I had published Havel when I was at Grove and Fred had carried on. There were three books of his. So, you know, what a wonderful juxtaposition and for Grove Press to be the proud publisher of both Beckett and Havel.

SOUTHGATE: Yes.

ROSSET: She wasn't interested. I said, "And she has an airplane." I said, "Fred, you know, it's just in case, and don't pin it on me or anything, but just in case she likes the idea and is going to do it you could ask her if she could take us with her." A 737, I mean, she flies to Europe.

SOUTHGATE: She has a 737?

ROSSET: Yes. That fell flat. So I told this to an attorney friend of mine, Martin Garbus, who had represented Sakharov and various other dissident writers and scientists and he thought it was a great idea and he said. "I'll go to Prague." And I said, "Well, I have to go to Paris. I'm going to go to see Beckett. Of course, by the time I got to Paris Beckett was in a coma so I was unable to do anything."

SOUTHGATE: This was late November?

ROSSET: In December. And I didn't feel like going to Prague. Marty called me from Prague. I got a hold of Havel's fax number and I knew I'd never get him on the phone, too busy. So I did fax a letter and it did get to him and he said, "yes, do come." So Marty went and he met Havel and he said it was one of the most exciting times of his life. And he stayed there for quite a while and he's been asked to help them write a new constitution of Czechoslovakia, and of Hungary and of East Germany, and he stayed for ten days and he kept saying, "Are you sure you don't want to come?" I just, I had no heart for it and I didn't. But this week, in the *The Voice*, this woman says this interesting thing was in Havel's office there, in this crazy, jumbled-up place, and I got my copy back, signed by Havel, saying that he was deeply touched by this...

SOUTHGATE: You got yours back?

ROSSET: Yes, I got mine back and I take it Marty has the third.

BLUE MOON

BLUE MOON BOOKS INC.

61 Fourth Avenue, New York, NY 10003, Phone (212) 505-6880

212
FAX-979-0809

East Hampton, Long Island
New York
December 8, 1989
PHONE AND FAX 516-324-5452

Dear Vaclav Havel,

It has been with an incredible sense of joy and revelation
that I and my friends have been "observers" of the unraveling
and rebinding of Czechoslovakia. At this moment (7:00 P.M.)
New York time I am watching Tom Brokaw on NBC showing Prague
tonight. Who knows what will have happened by the time this
letter is FAXED to you,

And in the midst of this, two weekends ago, I stumbled upon a
rolled up, lovely, one page, a very large page, almost a
"poster" of a limited edition of Samuel Beckett's play
CATASTROPHE, performed first in Avignon, then in New York,
published in New York by Grove Press, the firm I founded, and
all in 1983. But in addition to the foregoing, a Lord John Press
(which I shamefaceedly cannot identify right now, but I most
certainly will) did the limited edition, and as in the Grove
edition, it states that CATASTROPHE is "For Vaclav Havel".
The particular copy which I have is further personally
inscribed to you by Samuel Beckett himself. As if that were not
enough, beneath Beckett's name is inscribed "Vaclav Havel's copy."
Since 1983, I have been the guardian, albeit the unwitting one,
of your copy of what is perhaps Beckett's only political drama
written for the stage. Now it is time that it gets delivered
to you.

As courier, and a most fortunate one for us indeed, Martin Garbus
has volunteered for the job. I personally feel extremely happy
that he will make this journey because there can be no doubt
that Marty, who has represented and fought for the rights of such
people as André Sacharov, Anatoli Scharansky and Breyten
Bretenbach, is one of the leading Human Rights lawyers in the
world today. He has already spoken to Ivan Klima and Herb Gardner,
with whose blessings he goes. Furthermore, he goes on behalf of

P.E.N., and also, he hopes to write for the New York Times,
as he has done frequently in the recent past, plus a number of
other periodicals.

It is so seldom that we can feel ourselves witnesses to such a
rare and felicitous conjunction of the planets.

As a further and most favorable portent, it so happens that I
will be making a long planned visit to Paris next week to see my
old and most loved friend, Samuel Beckett, I will tell him about
all of the foregoing, and who knows, he might have a postscript
for you.

As your *one time* publisher at Grove, and as a great admirer of what you
and your fellow Czechs are accomplishing and will accomplish,
I take words out of Beckett's mouth and wish you "God Speed".

                    In peoplehood and solidarity,

                    Barney Rosset

My postscript: In the event you could withstand two "couriers"
and wish me to accompany Martin Garbus to Prague, I would be more
than willing to do so. Just send me the word. I'm leaving for
Paris Tuesday, December 12th. After that my office will be able
to reach me. Until then my office number and FAX number are
given above. Tomorrow, December 9 and Sunday (daytime) I can be
reached by phone or FAX - 516-324-5452.

Following is a brief description of a must appreciated award which
was given to me by P.E.N.

Self-typed by a typewriter which is having a hard time understanding
that the Stalinist Era is finally drawing expixture to a happy
and timely end.

PEN

American Center
Ninth Publisher Citation
to

Barney Rosset

for distinctive and continuous service to international letters, to the freedom and dignity of writers, and to the free transmission of the printed word across the barriers of poverty, ignorance, censorship and repression.

Conferred November 16, 1988
in New York City

Susan Sontag, President
PEN American Center

BECKETT *gave Rosset* Eleutheria *in 1986. Not wanting to translate it for publication, he wrote the letter below. Reminded many years later of the play, Rosset set out to publish* Eleutheria *but was denied permission to do so by Jérôme Lindon, Executor of the Beckett Estate and Beckett's French publisher (at Les Editions de Minuit). Lindon refused to grant permission on the grounds that Beckett had not wanted it published. In September 1994, Rosset organized a reading of the work (whose title means "freedom" in Greek) at his home in New York City, a reading with members of Actors Equity participating pro bono. The event provoked considerable attention in the press. Mel Gussow had this to say in the* New York Times:

> *Samuel Beckett's first full length play, "Eleutheria," previously unperformed, received its first staged reading yesterday afternoon at the home of Barney Rosset, a friend and publisher of the author. The play was read by a group of 13 actors under the direction of Peter Craze. In the audience were about 100 invited guests, including actors and directors as well as Beckett scholars.*
>
> *The unauthorized reading, initiated by Mr. Rosset, was to take place at the New York Theater Workshop, but because of legal complications resulting from the objection of the playwright's estate, the event was moved to a studio space in Mr. Rosset's apartment on Fourth Avenue in the East Village. Although this made it a quasi private affair, there*

was still some nervousness about legal questions, and a New York Times *photographer was not allowed to take pictures of the event.*

Despite the vast differences in opinion about the controversy, one thing was certain: The audience at the approximately three-and-a-half hour reading relished the script-in-hand performance. Beckett scholars hotly debated the issue and were clearly divided. There were those who felt the work—which contains so much of what was to come (both in Beckett's theatre and his fiction) and hence provides valuable insight into the evolution of the oeuvre—should be made available. And there were those who felt that respecting the playwright's wishes should be the only consideration. Indeed, as Gussow further noted,

> *Beginning in the late 1940's, Beckett's wife, Suzanne Deschevaux Dumesnil, took both "Eleutheria" and "Godot" to various Parisian directors and producers, including Roger Blin. Blin read both and chose "Godot" because it seemed less difficult to stage and also because he was "very impressed by the quality." "Godot" transformed Beckett's life and became the seminal play in 20th century experimental theatre.*

> *As Beckett followed "Godot" with "Endgame" and other plays, "Eleutheria" was put aside. On the cover*

of the original, manuscript, which is in the Beckett collection at the University of Texas, the author wrote, "Prior to Godot. 1947. Unpublished. Jettisoned." As late as March 1969, he wrote on a photocopy of the text, "Never edition of any kind if I can help it." (Sept. 27, 1994)

Subsequently, Lindon, noting that Beckett would not want the acrimonious situation between his two publishers to escalate even more and mindful that Rosset intended to publish the play and give it away at no cost, consented. But he did so with the proviso that Lindon (Minuit) would publish it first in French and then Rosset could publish it in English. The play appeared in a translation by Michael Brodsky in 1995, put out by Foxrock, Inc., the press Rosset founded with John Oakes and Dan Simon. Though no permission has ever been granted for the play to be performed, four staged readings took place—one shortly before the book's publication (as noted above) and three after, the first directed by Brian Tom O'Connor at the National Arts Club in New York, the second directed by Robert McNamara at the Scena Theater in Washington, D.C., and the third at the Classic Stage Company, also in New York, directed by Jonathan Rosenberg. In 2005, an Iranian translation of Eleutheria by Vahid Rahbani was performed in Tehran directed by Rahbani and Mohammadreza Jouze.

—ED.

Paris

25-6-86

Dear Barney,

Thanks for yours of 18th.

I had completely forgotten <u>Eleutheria.</u> I
have now read it again. With loathing. I cannot
translate it. Let alone have it published.
Another rash promise. Made with intent to lighten
your burden. Now I have added to it. It goes to
my heart to break this bad news. But I must. I'll
try to try writing something worth having for
you. If only a few pages. I feel unforgivable. So
please forgive me.

Much love from guilt-ridden Sam

For God's sake no more photos. Apologies to Tom
Victor.

ELEUTHERIA

by Samuel Beckett

***directed by* Peter Craze**
assistant to Mr. Craze: **John Zeitler**

☙

CAST

Jack the Servant	Keith Benedict
Madame Piouk	Laila Robins
Madame Meck	Lola Pashalinski
Olga Skunk	Emily Bly
Henri Clap	Austin Pendleton
Dr. Piouk	Richmond Hoxie
Victor Krapp	Scott Sears
The Window Man	James A. Stephens
The Spectator	Doug Stender
Michelle	Steven Petrasca
Madame Carl	Lynn Cohen
Tchoutchi/The Prompter	Steven Petrasca
Joseph/Thomas	Doug Stender

Mel Gussow
interviewing Barney
before first reading.
Photo by Astrid Rosset

Waiting for press
and invited audience
in front of New York
Theater Workshop.
Photo by Astrid Rosset

From Beckett, a farce predating 'Godot'

By JERRY TALLMER

It must have been like this in speakeasy days. You went to a closed door, said "Joe sent me," and either they let you in or they didn't.

In this case it should have been "Sam sent me." Or maybe Sam didn't. If you believe publisher Barney Rosset, Samuel Beckett would have wanted this reading. If you believe Edward Beckett, nephew of the man who wrote "Waiting for Godot," "Endgame," and "Krapp's Last Tape," he wouldn't have.

So there it was, Monday afternoon, and one presented oneself — as per invitation — at the doorway of the New York Theater Workshop, 79 E. Fourth St. in Manhattan's East Village. But the doorway was locked and shuttered. A young man stood outside. "Go to 61 Fourth Ave.," he said — or whispered. A gray-haired co-conspirator beside him on the sidewalk amplified: "Blumen Books, Eighth Street, third floor."

Ten blocks and 10 minutes later, another obscure door. Not Eighth Street but Ninth Street. Not the third floor — the second. Not Blumen Books — Blue Moon Books. And there, on folding chairs, some 70 people, gathered together with 13 actors and one director and Rosset for the first reading before any audience in the history of the world of "Eleutheria," the play Beckett had written two years before "Waiting for Godot." The one Edward Beckett, in Paris, doesn't want performed or published.

Because of his threat to sue, the New York Theater Workshop had asked Rosset, at the last minute, for a protective indemnity of $30,000. Hence the last-minute switch from Fourth Street to Fourth Avenue. Rosset, for his part, says Sam Beckett gave him "Eleutheria" in 1986 (three years before the playwright died, in Paris, at 83) with carte blanche to publish or whatever. What's he been doing with the work since?

"Sitting on it. I tried to get it produced by Long Wharf" — the New Haven, Conn., theater company — "but they were scared off."

It has been 39 years since, in a The Village Voice article, I hailed the arrival of "Waiting for Godot" as "the dramatic event of my generation," one of those path-finding "masterpieces [that] come along very seldom more than once in a lifetime."

"Eleutheria," written in French, translated by Albert Bermel, and directed at Monday's reading by Peter Craze, is perhaps not on that order of greatness, but it is very rich, very dense, very much Beckett for all that, and quite a lot funnier than "Godot." Godot's humor goes deeper. A memorandum supplied at the reading informs us that Suzanne Dumesnil — Mrs. Beckett — presented avant-garde director Roger Blin in Paris with two scripts back around 1949 or 1950, one for "Eleutheria," with 17 characters and three acts, one for "Godot," with five actors, two acts. Blin chose "Godot."

The central character of "Eleutheria" is a mordant young man, Victor Krap, some years later to be transmuted — with an additional "p" — into the not-so-young solo protagonist of "Krapp's Last Tape." Victor (Scott Sears in the reading) has given up trying to be a writer, left the family home, taken up digs of "squalid inertia" in a miserable rooming house where he mostly lies in bed. He's also ditched his fiancee, Olga Skunk, a young woman with a "very banal" face (Emily Bly, whose face is perfectly lovely).

The other characters include Victor's father, Henri Clap, lusty with approaching death (Austin Pendleton); Victor's battleship of a mother (Trish Connelly); another battleship, Mme. Meck (Lola Pashalinski); and Victor's Aunt Marguerite (Laila Robins), who has come back from Italy with her new husband, Dr. Andre Piouk (Richmond Hoxie).

This Piouk is a primordial Malthusian technician who would ban reproduction, make euthanasia obligatory, muster abortion troops to drown the newborn. He has no specialty; he's interested in mankind. "Where does he malpractice?" asks Henri Clap. There is also a butler (Keith Benedict), who when chastised by his employer for his obsequiousness, replies: "I like to grovel a bit."

Later in the play — which took a good three hours with intermissions — we meet the Window Man (James A. Stephens), a stoical *deus ex machina* who recalls the Button Maker of Ibsen's "Peer Gynt"; the Window Man's young son and hapless assistant (Stephen Petrarca); a couple of musclemen (both Doug Stender); Victor's dreadful landlady (Lynn Cohen); a Chinese torturer (Petrarca again); a French maid (Edie Avoli); a kid in the audience who yells: "This farce is too drawn out!" (Petrarca); and a character, The Spectator (Stender), who also from the audience climbs up on stage to say things like: "Incidentally, who's responsible for this turkey? Beckkay? Samuel Beck-kay? ... Hardly matters. On to the crawl."

So what's it all about, Alfie? It's about "life, death, liberty, the whole mess ... What can we do? The language hasn't been created to express those things, so let's keep our mouths shut."

Unless you're Samuel Beckkay, and you can't. It is also perfectly clear that after "Eleutheria," Beckett decided, after a try at it, to leave theater of the absurd to his colleague Ionesco. During intermission I asked Austin Pendleton what "Eleutheria" meant. "I have no idea," he said with a sheepish grin. It means freedom.

Jerry Tallmer writes regularly about movies and theater for this newspaper.

Eleutheria
Publication
National Arts
Club -1995

The President and The Board of Governors
of The National Arts Club
cordially invite you to celebrate
the long-awaited publication of

Samuel Beckett's First Play

ELEUTHÉRIA
(Foxrock, Inc.)

Translated by Michael Brodsky

Tuesday, May 30, 1995
6:00 - 8:00 PM

RSVP: The NAC Secretary's Office
(212) 475-3424

*Members who wish to have dinner following the
presentation must make reservations with
the Dining Room: (212) 477-2389*

The National Arts Club
15 Gramercy Park South
(20th Street East of Park Ave. South)
New York City

August 22, 1994
Mr. Edward Albee
c/o George Lane
William Morris Agency
13 50 Ave. of the Americas
New York, NY 10019

Dear Edward:

Long ago and far away—

Anyway, it is somehow interesting and comforting to be writing to you. It proves that we are both still alive. You especially, because of the wonderful and deserved reception for THREE TALL WOMEN.

As to this letter, I was urged on by John Oakes, who with Dan Simon, is the publisher of Four Walls and Eight Windows. John was an editor at Grove when I was rather rudely dismissed and he had the temerity to quit and, later, form his own company. Together we have been wrestling with a Beckett project. Sam's reaction to my dismissal from Grove was to give me his early play, ELEUTHERIA. Later he asked me if I would accept something new which he would write for me and thereby excuse himself from translating ELEUTHERIA, a task which both of us had conveniently overlooked. The new work, STIRRINGS STILL, was written, published and ELEUTHERIA was slipped into a drawer—and left there until Stan Gontarski, a Beckettian and a scholar of note, reminded me—and thus made available the reason for this letter:

I do not want to push any unnecessary reading material upon you, unless you would like to have it—so it is more or less as follows: First there is the text of ELEUTHERIA […]. I have Sam's original French text.

Second, a number of letters between Jérôme Lindon, publisher of Editions de Minuit and myself. They show the total impasse, extremely sad to me, which I have reached with Jérôme concerning the publication of the play.

John and I would be most pleased if you wanted to look at the material, and I would send it to you immediately if you wished to have it.
If you do wish to have it, and upon seeing it, are favorably impressed and agree with us that it should be published—I can say that as of now we have not acquired any foreword or introduction by anyone beyond ourselves. But don't let that put a burden on you.

I would be delighted if you just read the text. And if you feel that even that would be too burdensome I will certainly understand. At least I have had a good reason to communicate with you after all these years.

Best wishes,
Barney Rosset

LINCOLN CENTER THEATER

150 W 65th St NYC 10023 212 362 7600

October 24, 1994

Dear Barney:

There is absolutely no doubt in my mind: **ELEUTHERIA**
ought to be and must be seen. I wish you every
success in arranging for its production and I
promise to be in the front of the line when tickets
go on sale.

All the best regards,

Bernard Gersten
Executive Producer

Mr. Barney Rossett
61 Fourth Avenue
New York, New York 10010

DIRECTORS:
CHARLOTTE MOORE
CIARAN O'REILLY

November 2, 1994

Barney Rosset
Blue Moon Books
61 Fourth Ave
New York, NY 10003

Dear Barney:

Eleutheria has been on our minds since we first read the play last Spring. After reading Bermel's new translation, it has become an obsession. If the Beckett Estate were to give permission , we would love to be the company that gives it its world premiere. This would be especially thrilling if it could coincide with the opening of our new home in the Spring.. I know that you are familiar with our work but I enclose a history of our company for your perusal.

Rereading the play last evening, I find it difficult to understand why this play has never been produced. It is a fascinating play in its own right, rich in its characterizations and wit. I believe it is an important play. If an unpublished, unproduced play of Shakespeare's was discovered I think the public would demand to see it. Samuel Beckett is in that league and we would be deeply honored to bring this play to life on stage.

Sooner or later a play of this merit will be produced. We fervently hope it will be sooner rather than later and we hope it will be under the auspices of the Irish Repertory Theatre.

Thank you for your consideration and we look forward to hearing from you at your earliest convenience.

With best wishes,

Ciaran O'Reilly   &   Charlotte Moore

Barney setting up
video camera to record
Eleutheria reading at
National Arts Club,
NYC.
Photo by Astrid Rosset

La Maison Francaise, Washington, DC
on the anniversary of Samuel Beckett's
92th Birthday

SCENA Theatre presents

ELEUTHÉRIA
A play in three acts
By Samuel Beckett

Translated from the French by Michael Brodsky
Directed by Robert McNamara

CAST:

M. Henri Krap . . . . Brian Hemmingsen
Mme. Henri Krap . . . . . Kerry Waters
Victor Krap, their son . . Kryztov Lindquist
Madame Meck, friend of the Kraps
. . . . . Nancy Robinette
Dr. Andre Piouk . . . . . . Hugh Nees
Madame Andre Piouk . . . Stephanie Madden
Mademoiselle Olga Skunk, Victor's fiancee
. . . . . Kathryn Kelley
A Glazier . . . . Carter Jahncke
Michel, his son . . . . . . Christopher Henley
An Audience member . . William Largess
Tchoutchi, a Chinese torturer
. . . . Hugo Medrano
Madame Karl, Victor's landlady
. . . . . Jewel Orem
Jacques, manservant in the Krap home
. . . . . Didier Rousselet
Marie, maidservant in the Krap home,
Jacques's fiancee . . . . Holly Twyford
Thomas, Madame Meck's chauffeur
. . . . . Jim Zidar
Joseph, a thug . . . . Fred Strother
Prompter . . . . Richard Mancini

Place: Paris
Time: Three successive winter afternoons

STAFF:

Director . . . . Robert McNamara
Assistant Director . . Ellen Boggs
Publicity/Programs . Amy Schmidt
Cellist . . . . Cecilia Rossiter

SPECIAL THANKS: Barney Rosset, Astrid
Myers, Blue Moon Books, Inc., Embassy of
Ireland, Embassy of France, Mr. Michael
Maloney, Mr. Lazare Paupert, the French
Cultural Service, and SCENA Board Members
William Durkin, Otho Eskin and George Williams

A Note from the Director:

Eleutheria is Samuel Beckett's first play,
antedating, anticipating Waiting for Godot
and Endgame. Beckett very much sought
its production in the late 1940s world of
Paris pocket theatres. Twice, Eleutheria
was selected for production, by Jean Vilar
of the Theatre National Populaire (who
wanted to cut the play and then rejected it
when Beckett refused permission) and later
by director Roger Blin who had his choice
of either Eleutheria or Godot. After due
consideration, Blin chose the seemingly less
complicated text. Godot was produced to
acclaim while for years Eleutheria languished
in a trunk, accessible only to scholars and
specialists. With Beckett's death in 1989,
his early writings began to reach his public.
So to with Eleutheria. The near forgotten
"beginning of it all" was finally published

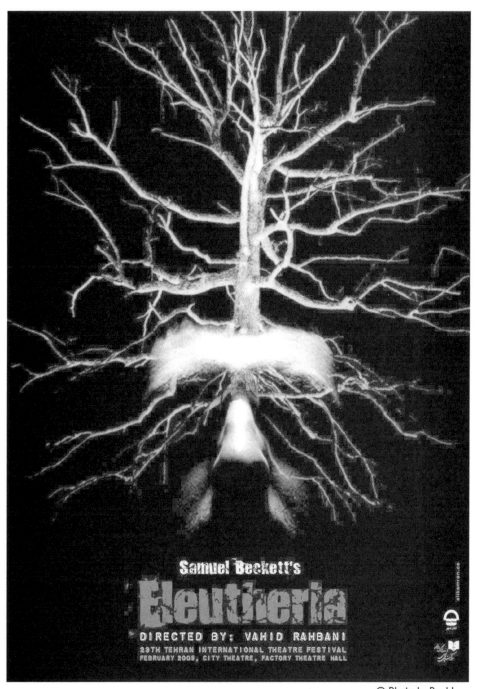

© Photo by Paul Lowe

BLUE MOON BOOKS INC.
61 Fourth Avenue,
New York, NY 10003
Phone (212) 5056680, Fax (212) 6731039

02 March 1993
M Jérôme Lindon
7, rue Bernard Palissy
75006 Paris, France

Cher Jérôme:

In July of 1985 you wrote to me, saying that "je crois être votre ami" and "les relations entre nos deux maisons sont anciennes et fondées sur des principes d'édition tres voisins." This letter is written in that spirit and I hope that you will read it that way, even if what I have to say, what I must say reflects the hurt which I have felt over the last few months. Nonetheless, I believe that the old feelings, from a previous time, can still prevail.

I've been puzzled over the last few months; after hearing of the publication plans for *Dream* that I had never been informed about them much less offered a chance to publish the book myself. Only very recently was I able to get a copy of the already printed book, *Dream of Fair to Middling Women*. I am frankly surprised that I, Samuel Beckett's sole American publisher for over 33 years, was not sent a courtesy copy by you, or John Calder or Eoin O'Brien.

I suspect I now know why some were not eager for me to see it. In his "Foreword" to *Dream* Eoin O'Brien states that in 1986 Sam "was considering . . . how best to help a friend to whom he wished to give a text for publication, and he asked me if it should be *Dream*." Eoin does not name me as that "friend," nor does he outline the circumstances of Sam's interest in helping this "friend," that in fact the "friend" had been Sam's American publisher for 33 years but had recently been discharged from the publishing house that he had built since 1952, a publishing house that made many a European writer readily available in the United States for the first time, chief among them Samuel Beckett. What is downplayed in O'Brien's "Foreword" is that Sam wanted to offer me something major to publish. It was the measure of his loyalty to his friend, publisher and dramatic agent who now had to start over with a new publishing house after having started and run Grove for more than 35 years.

Sam decided at the time not to give me *Dream* because it is a roman a clef, and some friends still living might have been hurt by its publication. He offered me instead *Eleutheria*, which he would try to translate himself. O'Brien goes on to note, "Shortly afterwards, he told me *Dream* should be published, but he did not want this to happen until he was 'gone for some little time.'" The conclusion from O'Brien's

"Foreword" seems inescapable; once it was time to publish *Dream of Fair to Middling Women*, it should have been offered to Sam's American publisher as Sam himself directed in 1986. That was certainly his intent. Somehow in recent negotiations to publish *Dream*, Sam's desire to make a gesture to his American publisher of 33 years was ignored, and I was left out of consideration entirely.

There is, regrettably, nothing that we can do about that now since the work is already in print and will shortly be published by an American publisher. But Sam gave me an inscribed copy of *Eleutheria* at that time—which I still have in my possession—to publish instead of *Dream*. Perhaps you can recall that Sam retreated to Ussy in 1986 to try and translate *Eleutheria* for me. In 1986 Sam already authorized major portions of the play to be published in the Samuel Beckett number of the *Revue d'Esthétique* (numéro special hors série) by Editions Privat, pp.lll-134. Sam could not finally bring himself to make the English translation. After translating a small part of the text he told me he simply could not face going back to the past, meaning the translation, and so dredge up too many memories. He was just not up to that effort. Instead he wrote Stirrings Still, which turned out to be his last prose text, at least in English. He dedicated the work to me and I published it, allowing John Calder to publish it in England. Thus *Eleutheria* became temporarily dormant.

....

In short, now is the time to publish *Eleutheria*, and I hope that we can do so in cooperation with each other and avoid the confusion, misunderstandings, and infighting surrounding the publication of *Dream*. You may recall that you were prepared to publish *Eleutheria* in 1953, and even announced it at that time. You may recall as well that Sam gave both *Waiting for Godot* and *Eleutheria* to Roger Blin for production, without preference for which should be staged first. Blin liked them both and chose to stage *Waiting for Godot* before *Eleutheria* only because with five actors *Godot* would be cheaper to mount. Some time thereafter Beckett withdrew *Eleutheria*, but at one time he thought (and Blin agreed) that it had equal value with *Godot*. As it turned out literary and publishing history was shaped less by the literary quality of the one play as much as by how much subsidy Blin was able to raise for a production.

Sam had given *Eleutheria* to you in 1953 for publication, and in my case, he offered it to me in 1986 for publication at that time and never withdrew it. For me at least, now is the time to publish Sam's only remaining major unpublished work, Eleutheria.

This fact is especially compelling in view of the publication of *Dream*, from which project I was excluded. And please be aware that even so, once I knew about it I worked hard to make that project possible in the U.S., albeit without me, and hopefully I succeeded.

A contract made up along the same lines as the one you made with John Calder for *Dream* would be acceptable to me. I would be very pleased if you would draw it up and send it to me. On the other hand, I would be happy to prepare it myself and send it to you.

Lastly I give you all my assurances that this project will be carried out without any of the squabbles and grief brought on by the publication of *Dream*.
I await your word.

Best regards,
Barney Rosset

Martin Garbus presenting
The Literarian Award to
Barney from The National
Book Foundation.

BLUE MOON BOOKS INC.

61 Fourth Avenue,

New York, NY 10003,

Phone (212) 5056680, Fax (212) 6731039

19 April 1993

M Jérôme Lindon

7, rue BernardPalissy

75006 Paris

France

FAX #331 4544 8236

Dear Jérôme:

Your letter of 6 April, which begins abruptly with a conclusion ("résumons"), seems
to imply that you have shut the door on what you take to have been negotiations
between us over permission to publish Samuel Beckett's first full-length play
Eleutheria.

I'm afraid, my dear Jérôme, that you misunderstood the intent of my recent
correspondence with you. You seem to be under the misapprehension that I have been
asking you for permission to publish the play. May I remind you that I already have
permission to do so, that from Sam himself.

The purpose of my recent communications was to extend the hand of cooperation to
you. I have been writing to you in hopes that our long and friendly relationship could
continue and out of respect for the publishing house which first published Samuel
Beckett in French. I was even willing to respect your wish that *Eleutheria* be published
first in French (although to my mind the bulk of it already has been published), but
I asked you at least to begin making the necessary preliminary arrangements and to
establish some sort of time table. That was a courtesy on my part, which I am still
willing to extend if a reasonable and mutually agreeable schedule can be established.
But do not confuse my gestures of friendship with requests for permissions.

On the matter of translation I thought again that I was offering a compromise.
You persist in alluding to unnamed accusers, and you never do explain how those
accusers could make pronouncements on an early draft—an incomplete version of the
manuscript. You offer not a single example of a translating problem. What you offer
instead is a summary dismissal. I have been (and still am) quite willing to listen to
reasonable analyses from you.

In the forty years of our relationship and of my publishing French writers I have never sought your permission for, nor approval of, any translation of French work, and I am not doing so now. However, let me remind you as well that I suggested in my last letter that I would publish no translation without having it gone over by several people. The first person I had in mind was Dick Seaver. I reminded you that to my knowledge he was one of the two people who Sam allowed to translate his work, and there are other possibilities as well. Any suggestions you might make for consultations would be carefully considered.

I am sure that you know by now that my decision to publish *Eleutheria* is a very serious and important matter for me.

I have already consulted with my attorneys and they have told me that I indeed do have the right to publish Sam's play. If you would like to pursue this line of inquiry further you are welcome to have your attorneys contact them. Their names are appended to the end of this letter.

However, I much prefer to go ahead with you in the same cooperative and friendly way as heretofore. It would be my full intent to conform to your desires on publishing matters to the fullest extent I can. It would give me great pleasure to work with you and not against you.

Cordially,

Barney Rosset

P.S. I appreciate very much your having translated your letters into English for my convenience. I regret not finding it feasible at this moment to do the same favor for you.

Attorneys: Martin Garbus & Robert Solomon Frankfurt, Garbus, Klein & Selz
488 Madison Ave.
9th Floor I New York, NY 10022
phone ; (212) 980.0120 fax: (212) 593.9175
cc: Edward Beckett. 21 April 1993

BLUE MOON BOOKS INC.

61 Fourth Avenue,

New York, NY 10003,

Phone (212) 5056680, Fax (212) 6731039

22 April 1993

Dear Edward,

It hurts me very much to go against Jérôme Lindon's decision and your wishes concerning the publication of *Eleutheria*. Your judgment as to what is right and wrong and your sense of what I should, and in this case not do, means a tremendous amount to me.

Eleutheria is an important seminal work by one of the greatest writers of this century, must be put into print or we who have been involved for so long in the dissemination of the work of Samuel Beckett shall all have to share a terrible burden of guilt. I have the right to publish it, it must be published and it will be published, if not by me, then eventually by somebody else. Whose orders am I marching under, those of a this time mistaken Jérôme Lindon or those which come from within me?

I agree completely with the chapter in the McMillan-Fehsenfeld book which eloquently states the importance of *Eleutheria* in the canon of the modern theater. In itself *Eleutheria* is a fine work. It is a key work to the understanding of the entire Samuel Beckett oeuvre. As the two writers said:

> Only with *Eleutheria* did Beckett complete a full-length play.... we...have in *Eleutheria* Beckett's own full statement on dramatic method—a statement which clearly influenced his later plays. Gogo and Didi did not spring onto the stage full blown from Beckett's brow. Though couched in the humorous language of dramatic parody, *Eleutheria* contains the serious theoretical underpinnings of the new kind of drama Beckett was to initiate in *Godot*.

Beckett himself sanctioned the publication of a major portion of it in *Revue d'Esthétique*—along with the essay, by McMillan-Fehsenfeld. At least to me personally, Sam did not criticize that essay, and beyond that we well know his great fondness and admiration for Martha Fehsenfeld.

I have stated over and over again my admiration for Jérôme Lindon personally, for his work as a publisher and for his political beliefs and how he acted in accordance with them, thus enduring terrible personal distress and danger. To me he has represented the best and purest qualities a book publisher can have. If he has made compromises in quality or from fear they certainly have not been apparent to me. I only wish that I could say the same for myself. And so I salute him. I give him my personal Medal of Honor, and following in that same direct lineage, I will not obey an unjust order even if he is the one issuing it. To follow it would ultimately be not only a terrible disservice to Samuel Beckett and his work, but also to him, to you, and all the rest of us.

In the very beginning (it seems of my life, but chronologically it was hardly that) Sam began discussing problems of translation and possibilities of putting back into print earlier books of his, then already lost from sight. All of this is poignantly reminiscent of the present situation.

Perhaps Jérôme has inadvertently aided me by saying in his letter of March 5, 1993 "Today, in an offhand manner, you break to me the news that you have had Eleutheria translated, that you intend to publish this translation." That statement was most certainly not true about my proposed publication of *Eleutheria*—nor of the many publishing efforts I made in the past and which were important to me. It forces me to remember how I made decisions in the past, just as with *Eleutheria*. My original decision to publish Beckett was not made lightly. It was made after a great deal of inner searching—and consultations with others. As I said in a letter to Sam in June of 1953:

> *Sylvia Beach is certainly the one you must blame for your future appearance*
> *on the Grove Press list. I went to see her with your work on my mind, and*
> *after she talked of you I immediately decided that what the Grove Press*
> *needed most in the world was Samuel Beckett....*
> *A second person was also very important. He is Wallace Fowlie. At my request*
> *he read the play and the two novels with great care and came back with the*
> *urgent plea for me to take on your work.*

Remember that I published Beckett before I published Lawrence's *Lady Chatterley's Lover* or Miller's *Tropic of Cancer*. My decisions in publishing *Lady Chatterly's Lover* and *Tropic of Cancer* were made in the same spirit as the one made to publish

Beckett—these books, these authors were important and their work was available to me. I really had no choice.

As for *Lady Chatterly's Lover*—the author D.H. Lawrence had published it himself in Italy in the 1920's, but Alfred Knopf, presumably one of the greatest American publishers, the one who certainly was thought of as of great importance in the bringing of European literature to America, published *Lady Chatterly's Lover* here but in an expurgated version. Lawrence is one of the greatest writers to even grace the English language, He, Knopf, published *Lady Chatterly's Lover* in an expurgated version and let it go at that.

If ever there was a book wherein its sexual content constituted its raison d'être it was this one, and Knopf cut it out. In effect Lawrence, a writer of towering importance, had been castrated by his own publisher. I greatly admire many of the things which Mr. Knopf had done, but that was not one of them. As a matter of fact it disgusted and infuriated me. It exposed a flaw, a running wound in our common psyche and I set about to heal it and I did. And I did not do it 'offhandedly' as Jérôme perceives me doing with *Eleutheria*. I sent a wonderful emissary, Prof. Mark Schorer, head of the English department at the University of California, to Lawrence's widow, Freida Lawrence Ravagli and got her permission to proceed, just before she died. Her agents then withdrew that permission. History tells how I treated that decision. I retained the finest attorneys who shared my belief in free speech I could find. We carefully organized a campaign for the publishing of the book. It went off like a well planned military expedition and it worked. But without any of the above, I would have done it anyway.

And it brought me congratulations from Samuel Beckett.

Before I knew of *Lady Chatterly's Lover*, before Grove Press existed, 11 years and a World War to be exact, I read *Tropic of Cancer* by Henry Miller. It made an enormous impact on me and on my entire life, an impact which was never diminished but rather became a part of me.

Without stating it to others, *Lady Chatterly's Lover* was my route to freeing *Tropic of Cancer*. There the battle plan went more than a bit awry, but we persevered, across and up and down the country. It was Grove Press's private Civil War. There were battles and skirmishes everywhere. My own highest moment came in my home town of Chicago when, as a witness, defending myself and Henry Miller, the state's attorney accused me of being a mercenary, someone fighting only for the gold lurking in the background. It gave me the opportunity to pull out of my jacket my college freshman English paper written some twenty years earlier, and it expounded my belief in the greatness of Henry Miller's vision of America and the superb quality of *Tropic of Cancer*. The jaundice in our eyes, but the presiding judge in Chicago decided otherwise and gave out a ringing decision, proclaiming the freedom to read.

The next great moment came in Paris when I took Henry Miller to a victory lunch with Samuel Beckett. My pantheon was complete and later, separately, each of my idols told me how much nicer the other had become since they had last met in the thirties.

Edward, I tell you all of this because it encompasses my Samuel Beckett world. As I gradually got to know Sam better and more intimately I got emboldened enough to argue more strongly with him—and very specifically to argue about publishing those earlier works of his which he said he absolutely wanted to have no further part of.

There was his little book on Proust, his book of short stories *More Pricks Than Kicks*, his novel *Murphy*, and his anthology of Latin American literature. We brought back a book Sam's poetry, which included his *Whoroscope* which won a much needed prize for him in 1930, and four poems from 1948 written in French with his own English translations. One by one he gave in on every single work and we published them.

It seemed to me that Jérôme Lindon perceived Samuel Beckett in a very different light than I did. For him, it was as if Sam was a monolithic genius, a block of unchangeable, albeit beautiful, marble. For me he was more of a changing, growing swaying, marvelous organism always in a state of transformation. Perhaps in this difference of perception, a transformation. Perhaps in this difference of perception, a subject fascinating in itself to Sam, lies the cause of our disagreement. What Sam said one day was subject to modification the next. Like the Oracle of Delphi, when you approached him you just might hear something you wanted to hear.

If Sam did not want *Eleutheria* published then why did so much of it get into Revue d'Esthétique, if he did not want it produced then why did he give it to his producer, R. Blin to do with it what he wished?

Lindon and Sam allowed Rick Cluchey to put on and film *Krapp's Last Tape* in Paris. I asked Sam, after showing him a video of Cluchey playing Krapp in New York, why he didn't tell Cluchey how to play the part. This was after Sam spoke the lines himself, in a beautiful, incredibly touching way. Sam said, "Oh, but he's not an actor." And so on.

In *Eleutheria* the name of the protagonist family is Krap. And the son of that family, Victor Krap, is reminiscent of Sam himself. *Eleutheria* was written in French. *Krapp's Last Tape* not only gives Krapp two r's but also it was written in English and further, it most certainly is directly autobiographical, whereas Victor Krap was more symbolical. So where does this dichotomy, so strongly espoused by Lindon, between the 'French' Beckett and the 'English' Beckett arise. Perhaps it was only in Jérôme's head. I urged Sam for a long time to write in English. Probably for my own selfish reasons—no more of that damned translating. Anyway he did just that, and then of course he had to translate his work back in to French. At least that way I was the first recipient.

And so Jérôme cannot escape responsibility for the publication of *Dream* because it was written in English, as he says in his letter of March 5, 1993, "Yet as *Dream* was originally written in English, I am in no way the publisher of this work." That's too easy and convenient.

And I cannot escape responsibility if *Eleutheria* is not now published, because it was written in French. No way.

When Sam gave me *Eleutheria* and offered to translate it and actually started to do so, he was but a short space of time from his death. As you know so well, he was a desperately tired man—trying so hard to please his friends.
He did not say to me it should not be translated. He said that he could not do it, it was simply too onerous a burden to go back all those years and look that piece in the eye again. To Sam, I know and believe that meant that, as always, he would have had to reconstruct the work, not translating in the usual sense. Whereas years before I would have urged him on, arguing and cajoling. This time I desisted. And Sam bribed me, he told me he would write something new for me if I left him off the hook on *Eleutheria*, if he did not have to translate it. My response was obvious. Later, after he had written two segments, which he called Fragments and which I liked tremendously, I asked him if I might publish *Fragments* as a book by itself, but also

putting it together with another short volume which Marguerite Duras had given me, in the same sympathetic way, that Sam had given me his work.

Sam, and only Sam, could have so gracefully and a little bit wickedly, said, well if you leave my little offering to be done separately I will write another section. The second bribe. And it worked. That was not a monolithic man at work.

When I commissioned him to write a motion picture script he did so and he came to New York to be present for the shooting of it. When a potentially disastrous mistake was made by the great cinematographer Boris Kaufman, Sam took it in stride and with hysteria all around him, calmly adjusted the script to meet the new condition.

I see Jérôme as basically not a very flexible person—for better or worse, and myself as more of the opposite type. Perhaps Sam saw that and adapted himself to each of us when he was dealing with us.

But I cannot adapt to Jérôme's inflexibility or make it on my own. Furthermore I can see no way to protect his sense of what is right by total capitulation on my part. All of us would be the losers. I have offered and continue to offer any way possible for me to cooperate with Jérôme—short of not publishing *Eleutheria*.
Edward, somehow I hope what I have had to say can give you the flavor of what I feel, and to what I feel compelled to do.

Notwithstanding the above, your friendship remains most valuable to me. The esteem of Jérôme is also very important to me, but I cannot desert either Sam or myself or all of the rest of us. Do try to bear with me, I will do my utmost to consider both of your desires. Why don't we allow this decision making 'cool off' for a period of time, let us say a month. During that time we can all try to think of some solution which would at least not destroy our ongoing relationship and hopefully might end in a constructive and cooperative undertaking.

Love,
Barney

Cc: Jérôme Lindon

The Samuel Beckett Estate

Carrigmor
Sheethanger Lane
Felden
Hemel Hempstead
Herts HP3 0BG
ENGLAND

30 September 1994

Mr. Barney Rosset
BLUE MOON BOOKS
61,Fourth Avenue
New York NY 10003 U.S.A.

Dear Barney,

You have announced to the press that,in spite of my interdiction,you are planning to publish a translation into English of *Eleutheria*.

Were you to persist in that intent and not give me your written assurance to the contrary,you would set yourself directly against me and the Estate.

Under those circumstances I could no longer let you be the representative in the United States of Samuel Beckett's interests.I will therefore ask you to voluntarily resign that function, failing which I will terminate our agreement under the terms of that agreement.

Yours sincerely.

Edward Beckett

SAMUEL BECKETT

Eleutheria

☆m

LES ÉDITIONS DE MINUIT

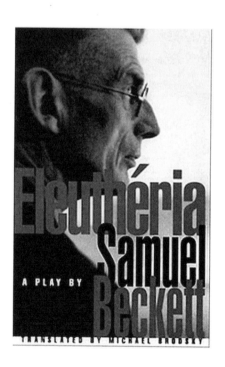

Dear Mr. Beckett

THE SAMUEL BECKETT ESTATE

November 8, 1994
Mr. Barney Rosset
BLUE MOON BOOKS
61, Fourth Avenue
New York, NY 10003 U.S.A.

Dear Barney,
I have asked Georges Borchardt to be the Estate's agent
in the U.S.A. and Canada. I am sorry that I had to take
this final step but under the circumstances I felt that I
had no alternative.

I would appreciate it if you could pass on to him any new
requests that you receive and give him what information
he might ask you for.

                    Yours,

                    Edward

Edward Beckett
and Barney Rosset
in East Hampton;
photo Astrid Rosset

E VERGREEN REVIEW *published many of the literary giants of the mid-to-late 20th Century. Among them, Susan Sontag. Rosset, who edited the magazine from 1957 to 1973 while at Grove Press and, again, when it reappeared in electronic format from 1998 until his death in 2012, included both Sontag and Beckett in the same issue (no. 34, December 1964), the former with her seminal essay "Against Interpretation," the latter with* Play. *Sontag would go on to direct a controversial* Waiting for Godot *in Sarajevo in 1993 and to support Rosset during his negotiations with the Beckett Estate when it opposed, in accordance with the author's wishes, his wanting to publish Beckett's* Eleutheria.

—ED.

January 16, 1995

TO: Barney Rossett
FROM: Susan Sontag

FAX #: 1/212/627-5002

PAGE 1 OF 1

Dear Barney,

As a member in good standing of the club of reverent but
independent-minded directors of Beckett's plays who have had
their wrists slapped by the Beckett estate, I hope you'll put
me on the list of people to whom you're sending copies of
Eleutheria. (I learned that, and how, you're publishing the
play in last week's *Voice*.)

My address is:

470 West 24th Street
New York, New York 10011

I send you New Year's greetings and warmest wishes for the
success of all your projects.

As ever,

Susan

Dear Susan,

Truly, truly, it gave me a great pleasure to get your FAX. It's been a long time since I first met you at Louis (Albert's?) restaurant on 6th Ave and 10th (maybe 11th) St. You were with Roger Strauss and you were wearing blue jeans (I'm sure of those two facts). Whoever was with me—no memory there—said that Roger really had a great belief in you. So - he was right.

Not so long ago I spoke to Deborah Karl concerning you. You wanted, I think, the right to do Happy Days (?). Anyway, I commiserated with her about you - and me. I had my orders - no rights to that Sontag. And here I was, thinking you had done something rather heroic, something Sam would have liked as much as he liked Godot being done in San Quentin. Maybe One Act in Sarajevo equaled two acts on the Champs Elysees. I can hear Sam saying—"Oh Barney, tell her to go ahead, but why don't You go and see it —let me know. Tell her "God Bless". And Edward and Jérôme said "never let her do another piece by Beckett." Well, they solved that, they fired me. No more agenting for me. It wasn't my métier anyway. But after 30 years or so you sort of get used to it.

So—I fired off Eleutheria this evening, using up every stamp we had. Now I will send you some of the lovely correspondence which has passed between Cher Jérôme and myself - and some accompanying documentation, which you can read—or put in your local dumpster—or pass on to my successor, Georges Borchardt (agent to agent).

The translation you are getting is by Albert Bermel—it followed one by Stan Gontarski, and now Michael Brodsky is doing another. Democracy at work. Anyway, I like them all. I will be happy to send on the French version—(i.e. the Beckett one—on a moment's notice.)

The VOICE piece was frighteningly accurate. [Jonathan] Kalb wrote it as he heard it.

The VOICE piece was frighteningly accurate. [Jonathan] Kalb wrote it as he heard it.

So, you could say that this is my little Sarajevo. That would make me proud.
Love to hear from you again—can't wait 40, 30, 20—even 10 years.

Very very best,

Barney

January 27, 1995

Dear Susan:

Seldom have I been so instantaneously and so deeply affected by another's words—yours. All I know is that if Lindon's turnaround with me holds good, there is a new Beckett world a-coming.

In 1986, Sam very strangely and interestingly re-signed a little contract with me saying not only was I to continue as his dramatic agent, but that I could be removed only by him. If that wish of his is honored again, I can only beg of you to do anything of Beckett you wish and if the forces of evil remove me again—so be it. It will have been worth it.

Years ago, Kenzaburo Oe and I watched a documentary together of the CIA's story—so prideful—of having killed Che Guevara. The officer said: he was a great soldier and goddamn, we got him. Kenzaburo and I—well, we both cried. Somehow your letter sent that same sorrow and anger through me.

I hope so much to sign a book publishing contract next week with Lindon and then comes the next act. If demanding *Eleutheria* got me fired as agent, does getting the former put me back in the same status as before? I think it should. Let's just cool this while I proceed further. I have a bad habit of "telegraphing my punch," but in this instance, I must at least reply to you and thereby confide my feelings which are too strong to suppress.

Incidentally, I had your Sarajevo piece and I lost it. Could you send me another?

It is so seldom in this world—or at least my corner of it— that things take a sudden good turn. It frightens me. I have never been prepared for that. But maybe this time I will be—your letter does it.

Maybe sometime we can give an interview together to announce a new Beckett production to be directed by one Susan Sontag.

Right now—"mum is the word" or "rumors sink ships." And by the way, I feel it was a singular honor to have received your letter.

Le votre (not Jerome's),

[signature]

P.S.
And it is comforting, after having seen and heard so many "ugly" Americans over the last 50 years, to now stumble over one beautiful one.

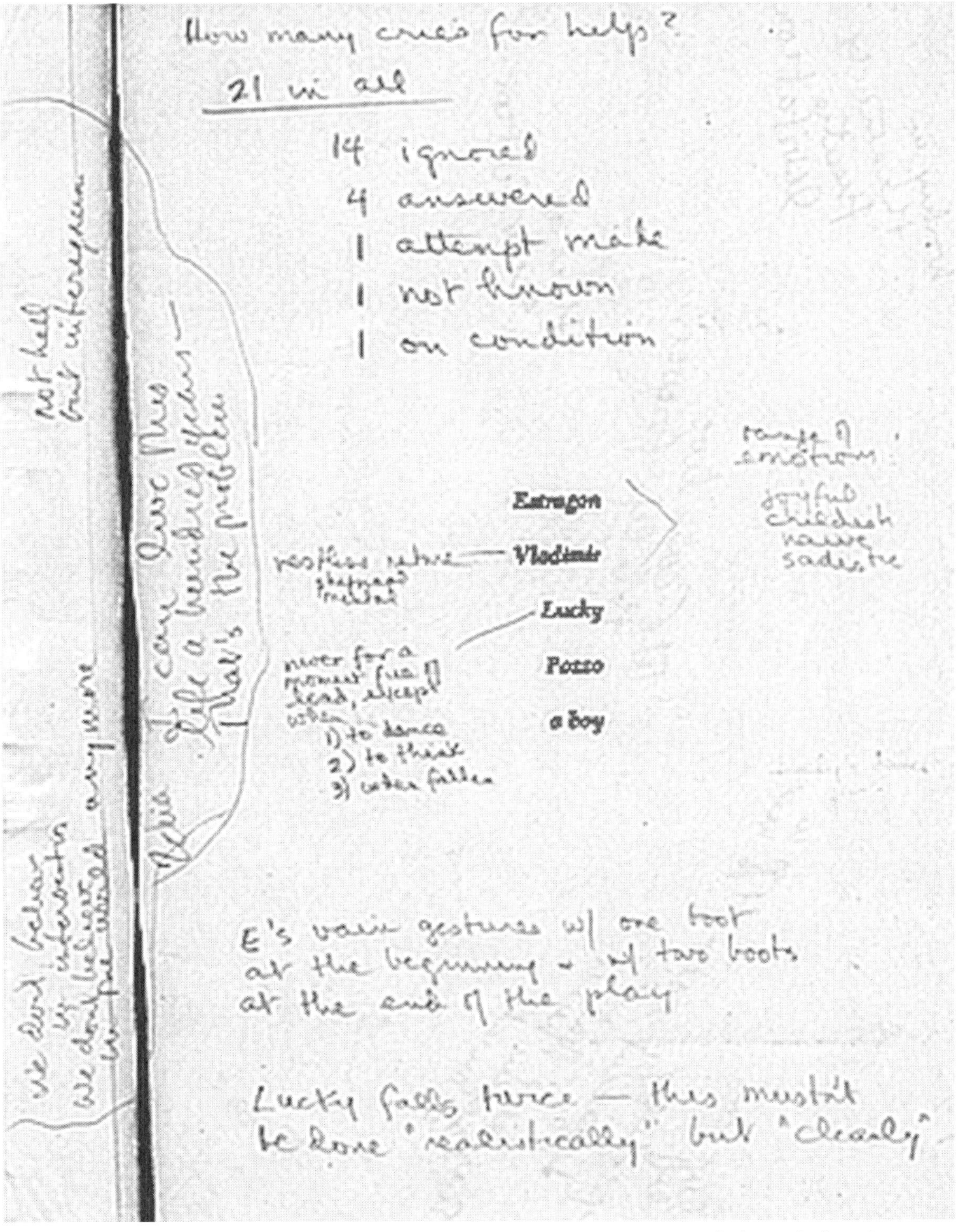

How many cries for help?

<u>21 in all</u>

14 ignored
4 answered
1 attempt made
1 not known
1 on condition

Estragon
restless nature ——— Vladimir
shattered intellect

never for a ——— Lucky
moment free ()
head, except ()
when
1) to dance   Pozzo
2) to think
3) when fallen   a boy

range of
emotions:
joyful
childish
naive
sadistic

E's vain gestures w/ one boot
at the beginning — w/ two boots
at the end of the play

Lucky falls twice — this mustn't
be done "realistically" but "clearly"

(left margin, vertical)
Glin I can cure this
Life a hundred years —
That's the problem

not hell
but purgatorie

we don't believe
in information
we don't believe
in the world anymore

Sontag production notes

26 August 1998

Dear Susan,

When you went to Sarajevo, taking Beckett's *Godot* with you, for me you were bringing to those people there what Joseph Needham, the British scientist and sinologist (and a left wing icon for me in my high school years), called "the sense of the numinous." Maybe that is what is also meant by the "holy spirit."

The Sarajevans become the Vladimirs and Estragons, who ultimately have to depend on their own resources, but if they hang on there is hope, as long as any of us have hope. For me, *Godot*'s epiphany" is in the sudden knowing that we all share the same dilemma in one way or another, and we will endure it, one way or another. "I can't go on, I'll go on."

When you went to Sarajevo and took the heart of Sam's work with you, you brought a creative and healing gift to those suffering people that has still not ceased to astonish and mesmerize me.

Yours,

Barney

Barney

WAITING FOR GODOT
IN SARAJEVO

Excerpts
Susan Sontag

I was not under the illusion that going to Sarajevo to direct a play would make me useful in the way I could be if I were a doctor or a water systems engineer. It would be a small contribution. But it was the only one of the three things I do—write, make films, and direct in the theatre—which yields something that would exist only in Sarajevo, that would be made and consumed there.

*   *   *

But isn't this play rather pessimistic, I've been asked. Meaning, wasn't it depressing for an audience in Sarajevo; meaning, wasn't it pretentious or insensitive to stage *Godot* there?—as if the representation of despair were redundant when people really are in despair; as if what people want to see in such a situation would be, say, *The Odd Couple*. The condescending, philistine question makes me realize that those who ask it don't understand at all what it's like in Sarajevo now, any more than they really care about literature and theatre.

*   *   *

Tripling the parts of Vladimir and Estragon, and expanding the play with stage business, as well as silences, was making it a good deal longer that it usually is. I soon realized that Act I would run at least ninety minutes. Act II would be shorter [...]. But even with a stripped-down and speeded-up Act II, the play would be two and a half hours long. [...] How could I ask the audience, which would have no lobby, bathroom, or water, to sit so uncomfortably, without moving, for two and a half hours?

I concluded that I could not do all of *Waiting for Godot.*

*   *   *

To respond to journalists' attentions, when one would rather be doing something else, is inevitably to find oneself saying things, or be reported as saying things, that seem inane or simpleminded. [...]

What are you trying to accomplish?

Make a small contribution to cultural life here.

Why *Waiting for Godot?*

Because it's a great play. And it resonates here.

Isn't it a metaphor? I know you've written about metaphor.

No, it's not a metaphor.

Well, then, what's the message of *Waiting for Godot?*

There is no message.

Well, what is your message in doing *Godot?*

I don't have a message.

[Same question, repeated more emphatically.]

That it's possible to come here. That other people should come and work here.

Weren't you afraid to come?

Anyone who isn't afraid is crazy.

Why don't you wear your flak jacket?

Nobody who lives here has a flak jacket. I think it would be indecent for me to wear mine.

Aren't you afraid?

[Sigh.]

Is this a political act?

I think of it as an act of conscience.

But you do have political opinions.

Who doesn't?

Are you for intervention?

Absolutely.

Why do you think other people like you don't come?

[Various diffident or testy answers.]

And so on.

*　　*　　*

Waiting for Godot opened, with twelve candles on the stage, on August 17th. There were two performances that day, one at 2:00 PM and the other at 4:00 PM. In Sarajevo there are only matinees; hardly anybody goes out after dark. Many people were turned away. For the first few performances I was tense with anxiety. But there was a moment, I think it was the third performance, when I began to stop worrying. The play now belonged to the actors, and I knew it was in good hands. And I think it was at the end of that performance—on Wednesday, August 18th at 2:00 PM—during the long tragic silence of the Vladimirs and Estragons which follows the messenger's announcement that Mr. Godot isn't coming today, but will surely come tomorrow, that my eyes began to sting with tears. [...] No one in the audience made a sound. The only sounds were those coming from outside the theatre: a UN APC thundering down the street and the crack of sniper fire.

Waiting for Godot in Sarajevo, 1993 © Paul Lowe

Dear Mr. Beckett

INTO-GAL, 2006, edited by Leo Edelstein & Judith Elliston

SARAJEVO:
SUSAN SONTAG'S PRODUCTION OF
WAITING FOR GODOT

BARNEY ROSSET: Susan Sontag and I formed an unusual relationship. It got to be close, and admiring without any really personal thing about it.

She put on *Godot* in Yugoslavia, Sarajevo, during a war there, when they were blowing the place to pieces. She kept putting it on, stubbornly. And of course taking great liberties. Sometimes she had two or three Pozzos, she switched parts, she did all sorts of things. Many of the people she used were both local and "amateurs". Many people entrenched in the hierarchy of academic studies complained bitterly, they said that she was distorting Beckett; I thought differently. I thought that she and the actors were putting their lives on the line every night…

We were both, almost at that very moment, honored by the French government by being made Commanders of Arts and Letters. I believe that the timing was a sheer coincidence, but it was very nice. There was something about what she was doing that I really, really admired.

Cérémonie de remise des insignes des arts et lettres

A GEORGES BORCHARDT, JOHN G.H. OAKES, BARNEY ROSSET, PHILIP ROTH, ET SUSAN SONTAG

MESDAMES ET MESSIEURS, LADIES AND GENTLEMEN

AS CULTURAL COUNSELOR OF THE FRENCH EMBASSY, I HAVE THE PLEASURE AND PRIVILEGE OF WELCOMING YOU TODAY TO THIS MEDAL CEREMONY OF THE ORDER OF ARTS AND LETTERS HONORING FIVE EMINENT LITERARY FIGURES: GEORGES BORCHARDT, JOHN G.H. OAKES, BARNEY ROSSET, PHILIP ROTH, AND SUSAN SONTAG. I MUST CONFESS, ON A MORE PERSONAL NOTE, THAT SINCE MY FIRST, QUITE INTIMIDATING, CEREMONY A FEW WEEKS AFTER MY ARRIVAL - THE GUEST OF HONOR AT THAT TIME WAS IN FACT ALSO A PUBLISHER - THE STATURE OF OUR HONORES TONIGHT MAKES THIS CEREMONY A SPECIALLY HUMBLING ONE.

BY WAY OF PREFACE TO OUR CEREMONY, I SHOULD LIKE TO SPEAK BRIEFLY ABOUT THE AWARD BEING GIVEN. FRANCE HAS A LONG HISTORY OF OFFICIAL GOVERNMENT DISTINCTIONS FOR EXCEPTIONAL ACHIEVEMENT. THESE DECORATIONS, AS THEY ARE CALLED AS A WHOLE, INCLUDE SUCH SOCIETIES, OR ORDERS, AS THE NATIONAL ORDER OF THE LEGION OF HONOR, THE ORDER OF ACADEMIC PALMS, AND OF COURSE THE ORDER WHOSE INSIGNIA THE HONOREES WILL RECEIVE TONIGHT, THE ORDER OF ARTS AND LETTERS.

THE ORDRE DES ARTS ET DES LETTRES WAS ESTABLISHED IN 1957 SPECIFICALLY TO RECOGNIZE OUTSTANDING

ARTISTIC WORK AND THE CULTURAL INFLUENCE OF ARTISTS AND WRITERS IN FRANCE AND THROUGHOUT THE WORLD. PREVIOUS TO THE CREATION OF THIS ORDER, ARTISTS AND WRITERS COULD BE OFFICIALLY RECOGNIZED ONLY THROUGH THE LEGION OF HONOR, (AND THAT IN VERY RESTRICTED NUMBERS), OR, THE ORDER OF ACADEMIC PALMS, IF THEY WERE CONNECTED WITH THE FIELD OF EDUCATION.

BOTH FOREIGNERS AND FRENCH NATIONALS CAN BE NAMED TO THIS ORDER, WHICH CONSISTS OF THREE RANKS (CHEVALIER, OFFICIER,

COMMANDEUR), AND IS GOVERNED BY CERTAIN AGE AND PROMOTION RESTRICTIONS. A COVETED AWARD, IT IS GIVEN OUT TWICE ANNUALLY TO ONLY A FEW HUNDRED PEOPLE WORLDWIDE.

REMISE DES INSIGNES DE COMMANDEUR DBS ARTS ET LETTRES A M. BARNEY ROSSET
(NEW YORK, 8 NOVEMBRE 1999)
OFTEN DO WE SEPARATE THE LIFE OF GREAT MEN FROM THEIR WORKS, HOWEVER ARTIFICIAL SUCH A DISTINCTION MAY BE. IN BARNEY ROSSET'S CASE, ONE CANNOT EVEN *DREAM* OF SEPARATING THE WORKS FROM THE LIFE OF ONE OF AMERICA'S FOREMOST PUBLISHERS OF THE XXth CENTURY.

FROM THE B MINUS YOU WERE GIVEN AT SWARTHMORE COLLEGE FOR THE ANTI-AMERICAN ESSAY YOU WROTE ON HENRY MILLER'S *TROPIC OF CANCER* TO THE NUMEROUS TRIALS YOU HAVE HAD TO FACE WHEN BECOME A FULLFLEDGED PUBLISHER, THE STORY OF YOUR LIFE AND

OF YOUR PUBLISHING LIFE IS ONE IN WHICH THE HERO CONSTANTLY FINDS HIMSELF AT ODDS WITH SOCIETY - OR MORE ACCURATELY WITH THE RULING INSTITUTIONS. FROM AN EARLY AGE, YOU HAVE ALWAYS LED AN ONGOING BATTLE FOR YOUR BELIEFS AND CONVICTIONS. THE YEARS YOU SPENT AT THE FRANCIS PARKER SCHOOL LED YOU TO TAKE UP A CRITICAL VIEW ON THE WORLD - A PERSPECTIVE WHICH YOU HAVE NEVER LOST. EVEN IF YOUR ATTEMPT AT ESCAPING SWARTHMORE FAILED AND YOU NEVER REACHED MEXICO AS YOU HAD PLANNED TO, YOU NEVERTHELESS MADE IT TO CHINA WHEN SERVING IN THE ARMY, IN CHARGE OF A PHOTOGRAPHIC UNIT. AFTER YOUR WORLD WAR II EXPERIENCE, YOU PRODUCED A FILM, *STRANGE VICTORY*, WHICH EPITOMIZES THE CRITICAL STANCE YOU WERE TAKING UP ON THE WORLD AND ON AMERICA.

IN 1952, YOU DECIDED TO BUY GROVE PRESS : THREE THOUSAND DOLLARS AND THREE SUITCASES FULL OF BOOKS WERE THE BEGINNING OF A GREAT STORY WHICH HAS CHANGED THE LITERARY AND CULTURAL MAP OF AMERICA. IT WAS ALSO THE CONTINUING STORY OF YOUR TROUBLES WHICH I MUST SAY YOU ALWAYS FACED WITH ASTUTENESS AND THE GREATEST SENSE OF HUMOUR.

WHEN FOR INSTANCE, YOU DECIDED TO PUBLISH *LADY CHATTERLEY'S LOVER*, YOU DECIDED TO PLAY HIDE AND SEEK WITH THE POST OFFICE BY HAVING THE UNABRIDGED VERSION SENT TO YOU IN THE MAIL SO THAT THE POST OFFICE WOULD SEIZE IT. THAT WAY YOU AVOIDED DEFENDING THE

BOOK IN A SMALL TOWN AND YOU THEN COULD DEFEND ITBEFORE A FEDERAL COURT AS YOU WANTED TO.

THE UNCEASING EFFORTS THAT YOU HAVE MADE TO SUPPORT LITERATURE HAVE MADE GROVE ONE OF THE BEST PUBLISHING HOUSES IN AMERICA. WHAT WAS SPECIFIC TO GROVE AND TO THE *EVERGREEN REVIEW* WHICH YOU FOUNDED IN 1957 WAS YOUR CONCEPTION OF PUBLISHING NOT ONLY AS THE JOB OF PRINTING A BOOK IN ORDER TO SELL IT BUT ALSO AS AN ART.

YOUR ART OF PUBLISHING ACTUALLY GOES BACK TO THE LATIN ROOTS OF THE WORD PUBLICARE, BRINGING A WORK OF ART INTO THE PUBLIC SPHERE, MAKING A BOOK AVAILABLE TO THE PUBLIC, TO ANYONE WILLING TO READ IT. THUS, GROVE PRESS AND THE *EVERGREEN REVIEW* DID NOT ONLY PROMOTE LITERATURE BUT AT THE SAME TIME DEFENDED A CULTURAL DIVERSITY BASED ON THE FREEDOM OF SPEECH. GROVE PRESS RELIED ON AND FOUGHT FOR DEMOCRACY IN CULTURE. WHEN ASKED WHY YOU PUBLISHED *LADY CHATTERLEY'S LOVER* WHEN YOU ADMITTED YOURSELF NOT BEING TOO FOND OF THE BOOK, YOU ANSWERED "IT WAS THERE, AND IT HAD TO BE PUBLISHED". PUBLISHING TO YOU IS THEREFORE A MATTER OF NECESSITY, ALMOST OF MORAL AND CIVIC RESPONSIBILITY TOWARDS YOUR FELLOW CITIZENS. THE SAME URGE LED YOU TO PUBLISH THE BOOKS WHICH ENDED UP BUILDING GROVE PRESS'S IMPRESSIVE BACKLIST. OVER THE YEARS YOU HAVE REMAINED TRUE TO YOUR ART OF PUBLISHING : YOU CONSIDERED THAT ANY BOOK WHICH

COULD BE PUBLISHED BY SOMEONE ELSE WAS NOT FOR GROVE TO PUBLISH. GROVE PRESS BOOKS WERE BOOKS WHICH HAD BEEN TURNED DOWN BY EVERYBODY; YOU HAVE SAID THAT "IF KNOPF COULD PUBLISH IT, THEN IT WAS A KNOPF BOOK NOT A GROVE BOOK. MANY OF THE BOOKS THAT [YOU]/ WE DID WERE REJECTED BY THIRTY OR FORTY PUBLISHERS. SOME OF THE BEST BOOKS IN FACT."

WAITING FOR GODOT BY BECKETT IS A CASE IN POINT. YOU DECIDED TO PUBLISH IT WHEN IT WAS BANNED IN THE USSR AND AT THE SAME TIME CONSIDERED BY SOME, HERE IN THE UNITED STATES, TO BE COMMUNIST PROPAGANDA. AGAINST ALL ODDS, YOU DECIDED TO MAKE AVAILABLE TO THE PUBLIC A WORK OF ART WITHOUT WHICH OUR CULTURE WOULD BE DIFFERENT TODAY. AND YOU SOLD... OVER 2 MILLION COPIES IN THE UNITED STATES !

SIMILARLY, WHEN THE POSTWAR CULTURAL ARENA SEEMED QUIETER THAN EVER, YOU MANAGED TO BRING THE INCREDIBLE DIVERSITY OF FRENCH POSTWAR LITERATURE AND CULTURE TO A BROAD PUBLIC. YOU TOOK THE WORD CULTURE IN ITS BROADEST SENSE RATHER THAN IN ITS SOMEWHAT HACKNEYED AND CANONICAL MEANING. INDEED, THE WORKS YOU PUBLISHED IN THE *EVERGREEN REVIEW* RANGED FROM EXISTENTIALIST PHILOSOPHY THE FIRST ISSUE FEATURED AN ESSAY BY JEAN-PAUL SARTRE TO CAMUS' APPEAL AGAINST CAPITAL PUNISHMENT, FROM THE THEATER OF THE ABSURD (EUGENE IONESCO, SAMUEL BECKETT) TO DRAWINGS BY TOMI UNGERER AND SINE.

YOUR ART OF PUBLISHING BECAME ONE OF TRANSLATION, IN ALL SENSES OF THE TERM: FROM ONE LANGUAGE TO ANOTHER, FROM ONE CULTURE TO ANOTHER; YOU EVEN BROUGHT WRITERS CONSIDERED MARGINAL INTO THE MAINSTREAM. WE ARE STILL REAPING THE FRUITS OF YOUR RELENTLESS EFFORTS AND ACHIEVEMENTS, AND SUCH IS YOUR LEGACY THAT THE AMERICAN PUBLIC IS INDEBTED TO YOU FOR MANY OF THE INTERESTING BOOKS IT READS. YOU HAVE RESHUFFLED THE CARDS AND ADDED NEW ONES, SUCH AS FANON, CENDRARS, CESAIRE, DAUMAL, DEBRAY, JARRY, LOUYS AND SO ON...

WE ARE AWARE OF THE HARDSHIPS YOU HAD TO GO THROUGH TO IMPOSE SUCH A CULTURAL "NEW DEAL" AND WE CAN ONLY PROFESS OUR ADMIRATION AND GRATITUDE FOR YOUR UNFLINCHING COURAGE. LAST BUT NOT LEAST, WE WANT TO THANK YOU FOR HAVING PAVED THE WAY FOR A GENERATION OF YOUNG PUBLISHERS, SUCH AS OUR FRIEND JOHN OAKES, PUBLISHERS WHO ARE TAKING THEIR CUES FROM YOU AND ARE CARRYING ON THE EXACTING MISSION YOU SET FOR YOURSELF. [YOU HAVE MANAGED TO PASS ON YOUR ART OF PUBLISHING].

MONSIEUR BARNEY ROSSET, AU NOM DU MINISTRE DE LA CULTURE, JE VOUS FAIS COMMANDEUR DANS L'ORDRE DES ARTS ET LETTRES.

Susan Sontag, Philip
Roth, Barney Rosset,
Georges Borchardt,
John Oakes,
and Pierre Buhler
Photo Astrid Rosset

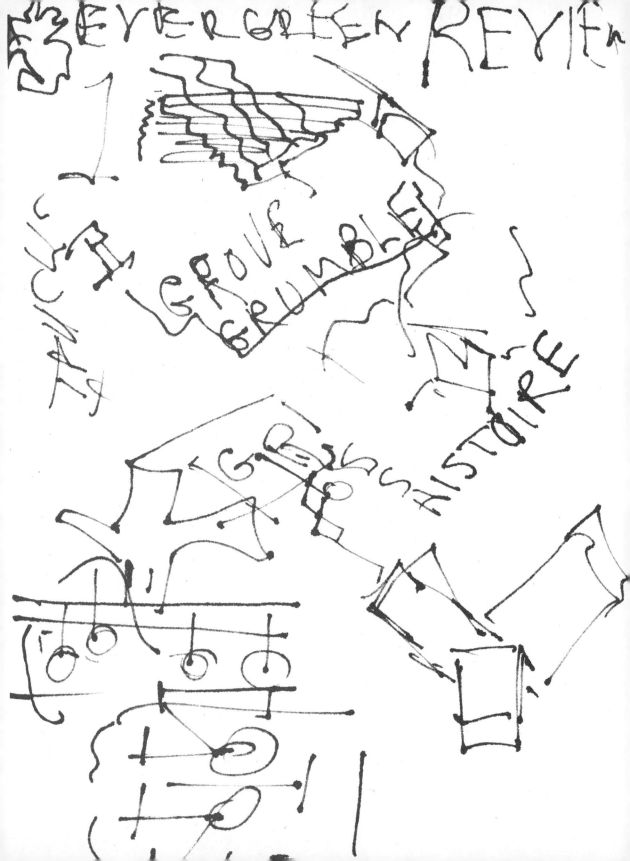

epilogue

*I*n 1987, Jan Jonson, who had directed Waiting for Godot at *Kumla Prison in his native Sweden, went to the United States to direct the play at San Quentin. Not only did he succeed in putting on the play at the oldest and most notorious correctional institution in California, but he did so with the full support—indeed, the blessings—of Samuel Beckett.*

Jan Jonson with Samuel Beckett, Paris, 1988. Photo Beppe Arvidsson

Act I of this volume contains, among others, the correspondence between Beckett and Rosset about Waiting for Godot, the play that made Beckett's name known throughout the Western world. It seems fitting to devote the final pages to what that production— and Beckett's work more generally—meant and continues to mean to one inmate at that prison, the "lifer" who played Pozzo, for Beckett understood how he related the experience of incarceration to the existential experience metaphorically defined by the play as shared by all humankind.

Spoon Jackson—himself a published writer who has been the recipient of awards from the William James Association's Prison Arts Project and the PEN American Center's Prison Writing Program—describes what "prison cannot touch": "that realness, love, and the magic of the theatre" that he "found and uncovered" in Beckett, in Jonson, in acting that play with his fellow inmates. From Lancaster Prison, where he was transferred, Jackson wrote in October 15, 2014, "Yes, waiting for the progress on my parole is tiring like Waiting *for Godot. Since I must do most of my legal work for myself and I am a fool for client. : -) I'll go on and on—"*

Barney Rosset, Beckett's friend and American publisher, was intrigued enough to travel from New York to California to see the 1988 production. He would then take a video of the performance to Paris where Beckett, in a nursing home, would watch it. Jonson has said of his own viewing of the video with Beckett, "Samuel Beckett took it to his heart and blessed our work by saying: 'I saw the roots of my play . . . go back to these people and continue the work you doing.'"

Jonson further relates, "When I was sitting with Sam Beckett in Paris a few weeks after our last performance at San Quentin and we saw our Godot *on video, he asked me: 'Who are you? Why have you done all this?' I answered him: 'I love the silence in your work; I even love the silence in your face...' Sam kissed my forehead and said: 'I saw the roots of my play, do me a favor—go back to these people and bring my* Endgame *with you!'"*

Rosset was later to publish Jackson's own writings in Evergreen Review. *For Longer Ago*, a collection of poems by Spoon, the following blurb appears on the back of the book:

> Spoon Jackson proves that Samuel Beckett's "I can't go on, I will go on" is still there. The evidence is in his internal journey which propels us to go with him to where "flying is the norm" and "the dreams are now." Spoon Jackson we are with you. And together we will go on.
>
> Barney Rosset

Like Jonson and Rosset, Beckett was moved by Jackson's poetry, which the would-be writer of poems, plays, and an autobiography began writing in 1985 in a poetry-writing course taught by Judith Tannenbaum at the prison. Jackson and Tannenbaum would ultimately co-author By Heart, a book Rosset endorsed as "so beautifully described, both objectively and emotionally" and one that "continues the path to freedom through art." The respect and admiration went both ways. "Barney will forever inspire me, like Samuel Beckett," Jackson has written. And "I always feel you Barney and Samuel Beckett's spirit with me."

—ED.

San Quentin production
of *Waiting for Godot*, 1988
Spoon Jackson as Pozzo (right)
Photo Beppe Arvidsson

HELLO! SAM, How are you? I thought
I'd write you this note to let you
know about the realness I have found
by playing the part of POZZO!
My name is SPOON JACKSON and playing
POZZO has introduce me to Parts of
my self I hadin't known and I have
grown tremendously as A human being!
I also found my wife by playing
the PART, she's A beautiful and real Person
inside and outside! She's A pair painter
from Sweden! Thank you for That!
I also been able to get my poetry out into
the world by being in the play and the people
seem to appreciate the truth and realness in
it! I have been trying to get A book of
my poems published but, the business people
are to afraid to take A chance on my
book so far! Hopefully they will soon!
anyway thank you! Sam for being
real and for allowing me to
find and share mine realness! Take care!
Thanks for enriching my life!

SPOON JACKSON

BOX B-92377

TAMAL, CA 94974

Stay Real
Brother!
Love
Spoon Jackson

EVERGREEN REVIEW, INC

September 17, 2012

Dear Spoon,

Thank you for sending me your poem <u>Go On</u> — your feelings are so clearly expressed and capture the sentiment of both Samuel Beckett and Barney.

I like when you said in your note — <u>STay Real</u> — and that is what I am trying to do. And I know that is what you have been doing all these years.

We know that we must go on even when we can'T go on. I send you warm wishes for all that you have achieved and will achieve. You are a fine poet.

Astrid Rosset

61 4th Avenue, 4th Floor, New York, NY 10003
Telephone: (212) 777-2480

Web: www.evergreenreview.com   Email: evergreen@nyc.rr.com

FOX ROCK

61 Fourth Avenue, New York City, New York 10003

December 19, 2013

Dear Spoon,

I was just looking at your letter
dated November 19 — and here it is already
December 17 — and in two weeks — a New Year!
And then in February it will be two years
since Barney passed away.

I really did think that I would have
moved by now, but it will be another few
months — or more — before all is settled.

I had a dream about Barney in Heaven —
he was negotiating with God about making
some changes — planting some trees and
bushes to make Heaven green and cool.
Barney was a master gardener and loved
his trees as much as his books. He
also suggested to God that he would

Phone 212-505-6880 | Fax 212-673-1039 | Email - evergreen@nyc.rr.com

61 Fourth Avenue, New York City, New York 10003

like to do some paintings to add some color to the white clouds! And a few more suggestions — and God was thinking about all these changes that Barney wanted to make and that maybe he made a mistake bringing him up to Heaven. I was amused by the dreams — feeling that Barney was doing alright — being active and pursuing his dreams!

I send all good wishes and thoughts to you for success in your petition for sentence reduction in 2014.

Staying Real.

Your friend — Astrid

Phone 212-505-6880 | Fax 212-673-1039 | Email - evergreen@nyc.rr.com

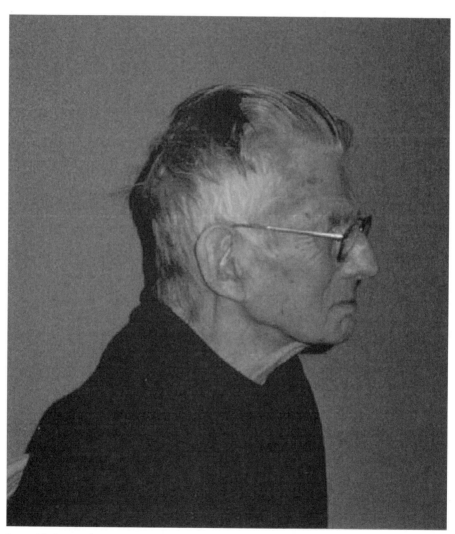

Samuel Beckett in rest home, December 1988. Photo Barney Rosset
Among the last photographs taken of Samuel Beckett

Samuel Beckett viewing San Quentin production of *Godot*.
Photo Barney Rosset

ROSSET PUBLICATIONS OF BECKETT

Works by Samuel Beckett published by Grove Press

- *Waiting for Godot*, 1954
- *Molloy*, 1955
- *Malone Dies*, 1956
- *Murphy*, 1957
- *All That Fall*, 1957
- *The Unnamable*, 1958
- *Endgame*, 1958
- *Molloy, Malone Dies, and The Unnamable: Three Novels,* 1958
- *Watt* 1959
- *Krapp's Last Tape and Other Dramatic Pieces*, 1960
- *Proust*, 1961
- *Happy Days*, 1961
- *Poems in English*, 1961
- *How It Is*, 1964
- *Stories and Text for Nothing*, 1967
- *Film: A Film Script*, with an essay by Alan Schneider, 1969
- *Cascando* and other short dramatic pieces, 1969
- *The Lost Ones*, 1972
- *More Pricks Than Kicks*, 1972
- *First Love and Other Stories*, 1974
- *Mercier and Camier*, 1975
- *Fizzles*, 1976
- *Ends and Odds*, 1976

- *I Can't Go On, I'll Go On*, 1977
- *Collected poems in English and in French*, 1977
- *Company*, 1980
- *Rockaby and Other Short Pieces*, 1981
- *Ill Seen, Ill Said*, 1981
- *Westward Ho*, 1983
- *DISJECTA: Miscellaneous Writings and a Dramatic Fragment*, 1984

By Samuel Beckett published by Blue Moon

- *Stirrings Still*, 1988

By Samuel Beckett published by Foxrock

- *Eleutheria*, 1995

Recent Samuel Beckett publications by Grove Press

- *The Grove Centenary Editions of Samuel Beckett*, ed. Paul Auster, 2006
- *The Collected Poems of Samuel Beckett*, ed. by Seán Lawlor and John Pilling, 2012
- *Echo's Bones,* ed. Mark Nixon, 2014

Works by Samuel Beckett published in *Evergreen Review*

- *Dante and the Lobster,* '57; 1
- *Echo's Bones,* '57; 1
- *From an Abandoned Work*; 3
- *Krapp's Last Tape,* summer '58; 5
- *Text for Nothing I,* summer '59; 9
- *Embers,* Nov/ Dec '59; 10
- *The End,* Nov/ Dec '60; 15
- *The Expelled,* Jan/ Feb '62; 22
- *Words and Music,* Nov/ Dec '62; 27
- *Cascando,* June '63; 30
- *Play,* Dec '64; 34
- *Imagination Dead Imagine,* Feb '66; 39
- *The Calmative,* June '67; 47
- *Lessness,* July '70; 80
- *The Lost Ones,* Spring '73; 96
- *Three Plays: Ohio Impromptu, Catastrophe, and What Where,* '84; 98

PERMISSION CREDITS

Grateful acknowledgment is made to the following publishers, individuals, estates, and agents for permission to reprint:

All reasonable efforts have been made to contact copyright holders. Should any omissions be made known to the publisher, they will be corrected in future editions.

Poster of Beckett Festival NYU, copyright © 1978, Estate of Paul Jenkins 2014.

Lincoln Center production photos of *Waiting for Godot*, copyright © 1988 by Brigitte Lacombe.

Susan Sontag material, copyright © by the Estate of Susan Sontag.

Sol LeWitt drawing, copyright © by Harper's Bazaar.

John Oakes interview with Barney Rosset, copyright © by John Oakes and *Review of Contemporary Fiction.*

Interview with Ken Jordan, copyright © by *The Paris Review.*

Petition in support of Barney Rosset, copyright © by Carin Kuoni and John Oakes.

Richard Avedon photo, copyright © by the Richard Avedon Foundation.

Barney Rosset article in INTO-GAL, copyright © 2006 by Leo Edelstein and Judith Elliston.

Photo by Bob Adelman, copyright © by Bob Adelman.

Photos by Richard Feldman, copyright © by Richard Feldman.

Article by Kenneth Rexroth, copyright © by The Nation.

Photo by John Minihan, copyright © by John Minihan.

Samuel Beckett letters, copyright © by the Estate of Samuel Beckett.

Letter dated 20 October 1964 from *The Letters of Samuel Beckett,*

Volume 3: 1957-1965, © The Estate of Samuel Beckett 2014, Introductions, translations, and notes © George Craig, Martha Dow Fehsenfeld, Dan Gunn, and Lois More Overbeck, published by Cambridge University Press, reproduced with permission.

Barney Rosset letters, photos, and documents, copyright © by the Estate of Barney Rosset.

Article by Jerry Tallmer, copyright © by the Estate of Jerry Tallmer.

Article by Howard Fertig, copyright © by Howard Fertig.

Grove Press ad, copyright © by Morgan Entrekin, Grove Press.

Letters of Spoon Jackson: located in Barney Rosset Papers, Rare Book and

index

A

B

L

M

W

Wainhouse, Austryn, 43, 58, 352

Waiting for Godot, 21, 39, 41, 42, 43, 49, 50, 59, 146, 185, 199, 200, 221, 231, 233, 299, 345, 369, 371, 415, 429, 437, 451, 453, 463

Watt, 68, 69, 116, 122, 230, 271, 350, 353, 355

Weidenfeld, George, 30, 34, 40, 43, 152, 155, 349, 350, 359, 360, 363, 365, 366, 367, 369

Wexler, Haskell, 32, 48, 219, 240

Whitelaw, Billie, 42, 43, 272, 273, 298, 301, 303, 304

Whoroscope, 121, 126, 131, 422

Wilber, Shirley, 43, 325

Wilder, Thornton, 43, 89, 93, 98, 100, 112

Williams, Robin, 43, 115, 331, 335, 412

Williamson, Nicol, 285

Winchell, Walter, 43, 230

Winters, Shelley, 43

Worth, Irene, 43, 299, 300, 307, 308, 311

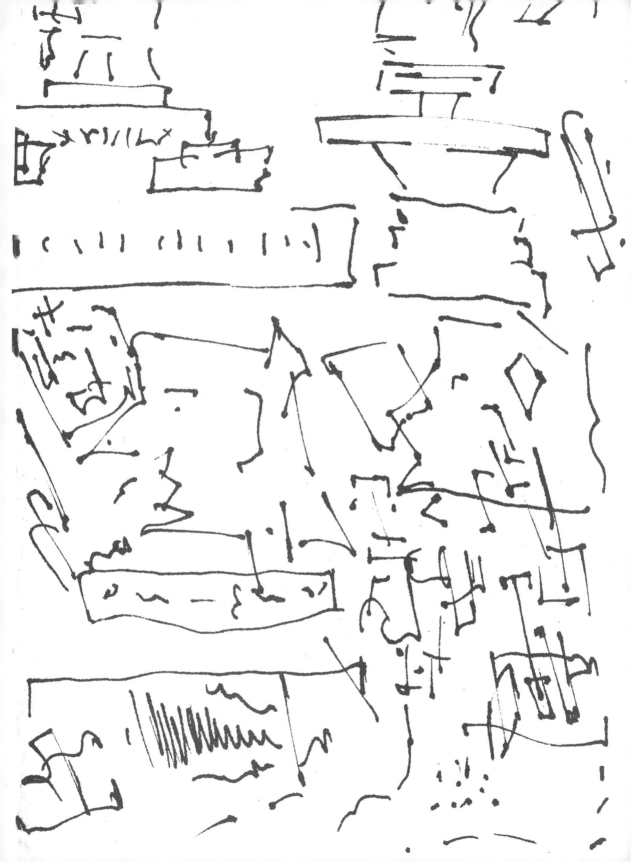

quelques parisien

LA RECHERCHE
LES TIGRES
LES CHAMEAUX CHIMPANS
L'ELEPHANTS